INVENTING THE FUTURE

INVENTING THE FUTURE

Postcapitalism and a World Without Work

Revised and Updated Edition

Nick Srnicek and Alex Williams

VERSO

London • New York

This revised and updated edition published by Verso 2016
First published by Verso 2015
© Nick Srnicek and Alex Williams 2015, 2016

1 3 5 7 9 10 8 6 4 2

Verso
UK: 6 Meard Street, London W1F 0EG
US: 20 Jay Street, Suite 1010, Brooklyn, NY 11201
www.versobooks.com

Verso is the imprint of New Left Books

ISBN-13: 978-1-78478-622-9
eISBN-13: 978-1-78478-098-2 (US)
eISBN-13: 978-1-78478-097-5 (UK)

British Library Cataloguing in Publication Data
A catalogue record for this book is available from the British Library

Library of Congress Cataloging-in-Publication Data
Names: Srnicek, Nick, author. | Williams, Alex, 1981– author.
Title: Inventing the future : folk politics and the struggle for
  postcapitalism / Nick Srnicek and Alex Williams.
Description: Brooklyn, NY : Verso Books, [2015]
Identifiers: LCCN 2015027996| ISBN 9781784780968 (PB) | ISBN 9781784780982
  (eISBN : US) | ISBN 9781784780975 (eISBN : UK)
Subjects: LCSH: Progress. | Radicalism. | Populism. | Social movements. |
  Capitalism. | Neoliberalism.
Classification: LCC HM891 .S76 2015 | DDC 303.44 – dc23
LC record available at http://lccn.loc.gov/2015027996

Typeset in Electra LT Std by Hewer Text UK Ltd, Edinburgh, Scotland
Printed and bound by CPI Group (UK) Ltd, Croydon, CR0 4YY

Contents

Acknowledgements

This book was authored not by two, but by many. We'd like to thank for their assistance during the preparation of this book: Alex Andrews, Armen Avanessian, Diann Bauer, Ray Brassier, Benjamin Bratton, Harry Cleaver, Nathan Coombs, Michael Ferrer, Mark Fisher, Sam Forsythe, Dominic Fox, Lucca Fraser, Craig Gent, Jeremy Gilbert, Fabio Gironi, Jairus Grove, Doug Henwood, Aggie Hirst, Amy Ireland, Joshua Johnson, Robin Mackay, Suhail Malik, Keir Milburn, Reza Negarestani, Matteo Pasquinelli, Patricia Reed, Rory Rowan, Michal Rozworski, Mohammed Salemy, Robbie Shilliam, Ben Singleton, Keith Tilford, James Trafford, Deneb Kozikoski Valereto, Pete Wolfendale, and the innumerable others who have shaped it through discussion. We'd also like to thank the team at Verso who helped make this a significantly better book in the process of editing: Rowan Wilson, Mark Martin, and Charles Peyton. And finally, Nick would like to thank his family for their constant support, and Helen Hester for her invaluable contributions on everything from the smallest grammatical change to the largest conceptual issue. Alex would like to thank his family for their continual support and advice, and Francesca Peck for her unswerving intellectual encouragement and tolerance throughout the writing of this book.

Introduction

Where did the future go? For much of the twentieth century, the future held sway over our dreams. On the horizons of the political left a vast assortment of emancipatory visions gathered, often springing from the conjunction of popular political power and the liberating potential of technology. From predictions of new worlds of leisure, to Soviet-era cosmic communism, to afro-futurist celebrations of the synthetic and diasporic nature of black culture, to post-gender dreams of radical feminism, the popular imagination of the left envisaged societies vastly superior to anything we dream of today.[1] Through popular political control of new technologies, we would collectively transform our world for the better. Today, on one level, these dreams appear closer than ever. The technological infrastructure of the twenty-first century is producing the resources by which a very different political and economic system could be achieved. Machines are accomplishing tasks that were unimaginable a decade ago. The internet and social media are giving a voice to billions who previously went unheard, bringing global participative democracy closer than ever to existence. Open-source designs, copyleft creativity, and 3D printing all portend a world where the scarcity of many products might be overcome. New forms of computer simulation could rejuvenate economic planning and give us the ability to direct economies rationally in unprecedented ways. The newest wave of automation is creating the possibility for huge swathes of boring and demeaning work to be permanently eliminated. Clean energy technologies make possible virtually limitless and environmentally sustainable forms of power production. And new medical technologies not only enable a longer, healthier life, but also make possible new experiments with gender and sexual identity. Many of the classic demands of the left – for less work, for an end to scarcity, for economic democracy, for the production of socially useful goods, and for the liberation of humanity – are materially more achievable than at any other point in history.

Yet, for all the glossy sheen of our technological era, we remain bound by an old and obsolete set of social relations. We continue to work long hours, commuting further, to perform tasks that feel increasingly meaningless. Our jobs have become more insecure, our pay has stagnated, and our debt has become overwhelming. We struggle to make ends meet, to put food on the table, to pay the rent or mortgage, and as we shuffle from job to job, we reminisce about pensions and struggle to find affordable childcare. Automation renders us unemployed and stagnant wages devastate the middle class, while corporate profits surge to new heights. The glimmers of a better future are trampled and forgotten under the pressures of an increasingly precarious and demanding world. And each day, we return to work as normal: exhausted, anxious, stressed and frustrated.

At a planetary level, things appear even more ominous. The breakdown of the global climate continues unabated, and the ongoing fallout from the economic crisis has led governments to embrace the paralysing death-spiral of austerity. Buffeted by imperceptible and abstract powers, we feel incapable of evading or controlling the tidal pulsions of economic, social and environmental forces. But how are we to change this? All around us, it seems that the political systems, movements and processes that dominated the last hundred years are no longer able to bring about genuinely transformative change. Instead, they have forced us onto an endless treadmill of misery. Electoral democracy lies in remarkable disrepair. Centre-left political parties have been hollowed out and sapped of any popular mandate. Their corpses stumble on as vehicles for careerist ambitions. Radical political movements bloom promisingly but are quickly snuffed out by exhaustion and repression. Organised labour has seen its power systematically taken apart, leaving it sclerotic and incapable of anything more than feeble resistance. Yet, in the face of these calamities, today's politics remains stubbornly beset by a lack of new ideas. Neoliberalism has held sway for decades, and social democracy exists largely as an object of nostalgia. As crises gather force and speed, politics withers and retreats. In this paralysis of the political imaginary, the future has been cancelled.[2]

This book is about how we got here, and where we might go next. Using an idea we call 'folk politics', we offer a diagnosis of how and why we lost the capacity to build a better future. Under the sway of folk-political thinking, the most recent cycle of struggles – from anti-globalisation to anti-war to Occupy Wall Street – has involved the fetishisation of local spaces, immediate actions, transient gestures, and particularisms of all kinds. Rather than undertake the difficult labour of expanding and consolidating gains, this form of politics has focused on building bunkers to resist the encroachments of global neoliberalism. In so doing, it has become a politics of defence, incapable of articulating or building a new world. For any movement that struggles to escape neoliberalism and build something better, these folk-political approaches are insufficient. In their place, this book sets out an alternative politics – one that seeks to take back control over our future and to foster the ambition for a world more modern than capitalism will allow. The utopian potentials inherent in twenty-first-century technology cannot remain bound to a parochial capitalist imagination; they must be liberated by an ambitious left alternative. Neoliberalism has failed, social democracy is impossible, and only an alternative vision can bring about universal prosperity and emancipation. Articulating and achieving this better world is the fundamental task of the left today.

Chapter 1

Our Political Common Sense: Introducing Folk Politics

The next move was ours, and we just stood there, waiting for something to happen, like good conscientious objectors awaiting our punishment after our purely symbolic point had been made.

Dave Mitchell

Today it appears that the greatest amount of effort is needed to achieve the smallest degree of change. Millions march against the Iraq War, yet it goes ahead as planned. Hundreds of thousands protest austerity, but unprecedented budget cuts continue. Repeated student protests, occupations and riots struggle against rises in tuition fees, but they continue their inexorable advance. Around the world, people set up protest camps and mobilise against economic inequality, but the gap between the rich and the poor keeps growing. From the alter-globalisation struggles of the late 1990s, through the anti-war and ecological coalitions of the early 2000s, and into the new student uprisings and Occupy movements since 2008, a common pattern emerges: resistance struggles rise rapidly, mobilise increasingly large numbers of people, and yet fade away only to be replaced by a renewed sense of apathy, melancholy and defeat. Despite the desires of millions for a better world, the effects of these movements prove minimal.

A FUNNY THING HAPPENED ON THE WAY TO THE PROTEST

Failure permeates this cycle of struggles, and as a result, many of the tactics on the contemporary left have taken on a ritualistic nature, laden with a heavy dose of fatalism. The dominant tactics – protesting, marching, occupying, and various other forms of direct action – have become part of a well-established narrative, with the people and the police each playing their assigned roles. The limits of these actions are particularly visible in those brief moments when the script changes. As one activist puts it, of a protest at the 2001 Summit of the Americas:

> On April 20, the first day of the demonstrations, we marched in our thousands towards the fence, behind which 34 heads of state had gathered to hammer out a hemispheric trade deal. Under a hail of catapult-launched teddy bears, activists dressed in black quickly removed the fence's supports with bolt cutters and pulled it down with grapples as onlookers cheered them on. For a brief moment, nothing stood between us and the convention centre. We scrambled atop the toppled fence, but for the most part we went no further, as if our intention all along had been simply to replace the state's chain-link and concrete barrier with a human one of our own making.[1]

We see here the symbolic and ritualistic nature of the actions, combined with the thrill of having done *something* – but with a deep uncertainty that appears at the first break with the expected narrative. The role of dutiful protestor had given these activists no indication of what to do when the barriers fell. Spectacular political confrontations like the Stop the War marches, the now-familiar melees against the G20 or World Trade Organization and the rousing scenes of democracy in Occupy Wall Street all give the appearance of being highly significant, as if something were genuinely at stake.[2] Yet nothing changed, and long-term victories were traded for a simple registration of discontent.

To outside observers, it is often not even clear what the movements want, beyond expressing a generalised discontent with the world. The contemporary protest has become a melange of wild and varied demands. The 2009 G20 summit in London, for instance, featured protestors marching for issues that spanned from grandiose anti-capitalist stipulations to modest goals centred on more local issues. When demands can be discerned at all, they usually fail to articulate anything substantial. They are often nothing more than empty slogans – as meaningful as calling for world peace. In more recent struggles, the very idea of making demands has been questioned. The Occupy movement infamously struggled to articulate meaningful goals, worried that anything too substantial would be divisive.[3] And a broad range of student occupations across the Western world has taken up the mantra of 'no demands' under the misguided belief that demanding nothing is a radical act.[4]

When asked what the ultimate upshot of these actions has been, participants differ between admitting to a general sense of futility and pointing to the radicalisation of those who took part. If we look at protests today as an exercise in public awareness, they appear to have had mixed success at best. Their messages are mangled by an unsympathetic media smitten by images of property destruction – assuming that the media even acknowledges a form of contention that has become increasingly repetitive and boring. Some argue that, rather than trying to achieve a certain end, these movements, protests and occupations in fact exist only for their own sake.[5] The aim in this case is to achieve a certain transformation of the participants, and create a space outside of the usual operations of power. While there is a degree of truth to this, things like protest camps tend to remain ephemeral, small-scale and ultimately unable to challenge the larger structures of the neoliberal economic system. This is politics transmuted into pastime – politics-as-drug-experience, perhaps – rather than anything capable of transforming society. Such protests are registered only in the minds of their participants, bypassing any transformation of social structures. While these efforts at radicalisation and awareness-raising are undoubtedly important to some degree, there still remains the question of exactly *when* these sequences might pay off. Is there a point at which a critical mass of consciousness-raising will be ready for action? Protests can build connections, encourage hope and remind people of their power. Yet, beyond these transient feelings, politics still demands the exercise of that power, lest these affective bonds go to waste. If we will not act after one of the largest crises of capitalism, then when?

The emphasis on the affective aspects of protests plays into a broader trend that has come to privilege the affective as the site of real politics. Bodily, emotional and visceral elements come to replace and stymie (rather than complement and enhance) more abstract analysis. The contemporary landscape of social media, for example, is littered with the bitter fallout from an endless torrent of outrage and anger. Given the individualism of current social media platforms – premised on the maintenance of an online identity – it is perhaps no surprise to see online 'politics' tend towards the self-presentation of moral purity. We are more concerned to appear right than to think about the conditions of political change. Yet these daily outrages pass as rapidly as they emerge, and we are soon on to the next vitriolic crusade. In other places, public demonstrations of empathy with those suffering replace more finely tuned analysis, resulting in hasty or misplaced action – or none at all. While politics always has a relationship to emotion and sensation (to hope or anger, fear or outrage), when taken as the primary mode of politics, these impulses can lead to deeply perverse results. In a famous example, 1985's Live Aid raised huge amounts of money for famine relief through a combination of heartstring-tugging imagery and emotionally manipulative celebrity-led events. The sense of emergency demanded urgent action, at the expense of thought. Yet the money raised actually extended the civil war causing the famine, by allowing rebel militias to use the food aid to support themselves.[6] While viewers at home felt comforted they were doing something rather than nothing, a dispassionate analysis revealed that they had in fact contributed to the problem. These unintended outcomes become even more pervasive as the targets of action grow larger and more abstract. If politics without passion leads to cold-hearted, bureaucratic technocracy, then passion bereft of analysis risks becoming a libidinally driven surrogate for effective action. Politics comes to be about feelings of personal empowerment, masking an absence of strategic gains.

Perhaps most depressing, even when movements have some successes, they are in the context of overwhelming losses. Residents across the UK, for example, have successfully mobilised in particular cases to stop the closure of local hospitals. Yet these real successes are overwhelmed by larger plans to gut and privatise the National Health Service. Similarly, recent anti-fracking movements have been able to stop test drilling in various localities – but governments nevertheless continue to search for shale gas resources and provide support for companies to do so.[7] In the United States, various movements to stop evictions in the wake of the housing crisis have made real gains in terms of keeping people in their homes.[8] Yet the perpetrators of the subprime mortgage debacle continue to reap the profits, waves of foreclosures continue to sweep across the country, and rents continue to surge across the urban world. Small successes – useful, no doubt, for instilling a sense of hope – nevertheless wither in the face of overwhelming losses. Even the most optimistic activist falters in the face of struggles that continue to fail. In other cases, well-intentioned projects like Rolling Jubilee strive to escape the spell of neoliberal common sense.[9] The ostensibly radical aim of crowdsourcing money to pay the debts of the underprivileged means buying into a system of voluntary charity and redistribution, as well as accepting the legitimacy of the debt in the first place. In this respect, the initiative is one among a larger group of projects that act simply as crisis responses to the faltering of state services. These are survival mechanisms, not a desirable vision for the future.

What can we conclude from all of this? The recent cycle of struggles has to be identified as one of overarching failure, despite a multitude of small-scale successes and moments of large-scale mobilisation. The question that any analysis of the left today must grapple with is simply: What has gone wrong? It is undeniable that heightened repression by states and the increased power of corporations have played a significant role in weakening the power of the left. Still, it remains debatable whether the repression faced by workers, the precarity of the masses and the power of capitalists is any greater than it was in the late nineteenth century. Workers then were still struggling for basic rights, often against states more than willing to use lethal violence against them.[10] But whereas that period saw mass mobilisation, general strikes, militant labour and radical women's organisations all achieving real and lasting successes, today is defined by their absence. The recent weakness of the left cannot simply be chalked up to increased state and capitalist repression: an honest reckoning must accept that problems also lie *within* the left. One key problem is a widespread and uncritical acceptance of what we call 'folk-political' thinking.

DEFINING FOLK POLITICS

What is folk politics? Folk politics names a constellation of ideas and intuitions within the contemporary left that informs the common-sense ways of organising, acting and thinking politics. It is a set of strategic assumptions that threatens to debilitate the left, rendering it unable to scale up, create lasting change or expand beyond particular interests. Leftist movements under the sway of folk politics are not only unlikely to be successful – they are in fact incapable of transforming capitalism. The term itself draws upon two senses of 'folk'. First, it evokes critiques of folk psychology which argue that our intuitive conceptions of the world are both historically constructed and often mistaken.[11] Secondly, it refers to 'folk' as the locus of the small-scale, the authentic, the traditional and the natural. Both of these dimensions are implied in the idea of folk politics.

As a first approximation, we can therefore define folk politics as a collective and historically constructed political common sense that has become out of joint with the actual mechanisms of power. As our political, economic, social and technological world changes, tactics and strategies which were previously capable of transforming collective power into emancipatory gains have now become drained of their effectiveness. As the common sense of today's left, folk politics often operates intuitively, uncritically and unconsciously. Yet common sense is also historical and mutable. It is worth recalling that today's familiar forms of organisation and tactics, far from being natural or pre-given, have instead been developed over time in response to specific political problems. Petitions, occupations, strikes, vanguard parties, affinity groups, trade unions: all arose out of particular historical conditions.[12] Yet the fact that certain ways of organising and acting were once useful does not guarantee their continued relevance. Many of the tactics and organisational structures that dominate the contemporary left are responses to the experience of state communism, exclusionary trade unions, and the collapse of social democratic parties. Yet the ideas that made sense in the wake of those moments no longer present effective tools for political transformation. Our world has moved on, becoming more complex, abstract, nonlinear and global than ever before.

Against the abstraction and inhumanity of capitalism, folk politics aims to bring politics down to the 'human scale' by emphasising temporal, spatial and conceptual immediacy. At its heart, folk politics is the guiding intuition that immediacy is always better and often more authentic, with the corollary being a deep suspicion of abstraction and mediation. In terms of temporal immediacy, contemporary folk politics typically remains reactive (responding to actions initiated by corporations and governments, rather than initiating actions);[13] ignores long-term strategic goals in favour of tactics (mobilising around single-issue politics or emphasising process);[14] prefers practices that are often inherently fleeting (such as occupations and temporary autonomous zones);[15] chooses the familiarities of the past over the unknowns of the future (for instance, the repeated dreams of a return to 'good' Keynesian capitalism);[16] and expresses itself as a predilection for the voluntarist and spontaneous over the institutional (as in the romanticisation of rioting and insurrection).[17]

In terms of spatial immediacy, folk politics privileges the local as the site of authenticity (as in the 100-miles diet or local currencies);[18] habitually chooses the small over the large (as in the veneration of small-scale communities or local businesses);[19] favours projects that are un-scalable beyond a small community (for instance, general assemblies and direct democracy);[20] and often rejects the project of hegemony, valuing withdrawal or exit rather than building a broad counter-hegemony.[21] Likewise, folk politics prefers that actions be taken by participants themselves – in its emphasis on direct action, for example – and sees decision-making as something to be carried out by each individual rather than by any representative. The problems of scale and extension are either ignored or smoothed over in folk-political thinking.

Finally, in terms of conceptual immediacy, there is a preference for the everyday over the structural, valorising personal experience over systematic thinking; for feeling over thinking, emphasising individual suffering, or the sensations of enthusiasm and anger experienced during political actions; for the particular over the universal, seeing the latter as intrinsically totalitarian; and for the ethical over the political – as in ethical consumerism, or moralising critiques of greedy bankers.[22] Organisations and communities are to be transparent, rejecting in advance any conceptual mediation, or even modest amounts of complexity. The classic images of universal emancipation and global change have been transformed into a prioritisation of the suffering of the particular and the authenticity of the local. As a result, any process of constructing a universal politics is rejected from the outset.

Understood in these ways, we can detect traces of folk politics in organisations and movements like Occupy, Spain's 15M, student occupations, left communist insurrectionists like Tiqqun and the Invisible Committee, most forms of horizontalism, the Zapatistas, and contemporary anarchist-tinged politics, as well as a variety of other trends like political localism, the slow-food movement, and ethical consumerism, among many others. But no single position embodies all of these dispositions, which leads us to a first qualification: as an uncritical and often unconscious common sense, folk politics comes to be instantiated to varying degrees in concrete political positions. That is to say, folk politics does not name an explicit position, but only an implicit tendency. The ideas that characterise this tendency are widely dispersed throughout the contemporary left, but some positions are more folk-political than others. This brings us to a second important qualification: the problem with folk politics is not that it starts from the local; all politics begins from the local. The problem is rather that folk-political thinking is content to remain at (and even privileges) that level – of the transient, the small-scale, the unmediated and the particular. It takes these to be sufficient rather than simply necessary moments. Therefore, the point is not simply to reject folk politics. Folk politics is a necessary component of any successful political project, but it can only be a starting point. A third qualification is that folk politics is only a problem for particular types of projects: those that seek to move beyond capitalism. Folk-political thinking can be perfectly well adapted to other political projects: projects aimed solely at resistance, movements organised around local issues, and small-scale projects. Political movements based around keeping a hospital open or preventing evictions are all admirable, but they are importantly different from movements trying to challenge neoliberal capitalism. The idea that one organisation, tactic or strategy applies equally well to any sort of struggle is one of the most pervasive and damaging beliefs among today's left. Strategic reflection – on means and ends, enemies and allies – is necessary before approaching any political project. Given the nature of global capitalism, any postcapitalist project will require an ambitious, abstract, mediated, complex and global approach – one that folk-political approaches are incapable of providing.

Combining these qualifications, we can therefore say that folk politics is necessary but insufficient for a postcapitalist political project. By emphasising and remaining at the level of the immediate, folk politics lacks the tools to transform neoliberalism into something else. While folk politics can undoubtedly make important interventions in local struggles, we deceive ourselves when we think these are turning the tide against global capitalism. They represent, at best, temporary respite against its onslaught. The project of this book is to begin outlining an alternative – a way for the left to navigate from the local to the global, and synthesise the particular with the universal. Such an alternative cannot simply be a conservative reversion to the working-class politics of the last century. It must instead combine an updated way of *thinking* politics (a shift from immediacy to structural analysis) with an upgraded means of *doing* politics (which directs action towards building platforms and expanding scales).

OVERWHELMED

Why did folk politics arise in the first place? Why is it that folk political tendencies, for all their manifest flaws, are so seductive and appealing to the movements of today? At least three answers present themselves. The first explanation is to see folk politics as a response to the problem of how to interpret and act within an ever more complex world. The second, related explanation involves situating folk politics as a reaction to the historical experiences of the communist and social democratic left. Finally, folk politics is a more immediate response to the empty spectacle of contemporary party politics.

Increasingly, multipolar global politics, economic instability, and anthropogenic climate change outpace the narratives we use to structure and make sense of our lives. Each of these is an example of what is termed a *complex system*, which features nonlinear dynamics, where marginally different inputs can cause dramatically divergent outputs, intricate sets of causes feedback on one another in unexpected ways, and which characteristically operates on scales of space and time that go far beyond any individual's unaided perception.[23] Globalisation, international politics, and climate change: each of these systems shapes our world, but their effects are so extensive and complicated that it is difficult to place our own experience within them. The global economy is a good example of this. In simple terms, the economy is not an object amenable to direct perception; it is distributed across time and space (you will never meet 'the economy' in person); it incorporates a wide array of elements, from property laws to biological needs, natural resources to technological infrastructures, market stalls and supercomputers; and it involves an enormous and intricately interacting set of feedback loops, all of which produce emergent effects that are irreducible to its individual components.[24] In other words, the interaction of an economy's parts produces effects that cannot be understood just by knowing how those parts work in isolation – it is only in grasping the relations between them that the economy can be made sense of. While we might have an idea of what an economy consists of, we will never be able to experience it directly in the same way as other phenomena. It can only be observed symptomatically through key statistical indexes (charting changes in inflation or interest rates, stock indexes, GDP, and so on), but can never be seen, heard or touched in its totality.

As a result, despite everything that has been written about capitalism, we still struggle to understand its dynamics and its mechanisms. Most importantly, we lack a 'cognitive map' of our socioeconomic system: a mental picture of how individual and collective human action can be situated within the unimaginable vastness of the global economy.[25] Recent decades have seen an increasing complexity in the dynamics that impinge upon politics. We might consider the imminent threat of anthropogenic climate change as a new kind of problem – one that is unamenable to any simple solution and that involves such intricately woven effects that it is hard to even know where to intervene. Equally, the global economy today appears significantly more complex in terms of the mobility of capital, the intricacies of global finance and the multiplicity of actors involved. How well do our traditional political images of the world map onto these changes? For the left at least, an analysis premised on the industrial working class was a powerful way to interpret the totality of social and economic relations in the nineteenth and early twentieth centuries, thereby articulating clear strategic objectives. Yet the history of the global left over the course of the twentieth century attests to the ways in which this analysis failed to attend to both the range of possible liberating struggles (based in gender, race or sexuality) and the ability of capitalism to restructure itself – through the creation of the welfare state, or the neoliberal transformations of the global economy. Today, the old models often falter in the face of new problems; we lose the capacity to understand our position in history and in the world at large.

This separation between everyday experience and the system we live within results in increased alienation: we feel adrift in a world we do not understand. The cultural theorist Fredric Jameson notes that the proliferation of conspiracy theories is partly a response to this situation.[26] Conspiracy theories act by narrowing the agency behind our world to a single figure of power (the Bilderberg Group, the Freemasons or some other convenient scapegoat). Despite the extraordinary complexity of some of these theories, they nevertheless provide a reassuringly simple answer to 'who is behind it all', and what our own role is in the situation. In other words, they act precisely as a (faulty) cognitive map.

Folk politics presents itself as another possible response to the problems of overwhelming complexity. If we do not understand how the world operates, the folk-political injunction is to reduce complexity down to a human scale. Indeed, folk-political writing is saturated with calls for a return to authenticity, to immediacy, to a world that is 'transparent', 'human-scaled', 'tangible', 'slow', 'harmonious', 'simple', and 'everyday'.[27] Such thinking rejects the complexity of the contemporary world, and thereby rejects the possibility of a truly postcapitalist world. It attempts to give a human face to power; whereas what is truly terrifying is the generally asubjective nature of the system. The faces are interchangeable; the power remains the same. The turn towards localism, temporary moments of resistance, and the intuitive practices of direct action all effectively attempt to condense the problems of global capitalism into concrete figures and moments.

In this process, folk politics often reduces politics to an ethical and individual struggle. There is a tendency sometimes to imagine that we simply need 'good' capitalists, or a 'responsible' capitalism. At the same time, the imperative to 'make it local' leads folk politics to fetishise immediate results and the concrete appearance of action. Delaying a corporate attack on the environment, for instance, is lauded as a success – even if the company simply waits out public attention before returning once again. Moreover, as Rosa Luxemburg pointed out long ago, the fetishisation of 'immediate results' leads to an empty pragmatism that struggles to maintain the present balance of power, rather than seeking to change structural conditions.[28] Without the necessary abstraction of strategic thought, tactics are ultimately fleeting gestures. Finally, the abjuring of complexity dovetails with the neoliberal case for markets. One of the primary arguments made against planning has been that the economy is simply too complex to be guided.[29] The only alternative is therefore to leave the distribution of resources to the market and reject any attempt to guide it rationally.[30] Considered in all these ways, folk politics appears as an attempt to make global capitalism small enough to be thinkable – and at the same time, to articulate how to act upon this restricted image of capitalism. By contrast, the argument of this book is that folk-political tendencies are mistaken. If complexity presently outstrips humanity's capacities to think and control, there are two options: one is to reduce complexity down to a human scale; the other is to expand humanity's capacities. We endorse the latter position. Any postcapitalist project will necessarily require the creation of new cognitive maps, political narratives, technological interfaces, economic models, and mechanisms of collective control to be able to marshal complex phenomena for the betterment of humanity.

OUTDATED

While the response to increasing complexity goes some way towards explaining the rise of folk-political thinking, it must also be situated in terms of the particular history of left politics in the twentieth century. In many respects, folk-political tendencies are understandable (if inadequate) responses to the challenges faced in the last fifty years – challenges that have emerged both within the left and in competition with conservative and capitalist forces.[31] In particular, folk politics emerged as a response to the collapse of the postwar social democratic complex that knitted together working-class institutions, social democratic parties, and the hegemony of embedded liberalism.[32] The breakdown of this social democratic bloc occurred across multiple lines of conflict and in various spheres: in the emergence of new forms of work, associated with the affective and cognitive; in the emergence of energy crises that disrupted geopolitical certainties; in the increasing difficulties capitalist enterprises faced in achieving profitability; in the proliferation of neoliberal ideology through the institutional networks of think tanks and university departments; in the explosion of new forms of political subjectivities, projects and demands; and in the widespread discrediting of nominally communist states. Each of these factors served to disrupt the foundation of the postwar social system in Europe and America. In this process, there was both an *outdating* of old left paradigms and an *outmanoeuvring* of the new ones.

Perhaps the most significant point in this destabilisation of the postwar settlement was in the late 1960s and early 1970s. The global revolts of 1968 gave both new prominence and new inspiration to a series of left movements that rejected the coordinates of struggle articulated by labour unions and political parties. These movements were driven partly by the emerging history of Stalinist repression, and when combined with the Soviet regime's suppression of democratising currents in Eastern Europe, this meant that communist parties were increasingly discredited in the eyes of young European leftists. This called into question the strategic validity of the Leninist programme of state-takeover by a revolutionary party leading a coalition of forces centred on the industrial working class.[33] If even 'successful' revolutions led to sclerotic technocracy and political repression in the long term, what then was to be the properly emancipatory course of action? Hierarchy and vanguardism in the communist party increasingly appeared opposed to the aims of the emerging social movements.

Beyond the difficulties of transitioning to postcapitalism under a communist administration, the prospects for state-takeover in the developed nations in the 1960s and 1970s seemed slight, especially given the divisions emerging on the left. The uprisings in France in May 1968, in which the French Communist Party notably failed to back the unionists and student groups, seemingly brought to an end any prospect of a political revolution. In addition, social democracy and its Keynesian-corporatist solutions to social inequity appeared increasingly content with the existing order, and unable or unwilling to move towards an emancipatory socialism. Though social democracy was capable of offering significant gains to certain groups, it retained an authoritarian establishment and a paternalistic cast, generally exclusive of women and ethnic minorities, and was dependent upon a mode of capitalist organisation (Fordism) that generated unusual levels of social cohesion. It was this social cohesion that was eroded in the late 1960s and early 1970s by the emergence of new mass desires (for increased flexibility in work, for example) and newly insistent demands (for racial and gender equality, for nuclear disarmament, for sexual freedoms, and against Western imperialism). By the late 1960s, these new problems could no longer be resolved with the existing set of leftist political agents, and electoral pressures were beginning to transform the social democratic party from a mass party of the working class into an increasingly coalition-based party of the middle class.[34] The remaining radical elements of social democratic parties were being slowly hollowed out.

The ongoing decline of the party form can be traced partly to the disastrous realities of rule in the nominally communist states and the disappointment of social democracy. At the same time, a series of well-founded critiques were marshalled from within the new left, prompted partly by the experiences of women in activist groups, who found their voices continued to be marginalised even in allegedly radical organisations. More hierarchical organisational forms, such as parties or traditional union organisations, continued to entrench the predominant patriarchal and sexist social relations prevalent in broader society. Considerable experimentation was therefore conducted to produce new organisational forms that could work against this social repression. This included the use of consensus decision-making and horizontal debating structures that would later come to worldwide fame with the Occupy Wall Street movement.[35] Outside of feminist groups, the new student left of the university campuses, while diverse in its manifestations, was often explicitly anti-authoritarian, anti-bureaucratic, and even anti-organisational.[36] Many of the tactics espoused by these groups emphasised the benefits of direct action and drew their influences from African-American civil rights movements and earlier student movements, as well as from the ideas of European Situationism, anarchist political currents, and the incipient environmental movement.[37] Here we can see the emergence of folk politics' basic strategic orientation and the modes of action that characterise it: from the occupation, sit-in, or squatted commune through to carnivalesque street protests and 'happenings'. Each of these tactics emerged in this period as a way to disrupt the functioning of everyday power, suspend the 'normal' forms of social regulation and promote egalitarian spaces for discussion. Beyond trying to change society, these interventions aimed at transforming the participants themselves and embodying the new forms of sociality to come.

The movements that crystallised in the period were therefore diverse in their makeup and outlook, operating across various subjectivities, territorial locations, and tactical and strategic forms. But each of them, in its own way, articulated new desires that could not readily be accommodated within the old forms of left-wing politics. One way to consider these movements is as part of a generalised 'antisystemic' political phenomenon of the time.[38] Across the globe, there was a tendency towards challenging and taking apart the power of bureaucratic hierarchies in favour of new modes of direct action, extending from the student, feminist and black power movements of the United States, through to the Situationist movement, student and allied labour movements of Europe, Prague's anti-Stalinists, the student revolts of Mexico and Tokyo, and China's Cultural Revolution.[39] At its most extreme, however, this antisystemic politics led towards the identification of political power as *inherently* tainted by oppressive, patriarchal and domineering tendencies.[40] This leaves something of a paradox. On the one hand, it could choose some form of negotiation or accommodation with existing power structures, which would tend towards the corruption or co-optation of the new left. But on the other hand, it could choose to remain marginal, and thereby unable to transform those elements of society not already convinced of its agenda.[41] The critiques many of these antisystemic movements made of established forms of state, capitalist and old-left bureaucratic power were largely accurate. Yet antisystemic politics offered few resources to build a new movement capable of contending against capitalist hegemony.

The legacy of these social movements was therefore two-sided. The ideas, values and new desires articulated by them had a significant impact on a global level; the dissemination of feminist, anti-racist, gay-rights and anti-bureaucratic demands remains their strongest achievement. In this, they represented an absolutely necessary moment of self-critique by the left, and the legacy of folk-political tactics finds its appropriate historical conditions here. Simultaneously, however, an inability or lack of desire to turn the more radical sides of these projects into hegemonic ones also had important consequences for the period of destabilisation that followed.[42] While capable of generating an array of new and powerful ideas of human freedom, the new social movements were generally unable to replace the faltering social democratic order.

OUTMANOEUVRED

Just as the new social movements were on the rise, the economic basis of the social democratic consensus was beginning to fall apart. The 1970s saw surging energy prices, the collapse of the Bretton Woods system, the growth of global capital flows, persistent stagflation and falling capitalist profits.[43] This effectively ended the basic political settlement that had supported the post-war era: that unique nexus of Keynesian economic policy, Fordist–corporatist industrial production and the broadly social democratic consensus that returned a part of the social surplus back to workers. Across the world, the structural crisis presented an opportunity for the forces of both the broad left and the broad right to generate a new hegemony that could resolve it.

For the right, the challenge was to restore capital accumulation and profitability. This challenge was eventually answered by the emergence of neoliberal thought on the global stage; but even before that, right-wing forces in the UK and the United States were experimenting with new ways to outmanoeuvre both the old and new left. One particularly important approach was a political-economic strategy to link the crisis of capitalism to union power. The subsequent defeat of organised labour throughout the core capitalist nations has perhaps been neoliberalism's most important achievement, significantly changing the balance of power between labour and capital. The means by which this was achieved were diverse, from physical confrontation and combat,[44] to using legislation to undermine solidarity and industrial action, to embracing shifts in production and distribution that compromised union power (such as disaggregating supply chains), to re-engineering public opinion and consent around a broadly neoliberal agenda of individual freedom and 'negative solidarity'. The latter denotes more than mere indifference to worker agitations – it is the fostering of an aggressively enraged sense of injustice, committed to the idea that, because I must endure increasingly austere working conditions (wage freezes, loss of benefits, a declining pension pot), then everyone else must as well. The result of these combined shifts was a hollowing-out of unions and the defeat of the working class in the developed world.[45]

While the right successfully faced the structural crisis by consolidating its political and economic power, the movements of the old and new left were unable to confront this new configuration of forces. In the 1970s, socialist and even communist political parties were gradually able to gain increasing ground in elections in Western Europe; but the old left simply tried to resolve the crisis by doubling down on the traditional corporatist agenda.[46] But the old Keynesian policy formulations were unable to kick-start growth, restrain unemployment or reduce inflation under these new economic conditions. As a result, left-wing governments coming to power in the 1970s, such as the British Labour Party, often ended up having to implement proto-neoliberal policies in frustrated attempts to foster a recovery.[47] The traditional labour movement, decrepit and stagnant, was by now being bested and co-opted by the forces of the right. In this context, the new left was a necessary critique that was essential to the left's revitalisation and progress. Yet, as we saw in the previous section, if the old labour organisations were in many senses bereft of ideas, the new left was unable to institutionalise itself and articulate a counter-hegemony. The result was a left that became increasingly marginalised.

As neoliberalism expanded and consolidated its common sense, the remaining social democratic parties increasingly came to accept neoliberalism's terms. With most major parties effectively signed up to its political and economic programme, and increasing numbers of public services being taken into private hands, the ability to achieve significant change at the ballot box was dramatically reduced. Widespread cynicism began to accompany a hollowed-out party politics that came to resemble the public relations industry, with politicians being reduced to the role of shopkeepers hawking undesirable wares.[48] Mass participation in electoral politics declined in tandem with the gradual acceptance of the neoliberal coordinates, and the age of post-politics was upon us. Mass voter disaffection is the result today, with voter turnout routinely at historic lows. Under these circumstances, the folk-political insistence on immediate results and small-scale participatory democracy has an obvious allure.

The position of the new social movements in this context was more ambiguous. By the 1990s, the positioning of the working class as privileged political subject had been fully broken down, and a much wider array of social identities, desires and oppressions had gained recognition.[49] Increasingly sophisticated attempts were made to develop the analysis of interacting power structures, giving rise to ideas of intersectional oppressions.[50] As a result of cultural dissemination and mainstream political endorsement, large parts of the programmes of feminist, anti-racist and queer political movements had become enshrined in law and embraced on a social level. But despite these successes, there had been a rollback from the kind of radical demands outlined in the 1970s, which envisaged a much more thorough transformation of society. Feminists, for example, have made significant gains in terms of pay equality, abortion rights and childcare policies, but these pale in comparison to projects for the total abolition of gender.[51] Similarly, for many black liberation movements, while anti-racist employment policies and anti-discrimination laws were widely enacted, they had not been accompanied by other radical programmes espoused by earlier movements.[52] Much of the success seen by the new social movements today is confined within the hegemonic terms established by neoliberalism – articulated around market-centred claims, liberal rights and a rhetoric of choice. What have been sidelined in the process are the more radical and anti-capitalist elements of these projects.

Looking back, we have the collapse of the traditional organisations of the left, and the simultaneous rise of an alternative new left predicated upon critiques of bureaucracy, verticality, exclusion and institutionalisation, combined with an incorporation of some of the new desires into the apparatus of neoliberalism. It was against this backdrop that folk-political intuitions increasingly sedimented as a new common sense and came to be expressed in the alter-globalisation movements.[53] These movements emerged in two phases. The first, appearing from the mid 1990s through to the early 2000s, consisted of groups such as the Zapatistas, anti-capitalists, alter-globalisers, and participants in the World Social Forum and global anti-war protests. A second phase began immediately after the 2007–09 financial crisis and featured various groups united by their similar organisational forms and ideological positions, including the Occupy movement, Spain's 15M and various national-level student movements. Both phases of the newest social movements sought to counter neoliberalism and its national and corporate avatars, with the first phase targeting global trade and governance organizations, and the latter focusing more on financialisation, inequality and debt.[54] Drawing influence from the earlier social movements, this latest cycle of struggles comprises groups that tend to privilege the local and the spontaneous, the horizontal and the anti-state. The apparent plausibility of folk politics rests on the collapse of traditional modes of organisation on the left, of the co-optation of social democratic parties into a choice-less neoliberal hegemony, and the broad sense of disempowerment engendered by the insipidness of contemporary party politics. In a world where the most serious problems we face seem intractably complex, folk politics presents an alluring way to prefigure egalitarian futures in the present. On its own, however, this kind of politics is unable to give rise to long-lasting forces that might supersede, rather than merely resist, global capitalism.

LOOKING FORWARD

The critique of folk politics advanced in this book is as much a warning as it is a diagnosis.[55] The existing tendencies in the mainstream and radical left are moving towards the folk-political pole, and we seek to reverse this trend. The aim of the first half of the book is therefore to disrupt an increasingly dogmatic set of principles about how to strategise and do politics today. Beginning with a critical take on existing politics, Chapter 2 seeks to diagnose and outline the limits of contemporary folk-political thinking. While the left has rejected the project of hegemony and expansion, Chapter 3 shows how neoliberalism successfully took the opposite path. In the place of folk politics, the second half will suggest an alternative leftist project organised around global and universal emancipation. Chapter 4 argues that a future-orientated left needs to reclaim the initiative for modernisation and its emphasis on progress and universal emancipation. Chapter 5 sets out an analysis of the tendencies of contemporary capitalism, emphasising the crisis of work and social reproduction. These tendencies demand a response, and our argument is that the left should begin mobilising a political project to direct these forces in a progressive manner. In contrast to today's dominant focus on debt and inequality, Chapter 6 envisions a post-work world. Chapters 7 and 8 examine some of the steps that will need to be taken to achieve this vision, which include building a counter-hegemonic movement and rebuilding the capacities of the left. Finally, the Conclusion takes a step back to examine the project of modernity from the perspective of a future-orientated left guided by the goal of universal emancipation. This book is predicated on a simple belief – that a modern left can neither continue with the current system nor return to an idealised past, but must instead face up to the task of building a new future.

Chapter 2

Why Aren't We Winning? A Critique of Today's Left

Goldman Sachs doesn't care if you raise chickens.

Jodi Dean

A key challenge facing the left today is to reckon with the disappointments and failures of the most recent cycle of struggles. From the anti-globalisation to the Occupy movements, we have seen a high point of folk-political practice. Why, despite a considerable mobilisation of people and passions, did these movements fail to achieve any significant change in the political status quo? Some writers have argued that the incapacity of contemporary leftist movements can be explained by their class basis, such as their alleged lack of a working-class component, or the infiltration of reformist liberal interests.[1] Others have argued that the problem lies with the nature of the system and the hurdles placed in front of any transformative project. Yet as we argued last chapter, this only partly explains the recent failures. By contrast, the argument of this chapter is that the problems lie more with the folk-political assumptions that shape the strategic horizon of recent left politics. We seek here to diagnose the limits posed by contemporary folk politics.

As was argued in Chapter 1, folk politics emerges at the junction between a generalised reaction to increasing social complexity and a specific history of leftist movements in the twentieth century. This chapter examines how the folk-political intuitions that were formed in the process have come to shape some of the dominant strands of contemporary leftist politics. We make no claim to cover the entire field of social movements here, but simply focus on what have been the most politically popular and significant moments of the radical left in the past fifteen years. We also do not claim that any of the particular political tactics used by these movements are inherently problematic. The merits of particular tactics are only legible when seen in the context of both the broader historical horizon and the strategy aimed at transforming it. It is in our current setting – of a world overwhelmingly determined by the imperatives of global capitalism, combined with folk-political strategies focused on the local and the spontaneous – that we locate the fundamental weakness of the contemporary left. We begin by examining one of the most popular political tendencies of the past fifteen years – horizontalism – before turning to widespread ideas centred on localism, and the general reactive thrust of most mainstream and radical leftist politics.

HORIZONTALISM

Crystallising in 1970s US social movements and thrust into prominence by the Zapatistas, alter-globalisation activists and the movement of the squares, horizontalism has become the dominant strand of today's radical left.[2] Responding to the twentieth-century failures of state-led political change, horizontalist movements instead advocate changing the world by changing social relations from below.[3] They draw upon a long tradition of theory and practice in anarchism, council communism, libertarian communism and autonomism, in order to – in the words of one proponent – 'change the world without taking power'.[4] At the heart of these movements lies a rejection of the state and other formal institutions, and a privileging of society as the space from which radical change will emerge. Horizontalism rejects the project of hegemony as intrinsically domineering, putting forth an affinity-based politics in its stead.[5] Rather than advocating an appeal to or takeover of the vertical power of the state, horizontalism argues for freely associating individuals to come together, create their own autonomous communities and govern their own lives. In broad terms, we can summarise these ideas in terms of four major commitments:

1. A rejection of all forms of domination
2. An adherence to direct democracy and/or consensus decision-making[6]
3. A commitment to prefigurative politics
4. An emphasis on direct action

Embedded within this set of commitments is a series of problems that constrain and limit their potential in the struggle against global capitalism.

Horizontalism's focus on domination in all its forms is perhaps its signal contribution.[7] Moving beyond the old left's traditional focus on the state and capital, it emphasises the various ways in which other types of domination continue to structure society (racial, patriarchal, sexual, ableist, and so on). It is a significant advance that many of today's radical left have adopted these ideas and centred their practice upon the complete removal of all forms of oppression – a commitment that we believe any serious leftist politics must adopt. Yet the means by which horizontalist movements attempt to overcome domination and oppression often end up being bound by the limits of folk politics. In seeking the direct and unmediated cancellation of social relations of domination, these movements either tend to ignore the more subtle forms of domination that persist, or else fail to construct persistent political structures able to maintain the new social relations in the long term.

The commitment to avoiding all forms of domination is closely tied to a critique of representation – both conceptual and political. In practice, this has led to a rejection of the more hierarchical structures that characterise representative politics.[8] Having experienced the history of corrupt trade unions and rapidly eroded liberal democracies, representation is seen as inevitably leading to self-serving and dominant elites. These structures are to be replaced by direct forms of democracy that privilege immediacy over mediation, invoking a more personal sense of politics.[9] The idea here is that a 'face-to-face democracy' is presumably more natural and authentic, and less prone to the emergence of hierarchies.[10] Political decisions are to be made not by representatives, but instead by individuals representing themselves in person.[11] Direct democracy ends up being taken as a basic value, underpinned by the folk-political intuition that what is immediate is better than what is mediated. Rather than majority rule, parliamentary procedure, or dictates from a central committee, it is consensus that is often the major aim of discussions.[12] Debate and governance should therefore be maximally inclusive, and the process of deliberation itself, as opposed to just its outcomes, is something to be valued.[13] Participatory democracy is understandably a major attraction for many people, particularly in light of the empty, ritualistic gestures of contemporary representative democracies.[14] Many participants speak of the feelings of empowerment they derive from participating in consensus decision-making processes.[15] Maximal inclusivity and consensus are therefore valorised, and the importance of tactics and process is placed above strategic objectives.

Direct democracy, consensus and inclusivity all form part of horizontalism's commitments to prefigurative politics, which aims to create in the here-and-now the world they would like to see. Prefigurative politics is a longstanding tradition on the left, from the anarchism of Kropotkin and Bakunin onwards, but it has only recently come to characterise the leading edges of left-wing politics. The earlier promise that, after the revolution, hierarchies and exclusions would evaporate was little consolation to the women and people of colour whose concerns were ignored by yet another white male leader. Rather than wait for a purported revolution, prefigurative politics attempts to instantiate a new world immediately – again relying on an implicit sense that immediacy is inherently superior to more mediated approaches. At its best, prefigurative politics attempts to embody utopian impulses in bringing the future into concrete existence today.[16] Yet at its worst, an insistence on prefiguration becomes a dogmatic assertion that the means must match the ends, accompanied by ignorance of the structural forces set against it.[17]

If the aim is to create the world we want in the here-and-now, and if recourse to mediating institutions is forbidden (or at least disavowed), then the appropriate form of practice has to be direct action. This is a form of practice that encompasses a wide range of possible tactics, ranging from theatrical protests in the vein of the Situationists, to wildcat strikes, to blockading ports, to burning down luxury housing developments. In these practices we can again see hints of folk politics – the privileging of the direct, the immediate and the intuitive. To be sure, direct action can sometimes be more effective and useful than protests – such as pouring concrete to destroy anti-homeless spikes, or using slow-down methods in workplace struggles.[18] Yet, as we will see, direct action often remains insufficient to secure long-standing change, and in isolation, is typically only a temporary impediment to the powers of state and capital.

Direct democracy, prefigurative politics and direct action are not, we hasten to add, intrinsically flawed.[19] Rather than being denounced in themselves, their utility needs to be judged relative to particular historical situations and particular strategic objectives – in terms of their ability to exert real power to create genuine lasting transformation. The reality of complex, globalised capitalism is that small interventions consisting of relatively non-scalable actions are highly unlikely to ever be able to reorganise our socioeconomic system. As we suggest in the second half of this book, the tactical repertoire of horizontalism can have some use, but only when coupled with other more mediated forms of political organisation and action. Following this broad overview of horizontalism's theoretical commitments and the general issues associated with them, we can now turn to two important sequences in twenty-first-century politics to highlight both the practical possibilities and the strong folk-political limits built into these models. In what follows, we examine two of the strongest cases for horizontalism: the Occupy movement emerging after the 2008 financial crisis and the Argentinean experience in the wake of the country's 2001 default. In each case, we can see both the real successes and the palpable limits of these approaches.

Occupy

The most significant recent embodiment of horizontalist principles occurred in the 'movement of the squares'. While occupations do not require horizontalist governance (indeed, the precursors to the tactic originally came from the military),[20] the vast majority of post-2008 occupations have been organised along such lines. This wave of occupations of public spaces spread rapidly to over 950 cities worldwide in 2011, each inflected with local political, economic, cultural and class concerns. Here we want to examine the failure of the Occupy movement in the Western world, in particular because it highlights the deficiencies of folk-political thinking in the core capitalist countries.[21] Notably, this failure occurred despite the vast range of approaches subsumed under the name of Occupy. In the United States, for example, from Occupy Wall Street to Occupy Oakland, this movement ranged from the dogmatically non-violent to the openly antagonistic, between an often confused liberalism and a militant libertarian communism.[22] Adding to this regional variation was the mixed ideological make-up of the participants, which spanned the political spectrum and included reformist liberals, anti-capitalists, insurrectionist anarchists, anti-state communists and union activists, along with a smattering of anti–Federal Reserve libertarians. In addition to this diversity, there was widespread resistance to the articulation of political demands, making the unity of the movement even more difficult to discern.

It is relatively easy to see why so many were motivated to join the movement. The horizontalist nature of Occupy gave people a means to express themselves in the face of societies that barely registered their voices.[23] Particularly in America, the structure of electoral democracy around two large parties has meant the window of political discourse has become incredibly narrow. The assortment of slogans and causes associated with Occupy testifies to an explosion of suppressed anger and a proliferation of political demands that otherwise went unheard. Even among those who did not directly participate in the occupations, Occupy provided a platform for the excluded in websites such as the 'We are the 99 Percent' Tumblr, with a chorus of voices protesting against economic immiseration and social exclusion.[24] Beyond any direct political result, the opportunity for the frustrations of the excluded to be publicly aired was inspiring and empowering for many.

Occupy also worked to disrupt the ordinary lives of both participants and observers, and allowed people to participate together in a shared political project. In the words of one observer, 'the practice of autonomy provides a lesson in one's own power'.[25] In places such as Oakland, activists frequently pushed towards more radical politics than the usual mediating organisations (such as non-profits) would have allowed. Occupy functioned, like many protest movements, as a way to radicalise those who were involved, especially when they were faced with disproportionately brutal police responses. Occupations were purported to prefigure a new world; but even if that new world has yet to emerge, the movements certainly showed participants what was possible with political solidarity.[26]

Beyond these internal benefits, occupied spaces functioned as bases for actions against the political system (as in protest camps against the G8).[27] The majority of these actions consisted of protest marches and rallies, with the spaces also operating as physical locations for collective decision-making. In relation to external actions, occupied spaces also worked as headquarters for skills training – for example, carrying out acts of civil disobedience, dealing with police repression or providing information on legal rights.[28] In a general sense, occupations worked as the most obvious real-world manifestation of the infrastructure for the overall movement. The occupations were also (though not always) a place for supporting the most marginal sections of society, particularly the homeless.[29] Perhaps most importantly, the occupations provided an insistent focal point for media attention – particularly the Zuccotti Park occupation in New York – and brought many otherwise sidelined issues to the attention of the government and the wider public.[30] At least for a limited time, Occupy was able to draw significant mainstream press and television news attention to issues of economic justice – a real achievement in a heavily neoliberalised media environment.

But despite these successes, there are important ways in which the occupations failed. Numerous commentators from within the movement have already noted a number of these, including the ways in which Occupy's rhetoric of inclusivity hid a series of exclusions based on race, gender, income and free time.[31] Folk-political constraints were contained in the practices and ideas of the movement, and it was these tendencies that ultimately left it incapable of expanding spatially, consolidating temporally or universalising itself. To be sure, some of the movements that made up Occupy had no intention of scaling up, persisting in time or universalising themselves. Many (though not all) horizontalist thinkers place an emphasis on the particular dynamism of relatively short-lived, spontaneous politics, holding that 'relative permanence is not necessarily a virtue'.[32] But whether intended or not, the movement's tendency in practice to prioritise spatial, temporal and conceptual immediacy weakened it collectively, leaving it unable to persist long enough to have a chance of seriously pursuing its basic objectives.

Drawing upon horizontalist principles, the Occupy movement was characterised chiefly by its adherence to direct democracy. While direct democracy can exist in a variety of different forms – from workers' councils to Swiss-style canton democracy – under Occupy it took the general assembly as the dominant organisational form.[33] In an era of declining democratic effectiveness, a new way of doing democracy was one of the most common aspirations articulated by participants in these protests.[34] Still, when fetishised as an end in itself, direct democracy inexorably imposes significant constraints. In the first place, the level of effort and involvement in politics that direct democracy demands leads to problems of sustainability. The participatory economics (Parecon) project, for instance, envisions direct democracy at every level of society; but this vision for a postcapitalist world translates into endlessly ramifying staff meetings over every detail of life – hardly the inspiring stuff of utopian visions.[35] Under Occupy, many general assemblies devolved into similar situations in which even the most mundane of issues had to be painstakingly addressed by a collective.[36] The acrimonious debates over drummers making too much noise in the Zuccotti Park occupation are just one particularly farcical example of this. The more general point is that direct democracy requires a significant amount of participation and effort – in other words, it entails increasing amounts of work. During brief moments of revolutionary enthusiasm, this extra work can become inconsequential; yet after the return to normality it is simply added to the ordinary pressures of everyday life.[37] The extra work of direct democracy is problematic especially because of the constitutive exclusions it entails – particularly for those who are unable to attend physically, those who do not feel comfortable in large groups and those who lack public speaking skills (with all the gendered and racialised biases inherent to these factors).[38] As the Occupy movement went on, the general assemblies simply collapsed, often under the weight of exhaustion and boredom. The conclusion to be drawn from this is that the problem of democracy today is not that people want a say over every single aspect of their lives. The real issue of democratic deficit is that the *most significant* decisions of society are out of the hands of the average person.[39] Direct democracy responds to this problem, but attempts to solve it by making democracy an immediate and bodily experience that rejects mediation. Similar preferences for immediacy in democracy also hold back its spatial scalability. To put it simply, direct democracy requires small communities. It is notable that the hundreds of thousands in Tahrir Square in Egypt did not have a general assembly, and that even at Occupy Wall Street, the general assembly consisted of only a small proportion of the total number of participants.[40] The very mechanisms and ideals of direct democracy (face-to-face discussion) make it difficult for it to exist beyond small communities, and make it virtually impossible to respond to problems of national, regional and global democracy. The spatial constraints of direct democracy also overlook the regressive aspects of small communities. These 'intimate' communities are often home to the most virulent forms of xenophobia, homophobia, racism, pernicious gossip, and all other varieties of backward thinking. Small communities of the kind required by direct democracy are not a suitable goal for a modern left movement. Moreover, participative democracy might well be constructed without them, particularly using the communications technologies available today.

Another folk-political constraint emerged with the emphasis on consensus as a basic goal of the process. The aim of consensus is to reach a decision that is acceptable to everyone, again reliant upon spatial immediacy. As anarchist David Graeber notes, 'It is much easier, in a face-to-face community, to figure out what most members of that community want to do, than to figure out how to convince those who do not to go along with it.'[41] Yet what works well on one scale (the face-to-face community) is much more difficult to make work on larger ones. Perhaps inevitably in the case of a relatively diffuse movement such as Occupy, consensus decision-making led to a lowest-common-denominator set of demands, where they emerged at all. There was also much rhetoric glorifying the absence of determinate demands as somehow radical. These arguments from within the movement identified the making of demands as alienating and divisive, as potentially reducing the role of the movement by appealing to outside powers – such as the state – and hence liable to lead towards the co-optation of the movement.[42] As critics of such views have argued, however, the divisive nature of demands is also a positive: while putting some participants off, they may equally mobilise those committed to achieving the demand in question. Moreover, they work to clarify the real political differences contained in the movement – differences often elided in practice, even where they might prove to be insurmountable.[43]

Further problems with Occupy emerged with its nominal rejection of any forms of organisational verticality. Most notably, this led to problems emerging in the relations between the movement and other similarly minded groups. Whereas the movement of the squares in Egypt and Tunisia built strong connections with existing labour movements, the Western world's Occupy movement largely rejected such associations.[44] This led to three tendencies. The first was a frequently paralysing decisional structure. When actions were taken by Occupy, they often came from a sub-group acting on their own, rather than from the general assembly making a consensus decision.[45] Actions, in other words, did not come from horizontalism. Second, evidence shows that hierarchical organisations are crucial in defending movements against the state. In Occupy, the maintenance of the occupied space against police repression was the result, not of horizontalism, but of vertical institutions that mobilised their members to support the occupation.[46] Similarly, in Egypt, football supporters and religious organisations were central to the defence of Tahrir Square against the violence of the state and reactionaries.[47] Finally, the rejection of verticality in all its forms meant a key mechanism for spatially and temporally expanding the movement was abandoned. Links to labour, social justice, and even political parties would have provided an infrastructure for Occupy to move beyond folk-political parameters. Organised workers, for instance, were crucial in Egypt for turning the general protest into a near general strike, shutting down the country as a result and providing the final blow to the Mubarak regime.[48] Links to political parties have also helped occupations in Iceland, Greece and Spain produce much broader successes. In the end, despite the clear desire to spread Occupy's ideas – and the real success in garnering public attention – the moves necessary to transform the social fabric were never taken.

More fundamentally, though, Occupy constrained itself by enforcing a rigidly prefigurative politics. The basic prefigurative gesture is to embody the future world immediately – to change our ways of relating to each other in order to live the postcapitalist future in the present. The role of occupations is a classic example of this: they often self-consciously aim to enact the space of a non-capitalist world through mutual aid, rejections of hierarchy and rigorous direct democracy. Yet these spaces are understood and built as explicitly temporary – not spaces for sustained change or the working-out of concrete alternatives, let alone ambitious competitors to global capitalism. Instead they are short-term spaces containing the transitory experiences of an immediate community.[49] A pamphlet from a precursor to the Occupy movement makes this particularly clear:

[Students who insisted on no demands] saw the point of occupation as the creation of a momentary opening in capitalist time and space, a rearrangement that sketched the contours of a new society. We side with this anti-reformist position. While we know these free zones will be partial and transitory, the tensions they expose between the real and the possible can push the struggle in a more radical direction.[50]

The acknowledgement that the occupation will be temporary is here combined with a naive belief that maybe this time it will spark a radical change. Prefigurative spaces face a continuous struggle against dissolution for good reasons. First, they require a variety of logistical supports, including housing, food, sanitation, healthcare, defence and legal advice. Most of this does not come from within the prefigurative community, but instead relies upon existing capitalist networks.[51] The social reproduction of encampments is difficult even under the most favourable conditions, and even established utopian communities (often religious in nature) typically find it impossible to remain independent and self-sustaining.[52] Second, prefigurative spaces are often subject to state and corporate repression – and if they are not, it is typically because they pose no threat to the existing social order. The Zapatistas, for example, are permitted to exist in relative freedom simply because the state and capital do not see them as a threat.[53] The moment a prefigurative space becomes a threat is the moment when repression weighs down on it, and when its fetishisation of horizontalism becomes a serious liability. Prefigurative politics, at its worst, therefore ignores the forces aligned against the creation and expansion of a new world. The simple positing and practising of a new world is insufficient to overcome these forces, as the repression faced by Occupy demonstrated.[54]

The immediate question that must be asked of any prefigurative politics is therefore: How can it be expanded and scaled up?[55] Even granting the problematic assumption that most people would want to live as the Occupy camps did, what efforts might be possible to physically and socially expand these spaces? When theorists face up to this question, vague hand-waving usually ensues: moments will purportedly 'resonate' with each other; small everyday actions will somehow make a qualitative shift to 'crack open' society; riots and blockades will 'spread and multiply'; experiences will 'contaminate' participants and expand; pockets of prefigurative resistance will just 'spontaneously erupt'.[56] In any case, the difficult task of traversing from the particular to the universal, from the local to the global, from the temporary to the permanent, is elided by wishful thinking. The strategic imperatives to expand, extend and universalise are left unfulfilled.

If Occupy was unsuccessful in expanding prefigurative spaces beyond the margins of society, these protest camps could still be useful as launching pads for direct action. Indeed, one of the most notable achievements of the Occupy movement was to establish a social and physical infrastructure that could act as a foundation for direct actions. In countries like Greece and Spain, debt strikes have been organised and picket lines formed for workers without the right to strike. Other Occupy movements supported squatters, provided food for the homeless, set up pirate media, mobilised to prevent evictions, protested against government cuts and provided humanitarian relief after natural disasters. But the influence of Occupy should not be overstated. For instance, many of the successful eviction and foreclosure movements have been extensions of pre-existing work done by movements such as the black activist–led Take Back the Land.[57] More broadly, the problem is that direct actions generally act on surface effects, patching the wounds of capitalism but leaving the underlying problems and structures intact. Foreclosures continue apace, consumer debt rises to new heights, workers are thrown out into the streets, and the homeless population surges. In the case of Occupy, what became apparent was the limits of a propaganda of the deed.[58] While direct action can have real successes, it remains localised and temporary, and in this it remains folk-political. Direct action can be effective in mitigating the worst excesses of capitalism, but it can never address the difficult problem of attacking a globally dispersed *abstraction*, often focusing instead on intuitive targets.[59] The project of an expansive left – a left aiming to transform capitalism in fundamental ways – remains absent.

The image of Occupy that emerges here is of a movement that was wedded to certain assumptions about the benefits of local spaces, small communities, direct democracy and temporary autonomy at the margins of society. In turn, these beliefs rendered the movement incapable of expanding spatially, establishing sustainable transformations and universalising itself. The Occupy movements achieved real victories in creating solidarity, giving a voice to disenchanted and marginalised people, and raising public awareness. But they nevertheless remained an archipelago of prefigurative islands, surrounded by an implacably hostile capitalist environment. The proximate cause for the movement's failure was state repression, in the form of police clad in riot gear ruthlessly clearing the occupied spaces across the United States. But the structural causes were built into the assumptions and practices of the movement. Without the central focus of the occupied spaces, the movement dispersed and fragmented. Ultimately, the organisational form of these movements could not overcome the problems of scalability and construct a form of persistent power capable of effectively resisting the inevitable reaction from the state.

What may work quite well on one scale – perhaps up to a hundred people – becomes increasingly difficult to operate effectively when extended beyond that.[60] If a truly ambitious left politics is to take on global actors – the neoliberal capitalist system and its governing institutions, leading governments and their armies and police forces, and an entire planet's worth of corporations and financial entities – then operating beyond the merely local is essential. While there is certainly much to learn from these movements, it is our contention that, on their own, they will remain ineffective at bringing about large-scale change.

Argentina

If any case from recent history offers hope for the sufficiency of horizontalism, it would appear to be Argentina, which achieved a large-scale national turn towards horizontalism and expansive worker control over factories. Yet a brief look at the Argentinean experience actually reveals new dimensions to the limits of folk-political approaches. In Argentina's circumstances, the immediate imperative for new social organisations came from the collapse of the national economy. Struck by a massive recession in 1998, the economy buckled and lost over a quarter of its GDP by 2002. Tensions reached a peak in December 2001, with government restrictions and financial chaos provoking the people into mass protests. The result was the collapse of the government and an eventual default on their debts. With the government both unable and unwilling to help its population, people were forced to find new ways to provide for themselves.

In the wake of these challenges, many of the Argentinean people took it upon themselves to self-organise and create new political and economic structures. To a significant degree, these responses were organised around explicitly horizontalist principles.[61] As with Occupy, there are a variety of benefits that can be identified in the horizontalist organising of Argentina. Perhaps most importantly, these movements were able to disrupt the common-sense norms of neoliberal society, moving beyond market individualism and negative solidarity. The fostering of bonds between individuals helped to overcome the antagonism that most protests and strikes often face from other parts of society. Like Occupy, but on a broader scale, Argentina's horizontal movements were also quickly able to provide the means for social reproduction under crisis conditions.[62]

But while these experiments with horizontalism brought about a number of achievements, its experience also revealed several further problems. Principal among these is the limitations faced by neighbourhood assemblies as an organisational form. Modelled on horizontalist principles, the neighbourhood assemblies arose in response to the immediate needs and possibilities opened up by the crisis. Like the general assembly of Occupy, they enabled people to have a newfound voice. But even when joined together in inter-neighbourhood assemblies, they never approached the point of replacing the state, or of being able to present themselves as a viable alternative. The functions of the state – welfare, healthcare, redistribution, education, and so on – were not about to be replaced by the horizontalist movement, even at its height of participation. It thus remained a localised response to the crisis. Further limitations surfaced as these assemblies could only function by either rejecting organised – which is to say, collective – interests, or incorporating them, and thus being overwhelmed.[63] Collective interests were incapable of being brought into the decision-making process without breaking it, since they often took control over discussion and debate. Problematically, these assemblies operated best on an individualistic basis.

Other organisational experiments in Argentina involved the spread of worker-controlled factories. In the wake of the economic crisis, some shuttered businesses were taken over and maintained by their employees. These factories helped to keep workers in jobs, and there is some evidence that they provided better pay for their workers. Unfortunately, despite the attention given to them, the total number of people involved was relatively small: in the most optimistic estimates, there were around 250 factories incorporating just under 10,000 workers.[64] With a labour force of over 18 million, this means far less than 0.1 per cent of the economy was participating in worker-controlled factories. Not only were these factories a minor part of the overall economy, but they also remained necessarily embedded within capitalist social relations. The dream of escape is just that: a dream. Tied to the imperative to create a profit, worker-controlled businesses can be just as oppressive and environmentally damaging as any large-scale business, but without the efficiencies of scale. Such problems are widespread across the worker-cooperative experience, having arisen not only in Argentina, but also in the Zapatista model and across America.[65]

Beyond these organisational limits, the key problem with Argentina as a model for postcapitalism is that it was simply a salve for the problems of capitalism, not an alternative to it. As the economy started to improve, participation in the neighbourhood assemblies and alternative economies drastically declined.[66] The post-crisis horizontalist movements in Argentina were built as an emergency response to the collapse of the existing order, not as a competitor to a relatively well-functioning order. Indeed, the more widespread problem with contemporary horizontalism is that it often sees emergency situations – in the wake of a hurricane, earthquake or economic meltdown – as representative of a better world.[67] It is a struggle, to say the least, to see how post-disaster conditions are an improvement for the vast majority of the world's population. A politics that finds its best expression in the breakdown of social and economic order is not an alternative, so much as a knee-jerk survival instinct. Equally problematic is the tendency for horizontalists to find political potential in the mundane ways we organise horizontally in everyday life – friends gathering together, parties, festivals, and so on.[68] The problem is that such modes of organising are not scalable beyond a small community – and, more to the point, are not useful for certain political goals. As the Argentinean example shows, these modes of organising can be valuable for basic neighbourhood survival and for creating a sense of solidarity between people. But horizontalism struggles to compete against more organised interests, to sustain itself once a base level of normality returns, and to achieve long-term and large-scale political goals such as providing universal healthcare, high-level education and social security. These approaches remain useful in exceptional circumstances and for a small range of goals, but they will neither revolutionise society nor genuinely threaten global capitalism.

In the case of both neighbourhood assemblies and worker-controlled factories, we see that the primary organisational models of horizontalism are insufficient. They are often reactive tactics that fail to compete in the antago-nistic environment of global capitalism. On a theoretical level, and in the actual experiences of Occupy and Argentina, the limits of horizontalism have repeatedly been made clear over the past decade. While recognising the important capacity of horizontalist tactics to provide small-scale support to communities and to temporarily disrupt certain exploitative practices, the commitment to fetishised versions of consensus, direct action, and particularly prefigurative politics, constrains the possibilities of expanding and overtaking existing social systems.

LOCALISM

Less politically radical than horizontalism, though no less ubiquitous, is local-ism. As an ideology, localism extends far beyond the left, inflecting the politics of pro-capitalists, anti-capitalists, radicals and mainstream culture alike, as a new kind of political common sense. Shared between all of these is a belief that the abstraction and sheer scale of the modern world is at the root of our present political, ecological and economic problems, and that the solution therefore lies in adopting a 'small is beautiful' approach to the world.[69] Small-scale actions, local economies, immediate communities, face-to-face interac-tion – all of these responses characterise the localist worldview. In a time when most of the political strategies and tactics developed in the nineteenth and twentieth centuries appear blunted and ineffectual, localism has a seductive logic to it. In all its diverse variants, from centre-right communitarianism[70] to ethical consumerism,[71] developmental microloans, and contemporary anar-chist practice,[72] the promise it offers to do something concrete, enabling politi-cal action with immediately noticeable effects, is empowering on an individ-ual level. But this sense of empowerment can be misleading. The problem with localism is that, in attempting to reduce large-scale systemic problems to the more manageable sphere of the local community, it effectively denies the systemically interconnected nature of today's world. Problems such as global exploitation, planetary climate change, rising surplus populations, and the repeated crises of capitalism are abstract in appearance, complex in structure, and non-localised. Though they touch upon every locality, they are never fully manifested in any particular region. Fundamentally, these are systemic and abstract problems, requiring systemic and abstract responses.

While much of the populist localism on the right can easily be dismissed as regressive macho fantasy (for example, secessionist libertarianism), sinister ideological cover for austerity economics (the UK Conservative Party's 'Big Society') or downright racist (the nationalist or fascist blaming of immigrants for structural economic problems), the localism of the left has been less thor-oughly scrutinised. Though undoubtedly well-meaning, both the radical and mainstream left partake in localist politics and economics to their detriment. In what follows we will critically examine two of the more popular variants – local food and economic localism – which in very different areas exemplify the problematic dynamics of localism in general.

Local food

With a cachet that reaches far beyond typical political circles, localism has recently come to dominate discussions of the production, distribution and consumption of food. Most influential here have been the interlinked movements known as 'slow food' and 'locavorism' (eating locally). The slow-food movement began in the mid 1980s in Italy, partly as a protest against the ever-increasing encroachment of fast-food chains. Slow food, as its name suggests, stands for everything McDonald's does not: local food, traditional recipes, slow eating and highly skilled production.[73] It is food that offers the most visceral embodiment of the benefits of the slow lifestyle, overcoming the vicissitudes of fast-paced capitalism by returning to an older culture of savouring meals and traditional production techniques.[74] But even its proponents admit that there are difficulties involved in living the slow-food lifestyle: 'Few of us have the time, money, energy or discipline to be a model Slow Foodie.'[75]

Without an assessment of how our lives are structured by social, political and economic pressures that make it easier to eat pre-prepared food than embrace the slow-food lifestyle, the end result is a variant of ethical consumerism with a hedonistic twist. It is patently correct that taking one's time to enjoy a well-prepared meal can be a pleasurable experience. Paying attention to a meal recasts the experience from one of pure utility into a more social and aesthetic experience. But there are structural reasons why we do not choose to do this often – reasons that are not the result of any individual moral failing. The structure of work, for example, is a primary reason why many of us are unable to enjoy slow eating, or meals prepared according to the ideals of the slow-food movement. Slow food might not always require money, but it always requires time. For those who have to work multiple jobs to support their families, time is at a premium. What is more, the gender politics of slow food are problematic, given that we live in patriarchal societies where the majority of food preparation is still presumed to be the task of wives and mothers.[76] While 'fast' food or pre-prepared meals might be unhealthy, their popularity enables the freeing up of women to live lives that are less marked by the everyday drudgery of feeding their families.[77] As innocent as it may at first seem, the slow-food movement, like many other forms of ethical consumerism, fails to think in large-scale terms about how its ideas might work within the broader context of rapacious capitalism.

Closely linked to the slow-food movement are locavorism and the '100-mile diet' – a food politics that emphasises eating locally. Locavorism holds that locally sourced food is not only more likely to be healthy, but is also a vital component of our efforts to reduce carbon outputs, and hence our impact on the environment. It situates itself, therefore, as a response to a global issue. Moreover, locavorism claims to be one way to overcome the alienation of our relationship to food under capitalism. By eating food grown or produced in our locality, so this logic runs, we will be able to get back in touch with the production of our food and reclaim it from the dead hands of a capitalism that has run amok.[78] Compared to the slow-food movement, locavorism positions itself more explicitly, and politically, against globalisation. In doing so, it appeals to a constellation of folk-political ideas relating to the primacy of the local as a horizon of political action, and of the virtues of the local over the global, the immediate over the mediated, the simple over the complex.

These ideas condense often complex environmental issues into questions of *individual* ethics. One of the most serious (and intrinsically collective) crises of our times is thus effectively privatised. This personalised environmental ethic is exemplified in localist food politics – in particular, in the moral (and price) premium placed on locally grown food. Here we find ecologically motivated arguments (for reducing energy expenditure by reducing the distances over which food is transported, for example) combined with class differentiation (in the form of marketing designed to promote identification with organic food). Similarly, complex problems are condensed into poorly formulated shorthand. For instance, the idea of 'food miles' – identifying the distances that food products have travelled, so as to reduce carbon outputs – appears a reasonable one. The problem is that it is all too often taken to be sufficient on its own as a guide to ethical action. As a 2005 report by the UK's Department of Agriculture and Food found, while the environmental impacts of transporting food were indeed considerable, a single indicator based on total food miles was inadequate as a measure of sustainability.[79] Most notably, the food-miles metric emphasises an aspect of food production that contributes a relatively small amount to overall carbon outputs. When it is simply assumed that 'small is beautiful', we can all too easily ignore the fact that the energy costs associated with producing food locally may well exceed the total costs of transporting it from a more suitable climate.[80] Even for the purpose of assessing the contribution of food transportation, food miles are a poor metric. Air freight, for example, makes up a relatively small portion of total food miles, but it makes up a disproportionately large slice of total food-related CO_2 emissions.[81] The energy consumption involved in putting food on our plates is important, but it cannot be captured in anything as simple as food miles, or in the idea that 'local is best'. Indeed, highly inefficient local food production techniques may be more costly than efficiently grown globally sourced foodstuffs. The bigger question here relates to the priorities we place on the types of food we produce, how that production is controlled, who consumes that food and at what cost.

Localist food politics flattens the complexities it is trying to resolve into a simplistic binary: global, bad; local, good. What is needed, by contrast, are less simplistic ways of looking at complex problems – an analysis that takes into account the global food system as a whole, rather than intuitive short-hand formulae such as food miles, or 'organic' versus non-'organic' foods. It is likely that the ideal method of global food production will be some complex mixture of local initiatives, industrial farming practices, and global systems of distribution. It is equally likely that an analysis capable of calculating the best means to grow and distribute food lies outside the grasp of any individual consumer, requiring significant technical knowledge, collective effort and global coordination. None of this is well served by a culture that simply values the local.

Local economics

Localism, in all its forms, represents an attempt to abjure the problems and politics of scale involved in large systems such as the global economy, politics and the environment. Our problems are increasingly systemic and global, and they require an equally systemic response. Action must always to some extent occur at the local level – and indeed some localist ideas, such as resiliency, can be useful. But localism-as-ideology goes much further, rejecting the systemic analysis that might guide and coordinate instances of local action to confront, oppose and potentially supplant oppressive instances of global power or looming planetary threats. Nowhere is the inability of localist solutions to challenge complex global problems more apparent than in movements towards localised business, banking and economics. Since the 2008 financial crisis, there have been a number of trends on the broad left towards reforming our economic and monetary systems. While much of this work is useful, one prominent strand has focused on transforming economic systems through localisation. The problem with big business, so the thinking goes, is not so much its inherently exploitative nature but the scale of the enterprises involved. Smaller businesses and banks would supposedly be more reflective of the local community's needs.

One popular recent campaign, the 'move your money' movement, centred on the idea that, if it was the scale of banks that was to blame for the financial crisis, then customers ought to move their funds collectively to smaller, more virtuous institutions. Ethical-consumerist campaigns like this offer a semblance of effective action – they provide a meaningful narrative about the problems of the system and indicate the simple and pain-free action necessary to resolve it. As with most folk-political actions, it has all the appearances and feeling of having done something. Major banks are positioned as the bad guys, and individuals can supposedly produce significant effects just by moving their money into smaller, local banks and credit unions. What this model neglects is the complex abstractions of the modern banking system. Money circulates as immediately global and immediately interconnected with every other market. In any situation where a small bank or credit union has more deposits than it is able to profitably reinvest within its locality, it will inevitably seek investments within the broader financial system. Indeed, a reading of the accounts of smaller banks in the United States reveals that they partake in and contribute to the same global financial markets as everyone else – investing in Treasury, mortgage or corporate bonds while often participating in socially destructive lending practices that equal those of the major banks.[82] While clearly a reformist measure, 'move your money' might at least have been expected to lead to some transformations in the composition of the US banking system. However, as of September 2013, total assets held by the six largest US banks had increased by 37 per cent since the financial crisis. Indeed, by every available measure the big US banks are larger today than at the beginning of the crisis, holding 67 per cent of all assets in the US banking system.[83] And while legislative efforts across the world have made some attempts to impose restraints on the activities that led to the crisis (requiring increased capital asset ratios and regular 'stress tests' designed to avoid further bailouts), risky lending continues,[84] and risky derivatives holdings remain at staggeringly high levels.[85]

If localist efforts to constrain the size of the largest banks appear doomed to failure, what are we to make of alternative campaigns to replicate some of the local banks that make up much of the continental European banking system? For example, 70 per cent of the German banking sector consists of community or smaller-sized banks.[86] German and Swiss community banks, their proponents argue, pool risks collectively and are mutually owned, with high degrees of autonomy to take advantage of local knowledge, and as a result generally remained profitable throughout the financial crisis.[87] It is also argued that local banks of this type are more likely to lend to small businesses than the larger institutions that are more common in the United States and the UK. There are advantages to some local banking models, but their stability is often overstated. For example, despite being highly localised and under community control, Spain's community banks (the *cajas*) took significant risks in the property market and other speculative investments in the 2000s, necessitating thoroughgoing financial restructuring after the 2008 crisis. Though under the alleged control of boards with community representation, investment decisions were effectively taken with little proper oversight. Localisation here meant the politicisation of allegedly disinterested governance boards, turning some *cajas* into platforms for local government investment in speculative property schemes, as a culture of cronyism took hold.[88] With the worst of Spain's banking crisis centred on the local banks, restructuring meant the merging of local banks to form larger institutions. Even in Germany, often touted as having the best localised banking system in the world, there were issues with some regional banks. The Landesbanken, for example, were heavily invested in structured credit products that performed particularly poorly during the financial crisis.[89] The lesson to draw from this is that there is nothing inherent in smaller institutions that will enable them to resist the worst excesses of contemporary finance – and that the idea of cleanly separating the local from the global is today impossible. Political capture, the need to seek profitable investments beyond those available in the local area, and simply the high returns of more risky investments, are all factors leading local banks to participate in the broader financial system. Even mutual ownership is no guarantee of financial probity, as demonstrated by the recent travails of the UK's Co-operative Bank, which almost collapsed entirely following an ill-conceived takeover of a building society in 2009.[90] The systemic problems of the financial system can only be properly dealt with by taking apart financial power, whether by means of broad regulation (as was briefly achieved under postwar Keynesianism) or more revolutionary methods. Fetishising the small and the local seems to be a means of simply ignoring the more significant ways in which the system could be transformed for the better.

RESISTANCE IS FUTILE

A folk-political sentiment has manifested itself in both radical horizontalist and more moderate localist movements, yet similar intuitions underpin a broad range of the contemporary left. Across these groups, a series of judgments are widely accepted: small is beautiful, the local is ethical, simpler is better, permanence is oppressive, progress is over. These kinds of ideas are favoured over any counter-hegemonic project – a politics that might contend with capitalist power at the largest scales. At its heart, much of contemporary folk politics therefore expresses a 'deep pessimism: it assumes we can't make large-scale, collective social change'.[91] This defeatist attitude runs amok on the left – and perhaps with good reason, considering the continued failures of the past thirty years.

For centre-left political parties, nostalgia for a lost past is the best that can be hoped for. The most radical content to be found here consists of dreams of social democracy and the so-called 'golden age' of capitalism.[92] Yet the very conditions which once made social democracy possible no longer exist. The capitalist 'golden age' was predicated on the production paradigm of the orderly factory environment, where (white, male) workers received security and a basic standard of living in return for a lifetime of stultifying boredom and social repression. Such a system depended on an international hierarchy of empires, colonies and an underdeveloped periphery; a national hierarchy of racism and sexism; and a rigid family hierarchy of female subjugation. Moreover, social democracy relied on a particular balance of forces between classes (and a willingness for compromise between them), and even this was only possible in the wake of the unprecedented destruction caused by the Great Depression and World War II, and in the face of external threats from communism and fascism. For all the nostalgia many may feel, this regime is both undesirable and impossible to recover. But the more pertinent point is that even if we could go back to social democracy, we should not. We can do better, and the social democratic adherence to jobs and growth means it will always err on the side of capitalism and at the expense of the people. Rather than modelling our future on a nostalgic past, we should aim to create a future for ourselves. The move beyond the constraints of the present will not be achieved through a return to a more humanised capitalism reconstructed from a misty-eyed recollection of the past.

While nostalgia for a lost past is clearly not an adequate response, neither is today's widespread glorification of resistance. Resistance always means resistance against another active force. In other words, it is a defensive and reactive gesture, rather than an active movement. We do not resist a new world into being; we resist in the name of an old world. The contemporary emphasis on resistance therefore belies a defensive stance towards the encroachments of expansionary capitalism. Trade unions, for instance, position themselves as resisting neoliberalism with demands to 'save our health system' or 'stop austerity'; but these demands simply reveal a conservative disposition at the heart of the movement. According to these demands, the best one can hope for is small impediments in the face of a predatory capitalism. We can only struggle to keep what we already have, as limited and crisis-ridden as it may be. Even in left-leaning Latin America this trend is visible, with the most significant successes largely around efforts to impede transnational corporations, particularly in relation to mining.[93] In many circles resistance has come to be glorified, obscuring the conservative nature of such a stance behind a veil of radical rhetoric. Resistance is seen to be all that is possible, while constructive projects are nothing but a dream.[94] While it can be important in some circumstances, in the task of building a new world, resistance is futile.

Other movements argue for an approach of withdrawal, whereby individuals exit from existing social institutions. Horizontalism is closely linked to this approach, being predicated on the rejection of existing institutions and the creation of autonomous forms of community. Indeed, the recent history of activism has tended towards such approaches.[95] Often these approaches are explicitly opposed to complex societies, meaning that the ultimate implied destination is some form of communitarianism or anarcho-primitivism.[96] Others suggest making oneself invisible in order to evade detection and repression by the state.[97] At the extreme, some argue for what amounts to a left-wing survivalism: civilisation is in catastrophe,[98] and we should therefore become invisible,[99] retreat to small communes,[100] and learn how to grow food, hunt, heal and defend ourselves.[101] If left at the level of survivalism, these kinds of positions, while perhaps unappealing, would at least have some consistency. They at least have the virtue of being open about their implications. However, arguments for withdrawal and exit too easily confuse the idea of a social logic *separate* from capitalism with a social logic that is *antagonistic* to capitalism – or, in an even stronger claim, that *poses a threat* to capitalist logics.[102] Yet capitalism has been and will continue to be compatible with a wide range of different practices and autonomous spaces. The Spanish town of Marinaleda offers a useful example of this. Over the course of three decades, this small community (pop. 2,700) has built up a 'communist utopia' that has expropriated land, built its own housing and co-operatives, kept living costs low, and provided work for everyone. Yet the limits of such an approach for transforming capitalism are quickly revealed: housing materials are provided by the regional government, agricultural subsidies come from the European Union, jobs are sustained by the rejection of labour-saving devices, income still comes from selling goods on wider capitalist markets, and businesses remain subjected to capitalist competition and the global financial crisis.[103] Marinaleda is but one example of how the project of withdrawing, escaping or exiting from capitalism is still contained within a folk-political horizon, within which defending small bunkers of autonomy against the onslaught of capitalism is the best that can be hoped for. Yet we would argue not only that more can be hoped for (and achieved), but that, in the absence of broad and systematic contention, even those small pockets of resistance are likely to be swiftly eradicated.

ALL POLITICS IS LOCAL?

Horizontalism, localism, nostalgia, resistance and withdrawal all embody, to greater or lesser degrees, folk-political intuitions about how to do politics. And they all remain inadequate for the task of transforming capitalism. But this is not to say that they should be rejected in their entirety. As the rest of the book will make clear, there are a number of important elements to retain from these approaches. Rather than being intrinsically malign, folk politics is simply partial, temporary and insufficient. Various horizontalist approaches, for example, have raised important questions about power, domination and hierarchy – but they have not developed adequate responses to them. Folk politics as a tendency retreats from the difficulty of these problems by attempting to dispel them from the outset. Yet, in a world where dominance, power, hierarchy and exploitation are imposed upon us, such questions must be confronted directly, rather than retreated from.[104] Likewise, in a banal sense, all politics is local. We act upon things in our immediate vicinity in order to change larger political structures. We cannot simply reject the local. But today's folk-political tendencies invoke a stronger sense of local politics: a retreat into the local in order to avoid the problems of a complex and abstract society; an assumption about the authenticity and naturalness of the local; and a neglect of scalable and sustainable practices that might go beyond the local. While all politics begins within the local, folk politics *remains* local.

In the end, a significant part of the problem with folk politics lies less in the particular tactics and practices it tends to adhere to than in the overarching strategic vision into which it is placed. Protests, marches, occupations, sit-ins and blockades all have their place: none of these tactics in themselves are fundamentally folk-political. But when they are marshalled by a strategic vision that sees temporary and small-scale changes as the horizon of success, or when they are extrapolated beyond the particular conditions that made them effective, they are inevitably going to be bound up within folk-political thinking. If the tactic of occupation, for example, is employed in order to create exemplars and temporary spaces of non-capitalist social relations, it will inevitably fail to achieve substantial change. If, on the other hand, it is understood as a mechanism to produce solidarity networks and mobilise them for further action, then it may still have use within broader counter-hegemonic strategies. But this sort of strategic reflection about the virtues and limits of any particular action is what is absent from too much of the left today. The numerous protests and marches and occupations typically operate without any sense of strategy, simply acting as dispersed and independent blips of resistance. There is far too little thought given to how to combine these various actions, and how they might function together to collectively build a better world. Instead we are left with actions that sometimes succeed but which rarely have an overarching eye to how this contributes to medium- and long-term goals.[105] In the next chapter, we look at how the right undertook such strategic reflection and orchestrated a situation in which neoliberalism became the dominant common sense of our time.

Chapter 3

Why Are They Winning?
The Making of Neoliberal Hegemony

We are all Keynesians now.

Milton Friedman

If our era is dominated by one hegemonic ideology, it is that of neoliberalism. It is widely assumed that the most effective away to produce and distribute goods and services is by allowing instrumentally rational individuals to exchange via the market. State regulations and national industries are, by contrast, seen as distortions and inefficiencies holding back the productive dynamics inherent to free markets. Today, this vision of how economies should operate is what both its critics and proponents take as a baseline. Neoliberalism sets the agenda for what is realistic, necessary and possible. While the economic crisis of 2008 has upset the blind belief in neoliberalism, it nevertheless remains an entrenched part of our worldview – so much so that it is difficult even for its critics to picture coherent alternatives. Yet this ideology of neoliberalism did not emerge fully formed from the minds of Milton Friedman or Friedrich Hayek, or even the Chicago School, and its global hegemony did not arise inevitably from capitalism's logic.

In its origins, neoliberalism was a fringe theory. Its adherents found it difficult to gain employment, were often untenured, and were mocked by the Keynesian mainstream.[1] Neoliberalism was far from being the world-dominating ideology it would eventually become. The question this chapter will focus on is: How did a small band of neoliberals manage to reshape the world so radically? Neoliberalism was never a given, never a necessary endpoint of capitalist accumulation. Rather, it was a political project from the beginning, and a massively successful one in the end. It succeeded by skilfully constructing an ideology and the infrastructure to support it, and by operating in a non–folk-political manner. This chapter aims to show that neoliberalism functioned as an expansive universal ideology. From humble beginnings, the universalising logic of neoliberalism made it capable of spreading across the world, infiltrating the media, the academy, the policy world, education, labour practices, and the affects, feelings and identities of everyday people. This chapter therefore focuses primarily on how neoliberal hegemony was constructed, rather than on the specific content of neoliberalism. What is of greatest interest is how it was able to transform the ideological and material fabric of global society.

What standard histories of neoliberalism often neglect is the ways in which the main components of this ideological architecture were systematically and painstakingly set in place in the decades prior to the 1970s.[2] It is in this prehistory of the neoliberal era that we can discern an alternative mode of political action – one that evades the limits of folk politics. This is not to say that this prehistory provides a model for any future leftist programme simply to copy; rather, it is an instructive case study in how the right was able to move beyond folk politics and create a new hegemony. The history of neoliberalism has been one of contingencies, struggle, concentrated action, patience and grand-scale strategic thinking. It has been a flexible idea, actualised in various ways according to the specific circumstances it encountered: from Germany in the 1940s, Chile in the 1970s and the UK in the 1980s, to post-Hussein Iraq in the 2000s. This versatility has made neoliberalism a sometimes contradictory project, but one that succeeds precisely by transforming these contradictions into productive tensions.[3]

These tensions and variations have led some to believe that the term 'neoliberalism' is meaningless and should be relegated to polemics. But the term has some validity, even if it is often used loosely. In popular perception, neoliberalism is usually identified with a glorification of free markets – a position that also entails a commitment to free trade, private property rights and the free movement of capital. Defining neoliberalism as the veneration of free markets is problematic, however, because many ostensibly neoliberal states do not adhere to free-market policies. Others have argued that neoliberalism is predicated upon instilling competition wherever possible.[4] This makes sense of the drive towards privatisation, but it fails to explain the debates within neoliberalism about whether competition is an ultimate good or not.[5] Some take into account these tensions within neoliberalism and recognise it as the political, rather than economic, project of a particular class.[6] There is certainly some truth to this claim, but, taken at face value, it cannot explain why neoliberal ideology was rejected for so long by the capitalist classes that purportedly benefit from it.

Our view is that, contrary to its popular presentation, neoliberalism differs from classical liberalism in ascribing a significant role to the state.[7] A major task of neoliberalism has therefore been to take control of the state and repurpose it.[8] Whereas classical liberalism advocated respect for a naturalised sphere supposedly beyond state control (the natural laws of man and the market), neoliberals understand that markets are not 'natural'.[9] Markets do not spontaneously emerge as the state backs away, but must instead be consciously constructed, sometimes from the ground up.[10] For instance, there is no natural market for the commons (water, fresh air, land), or for healthcare, or for education.[11] These and other markets must be built through an elaborate array of material, technical and legal constructs. Carbon markets required years to be built;[12] volatility markets exist in large part as a function of abstract financial models;[13] and even the most basic markets require intricate design.[14] Under neoliberalism, the state therefore takes on a significant role in creating 'natural' markets. The state also has an important role in sustaining these markets – neoliberalism demands that the state defend property rights, enforce contracts, impose anti-trust laws, repress social dissent and maintain price stability at all costs. This latter demand, in particular, has greatly expanded in the wake of the 2008 crisis into the full-spectrum management of monetary issues through central banks. We therefore make a grave mistake if we think the neoliberal state is intended simply to step back from markets. The unprecedented interventions by central banks into financial markets are symptomatic not of the neoliberal state's collapse, but of its central function: to create and sustain markets at all costs.[15] Yet it has been an arduous and winding path from neoliberalism's origins to the present, in which its ideas hold sway over those injecting trillions of dollars into the market.

THE NEOLIBERAL THOUGHT COLLECTIVE

The origins of neoliberalism are disparate, both geographically and intellectually. Elements of what would become the neoliberal project can be found in 1920s Vienna, 1930s Chicago and London, and 1930s and 1940s Germany. Throughout these decades, national movements worked on the margins of academia to maintain liberal ideas. It was not until 1938 that these independent movements were to gain their first transnational organisation, resulting from the Walter Lippmann Colloquium held in Paris just before the eruption of World War II. For the first time, this event brought together the classical liberal theorists, the new German ordoliberals, the British LSE liberals, and Austrian economists such as Friedrich Hayek and Ludwig von Mises. It focused on the historical ebbing of classical liberalism in the face of rising collectivism, and it was here that the first steps were made in consolidating a group of new liberal thinkers. Out of this event a new organisation – Centre International d'Études pour la Rénovation du Libéralisme – arose with the explicit aim of developing and spreading a new liberalism. The outbreak of World War II quickly put an end to the ambitious aims of this organisation, but the network of people involved would continue to work towards developing a *neo*liberalism. The seeds of the global neoliberal infrastructure had been planted.

It was an idea of Hayek's that ultimately mobilised this infrastructure into a 'neoliberal thought collective' and inaugurated the slow rise of the new hegemony.[16] Since the Walter Lippmann Colloquium had been buried in the onslaught of World War II, the transnational infrastructure of an incipient neoliberalism had to be reconstructed. A chance meeting with a Swiss businessman in 1945 gave Hayek the financial means to put his ideas into action.[17] Thus was born the Mont Pelerin Society (MPS): a closed intellectual network that provided the basic ideological infrastructure for neoliberalism to ferment.[18] It is no exaggeration to say that almost all of the important figures in the postwar creation of neoliberalism were in attendance at its first meeting in 1947, including the Austrian economists, the UK liberals, the Chicago School, the German ordoliberals and a French contingent.[19]

From its beginnings, the MPS was consciously focused on changing political common sense and sought to develop a liberal utopia.[20] It explicitly understood that this intellectual framework would then be actively filtered down through think tanks, universities and policy documents, in order to institutionalise and eventually monopolise the ideological terrain.[21] In a letter to those he had invited, Hayek wrote that the purpose of the MPS was

> to enlist the support of the best minds in formulating a programme which has a chance of gaining general support. Our effort therefore differs from any political task in that it must be essentially a long-run effort, concerned not so much with what would be immediately practicable, but with the beliefs which must gain ascendance if the dangers are to be averted which at the moment threaten individual freedom.[22]

The Society thus made a 'commitment to a long-run *war of position* in the "battle of ideas" ... Privatized, strategic, elite deliberation was therefore established as the modus operandi.'[23] Opening the ten-day event, Hayek diagnosed the problem of the new liberals: a lack of alternatives to the existing (Keynesian) order. There was no 'consistent philosophy of the opposition groups' and no 'real programme' for change.[24] As a result of this diagnosis, Hayek defined the central goal of the MPS as changing elite opinion in order to establish the parameters within which public opinion could then be formed. Contrary to a common assumption, capitalists did not initially see neoliberalism as being in their interests. A major task of the MPS was therefore to educate capitalists as to why they should become neoliberals.[25] In order to achieve these goals, the vision of effective action was one of operating on the invisible framework of political common sense that was formed by the ideas circulating in elite networks. From its origins, the MPS eschewed folk politics by working with a global horizon, by working abstractly (outside the parameters of existing possibilities) and by formulating a clear strategic conception of the terrain to be occupied – namely, elite opinion – in order to change political common sense.

Behind this set of goals there lay a consistent but highly flexible account of what was new about *neo*liberalism. Divisions arose, in particular, over the role of the state in maintaining a competitive order; some argued that intervention was necessary to sustain competition, and others that intervention was the source of monopolies and centralisation.[26] There were less divisive arguments over other particular policy positions, indicating that this was far from a homogeneous or unified group. In many ways, the common element was simply the social network itself, with its commitment to building a new liberalism.[27] Yet this inbuilt plurality allowed neoliberalism to foster and mutate as it spread around the world, giving it hegemonic strength in its adaptations to the particularity of each space.[28] Its flexibility as an ideology allowed it to excel in carrying out its hegemonic function of incorporating different groups into an overarching consensus.[29]

These debates also extended to questions of strategy. Many members and financiers of Mont Pelerin were impatient with Hayek's long-term approach and wanted to start producing books and other publications immediately, in order to influence the public.[30] In the midst of Keynesian dominance, stable growth and low unemployment, Hayek keenly recognised the unlikelihood of changing public opinion. The Society's strategy was self-consciously long-term, and Hayek's view eventually won out within its meetings. Outside these meetings, the networks surrounding the MPS began actively to construct an extensive transnational infrastructure of ideological diffusion. Hayek had been planning since at least the mid 1940s to establish a system of think tanks propounding neoliberal ideas, while at the same time working to place Society members in government positions (a strategy that eventually produced three heads of state and a large number of cabinet ministers).[31] It was the 1950s, in particular, that saw the proliferation of think tanks allied to the Society, and the subsequent diffusion of neoliberal ideas into the academic and policy worlds.

In the UK, the aims of the MPS were pursued by a network of think tanks and other organisations, such as the Institute of Economic Affairs, the Adam Smith Institute, the Centre for Policy Studies, and an array of smaller groups. Members of the MPS were to enter into US politics, first via think tanks like the American Enterprise Institute, and then through more formal positions such as Milton Friedman's role as economic advisor to Barry Goldwater in his presidential run. Yet it was in Germany that neoliberalism would first achieve both organisational and policy success.

NOT SO TENTATIVE STEPS

In the wake of World War II, the world was primed for significant changes in economic ideas. Yet it was Germany that faced a unique set of economic difficulties – both the well-known hyperinflation problems of the Weimar

Republic and the arduous post–World War II reconstruction effort. While most of the world adopted Keynesian policies, Germany took a different pathway, guided by some of the same neoliberals who had convened at the Walter Lippmann Colloquium. Given the utter collapse of the German state, the problem facing postwar reconstruction planners was how to reconstitute the state – specifically, how to produce legitimacy without having a functional state infrastructure already in place. The answer was found in the ideas propounded by the early ordoliberals: establish a space of economic freedom. This in turn generated a web of connections between individuals which produced the legitimacy of a nascent postwar German state. Rather than a legal legitimacy, the state was seen to derive its legitimacy from a well-functioning economy.[32] It was this idea that would provide the grounding for neoliberalism's first policy experiments.

Following World War II, the ordoliberals began to move into government positions and implement their ideas, establishing the material and institutional foothold from which to shape economic ideology. The first, and perhaps most historically significant position, was the appointment of Ludwig Erhard to the directorate of economics in the postwar administrative zone of the British and US militaries. With the support of a fellow ordoliberal, Wilhelm Röpke, Erhard simultaneously eliminated all existing price and wage controls, and drastically cut income and capital taxes. This was a radical deregulatory move, and one that compelled the Soviet Union to establish a blockade on Berlin and inaugurate the Cold War.[33] In the decades that followed, ordoliberals would come increasingly to populate significant positions in the German Ministry of Economics, with Erhard himself becoming Chancellor in 1963. But despite their intentions, the ordoliberals lacked a principled distinction between legitimate and illegitimate government interventions – an ambiguity which facilitated the German economy's transformation into increasingly Keynesian forms. Interventions to maintain competition shaded into interventions to provide welfare, and by the 1970s Germany had become a standard social democratic state. The difficulties encountered in the policy world did not stop neoliberalism from innovating on other terrains, though – in particular, the space of the so-called 'second-hand dealers' in ideas.

SECOND-HAND DEALERS

Neoliberals had long emphasised the importance of using a variety of venues to influence elites and construct a new common sense. In the postwar era, this approach spanned academia, the media and the policy world. But one of the primary innovations for neoliberal consolidation of the ideological sphere was the use of think tanks. While they had existed for over a hundred years, the extensive use made of them by the MPS was a novelty. It involved developing policy arguments, building policy solutions and homing in on economic culprits. An informal division of labour was established, with some think tanks focusing on the large philosophical ideas, targeting the very assumptions and rationale of the orthodox Keynesian position – this was the task adopted by the Manhattan Institute for Policy Research (MIPR) in the 1970s, for example – while others aimed to produce more immediate public policy proposals. These were explicit attempts to unhinge the dominant worldview in order to subsequently introduce specific policy solutions that were grounded upon the neoliberal view.

The figure of Antony Fisher was vital in the building of neoliberalism's ideological hegemony.[34] One of the founders of the UK's first neoliberal think tank – the Institute of Economic Affairs (IEA) – Fisher explicitly argued that the most difficult part of changing ideas lay not in their production, but in their diffusion. As a result of this belief, Fisher would be heavily involved in establishing conservative think tanks not only in the UK, but also in Canada (the Fraser Institute) and the United States (the MIPR). The IEA itself was focused on 'those whom Hayek had called the "second-hand dealers" in ideas, the journalists, academics, writers, broadcasters, and teachers who dictate the long-term intellectual thinking of the nation'.[35] The explicit intention was to change the ideological fabric of the British elite, infiltrating and subtly altering the terms of discourse. This also extended shrewdly to the mission of the IEA itself, which maintained a deceptive position on its own aims, presenting itself as an apolitical organisation focusing on research into markets in general.[36] In line with this vision of ideological takeover, the IEA produced short pamphlets intended to be as accessible as possible to a mainstream audience.[37] Moreover, these texts were written in a somewhat utopian fashion, without regard for whether a policy was capable of being implemented at that moment.[38] The goal, as always, was the long-term redefinition of the possible. Over the course of decades, these various interventions developed a wide-ranging neoliberal worldview. More than just single-issue responses to the fashionable problems of the day, what the IEA and its associates had constructed was a systematic and coherent economic perspective.[39] Think tanks instilled this worldview by educating and socialising rising members of political parties. Numerous members of what would become Thatcher's administration passed through the IEA during the 1960s and 1970s.[40] The outcome of the IEA's efforts was not only to subtly transform the economic discourse in Britain, but also to naturalise two particular policies: the necessity of attacking trade union power, and the imperative of monetary stability. The former would purportedly let markets freely adapt to changing economic circumstances, while the latter would provide the basic price stability needed for a healthy capitalist economy.

In the United States, too, think tanks and academic research groups were built to push for a broadly neoliberal agenda, the Heritage Foundation and the Hoover Institute being two of the most notable.[41] The MIPR aimed to redefine political common sense by writing books on neoliberal economics that were intended for a popular audience, some of which eventually sold over 500,000 copies. Other books, such as Charles Murray's *Losing Ground*, laid the foundations for the policy shift which today identifies welfare dependency rather than poverty itself as the central social problem. Numerous other widespread policy ideas, such as zero-tolerance policing and workfare, stemmed from the policy factory of the MIPR. Its books succeeded in their objective of changing the common sense of the political classes and the public. The think tank, as an organisational form, was so integral to neoliberalism's ideological success that the very process of creating think tanks was itself institutionalised. The Atlas Economic Research Foundation, founded in 1981 by Fisher, declared as its explicit aim 'to institutionalise this process of helping start up new think tanks'. Atlas today boasts of having helped create or connect over 400 neoliberal think tanks in more than eighty countries. The sheer scale of the neoliberal ideological infrastructure is made fully transparent here.

Beyond think tanks, a variety of other mechanisms were used to build up a hegemonic discourse. In working to install the Chicago brand of neoliberalism as the dominant alternative, Milton Friedman wrote extensive op-eds and newspaper columns, and made use of television interviews in a way that was unprecedented for an academic. Businesses funded projects to turn his work into popular television shows, taking the media terrain by storm.[42] These technological tools were the essential means he used to diffuse his economic vision to policymakers and the public. Newspapers such as the *Wall Street Journal*, *Daily Telegraph* and *Financial Times* paralleled this effort, shaping the public's perspective by invoking neoliberal policies at every opportunity.[43] Business schools and management consultancies also began to adopt and spread neoliberal ideas about corporate forms, and the Chicago School became a global beacon of neoliberal thought.[44] Such institutions were crucial for the spread of neoliberal hegemony, since they were often the training grounds of the global elite.[45] Individuals would come to these neoliberal US schools and then return to their own countries with the neoliberal ideology inculcated in them. By the 1970s, therefore, a full-spectrum infrastructure had developed to promulgate neoliberal ideas. Think tanks and utopian proclamations organised long-term thinking; public-facing speeches, pamphlets and media efforts framed the general outlines of the neoliberal common sense; and politicians and policy proposals made tactical interventions into the political terrain.[46] Yet, despite their increasingly hegemonic potential, a mere decade prior to the arrival in office of Thatcher and Reagan, Keynesianism still reflected the most widely accepted approach to organising states and markets. The ideas of this group of neoliberal intellectuals were still often seen as senseless throwbacks to the failed policies of the pre–Great Depression era. But this would all change by the 1980s – a decade that would leave Keynesianism in disarray and enshrine neoliberalism as the preeminent model for economic modernisation.

GRASPING THE WHEEL

Having made national inroads, neoliberalism first gained serious international prominence in the 1970s, as a response to the combined pressures of high unemployment and high inflation – both of which had originated in oil shocks, general commodity price rises, wage increases and the expansion of credit. The dominant Keynesian approach to the economy had argued that governments should stimulate the economy by putting money into it when unemployment was rising, but, when inflation was rising, take money out of the economy, to slow down price rises. In the 1970s, however, both problems arose simultaneously – rising inflation and rising unemployment, or 'stagflation'. The traditional Keynesian policy solutions were incapable of dealing with this conjunction, thus seemingly dictating a turn to alternative theories. It is important to be clear that, at this point, multiple interpretations of the economic problem were possible. The production of inflation through wage rigidities and trade union power was not the only possible framing of the problem, and neoliberalism was not the only possible solution. Alternative interpretations were available, alternative answers possible; in the moment, no one knew what the way out would be.[47] The neoliberal narrative of the crisis, for instance, plays down the role of banking deregulation by UK Chancellor Anthony Barber in the early 1970s and the breakdown of the Bretton Woods system. These deregulations sparked a surge in the monetary base and a subsequent surge in price inflation, and then wage inflation.[48] In other words, an alternative narrative was possible in which the problem was not strong unions, but rather deregulated finance.

That the neoliberal story won out is in no small measure because of the ideological infrastructure that adherents to its ideas had constructed over decades. The neoliberals found themselves well placed, since they had routinely argued that inflation was a necessary outcome of the welfare state's unwillingness to break wage and price rigidities. They had both a diagnosis of the problem and a solution. Government officials who were uncertain about what to do in the face of crisis found a plausible story in neoliberalism.[49] It was thus the long-term construction of intellectual hegemony by the neoliberal thought collective that left them well positioned to leverage their ideas into power.[50] As Milton Friedman famously put it, 'Only a crisis – actual or perceived – produces real change. When that crisis occurs, the actions that are taken depend on the ideas that are lying around. That, I believe, is our basic function: to develop alternatives to existing policies, to keep them alive and available until the politically impossible becomes the politically inevitable.'[51] This programme spells out exactly what happened in the 1970s crisis. If alternative analyses of the crisis had been accepted, it would have entailed a policy response different from that of neoliberalism. Rather than attacking the power of labour, for example, politicians could have responded by re-regulating credit creation. In other words, neoliberalism was not a necessary outcome, but a political construction.[52]

While Keynesian approaches were eventually able to develop an explanation of stagflation, by then it was too late, and the neoliberal approach had taken over academic economics and the policy world. In short, neoliberalism had become hegemonic. The decade after 1979 saw Margaret Thatcher elected as the British prime minister, Paul Volcker appointed as chairman of the Federal Reserve, and Ronald Reagan elected president of the United States. The IMF and World Bank, facing identity crises after the breakdown of the Bretton Woods system, were rapidly infiltrated and converted into crucibles of the true neoliberal faith by the 1980s. France undertook a neoliberal turn during the Mitterrand administration in the early 1980s, and the major economies of Europe became bound by the neoliberal policies embodied in the constitution of the European Union. In the United States and UK, a wave of systematic attacks were launched against the power of labour. Piece by piece, trade unions were demolished and labour regulations dismantled. Capital controls were loosened, finance was deregulated, and the welfare state began to be scavenged for profitable parts.

Outside Europe and North America, neoliberalism had already been forced on Chile and Argentina in the aftermath of military coups in the 1970s. The developing world debt crisis of the 1980s acted as a key moment to break traditional proto-socialist hegemonies and institute a turn to neoliberalism across the world.[53] Moreover, with the breakdown of the USSR, Eastern Europe saw a wave of neoliberalising trends that were spurred on by Western economic advisors. It is estimated that these privatising policies in former Soviet nations led to a million deaths, proving that privatisation could be just as deadly as collectivisation, and that the expansion of neoliberalism was a far from bloodless affair.[54] Misery, death and dictatorships lay in the wake of its advances across the globe. This was a normative regime that had forced itself into the everyday psychic and bodily reality of the world's population. By the mid 1990s, with the collapse of the USSR, neoliberalism's extension via IMF structural adjustment policies, its consolidation in the UK's New Labour and Clinton's US administration, and its ubiquity in the academic field of economics, neoliberalism had reached its hegemonic peak. The novel conjunctural moment of the 1970s was quickly forgotten by the public, and neoliberalism took on the universal and natural qualities that Thatcher's doctrine of 'there is no alternative' had espoused. Neoliberalism had become a new common sense, accepted by every party in power. It mattered little whether the left or right won; neoliberalism had stacked the deck.

THE IMPOSSIBLE BECOMES INEVITABLE

As we have seen, neoliberalism propagated its ideology through a division of labour – academics shaping education, think tanks influencing policy, and popularisers manipulating the media. The inculcation of neoliberalism involved a full-spectrum project of constructing a hegemonic worldview. A new common sense was built that came to co-opt and eventually dominate the terminology of 'modernity' and 'freedom' – terminology that fifty years ago would have had very different connotations. Today, it is nearly impossible to speak these words without immediately invoking the precepts of neoliberal capitalism.

We all know today that 'modernisation' translates into job cuts, the slashing of welfare and the privatisation of government services. To modernise, today, simply means to neoliberalise. The term 'freedom' has suffered a similar fate, reduced to individual freedom, freedom from the state, and the freedom to choose between consumer goods. Liberal ideas of individual freedom played an important role in the ideological struggle with the USSR, priming the population of the Western world to mobilise behind any ideology that purported to value individual freedoms. With its emphasis on individual freedoms, neoliberalism was able to co-opt elements of movements organised around 'libertarianism, identity politics, [and] multiculturalism'.[55] Likewise, by emphasising freedom from the state, neoliberalism was able to appeal to anarcho-capitalists and the movements of desire that exploded in May 1968.[56] Lastly, with the idea of freedom being limited to a freedom of the market, the ideology could co-opt consumerist desires. At the level of production, neoliberal freedom could also recruit emerging desires among workers for flexible labour – desires that were soon turned against them.[57] In struggling for and successfully seizing the ideological terrain of modernity and freedom, neoliberalism has managed to wind its way inexorably into our very self-conceptions. In arrogating the meaning of terms such as modernisation and freedom, neoliberalism has proved itself to be the single most successful hegemonic project of the last fifty years.

Neoliberalism has thus become 'the *form of our existence* – the way in which we are led to conduct ourselves, to relate to others and to ourselves'.[58] It is, in other words, not just politicians, business leaders, the media elite and academics who have been enrolled into this vision of the world, but also workers, students, migrants – and everyone else. In other words, neoliberal-ism creates subjects. Paradigmatically, we are constructed as competitive subjects – a role that encompasses and surpasses industrial capitalism's productive subject. The imperatives of neoliberalism drive these subjects to constant self-improvement in every aspect of their lives. Perpetual education, the omnipresent requirement to be employable, and the constant need for self-reinvention are all of a piece with this neoliberal subjectivity.[59] The competitive subject, moreover, straddles the divide between the public and the private. One's personal life is as bound to competition as one's work life. Under these conditions, it is no surprise that anxiety proliferates in contem-porary societies. Indeed, an entire battery of psychopathologies has been exacerbated under neoliberalism: stress, anxiety, depression and attention deficit disorders are increasingly common psychological responses to the world around us.[60] Crucially, the construction of everyday neoliberalism has also been a primary source of political passivity. Even if you do not buy into the ideology, its effects nevertheless force you into increasingly precarious situations and increasingly entrepreneurial inclinations. We need money to survive, so we market ourselves, do multiple jobs, stress and worry about how to pay rent, pinch pennies at the grocery store, and turn socialising into networking. Given these effects, political mobilisation becomes a dream that is perpetually postponed, driven away by the anxieties and pressures of every-day life.

At the same time, we should recognise that this production of subjectivity was not simply an external imposition. Hegemony, in all its forms, operates not as an illusion, but as something that builds on the very real desires of the population. Neoliberal hegemony has played upon ideas, yearnings and drives already existing within society, mobilising and promising to fulfil those that could be aligned with its basic agenda. The worship of individual freedom, the value ascribed to hard work, freedom from the rigid work week, individual expression through work, the belief in meritocracy, the bitterness felt at corrupt politicians, unions and bureaucracies – these beliefs and desires pre-exist neoliberalism and find expression in it.[61] Bridging the left–right divide, many people today are simply angry at what they see as others taking advantage of the system. Hatred for the rich tax evader combines easily with disgust for the poor welfare cheat; anger at the oppressive employer becomes indistinguishable from anger at all politicians. This is linked with the spread of middle-class identities and aspirations – desires for home ownership, self-reliance and entrepreneurial spirit were fostered and extended into formerly working-class social spaces.[62] Neoliberal ideology has a grounding in lived experience and does not exist simply as an academic puzzle.[63] Neoliberalism has become parasitical on everyday experience, and any critical analysis that misses this is bound to misrecognise the deep roots of neoliberalism in today's society. Over the course of decades, neoliberalism has therefore come to shape not only elite opinions and beliefs, but also the normative fabric of everyday life itself. The particular interests of neoliberals have become universalised, which is to say, hegemonic.[64] Neoliberalism constitutes our collective common sense, making us its subjects whether we believe in it or not.[65]

A MONT PELERIN OF THE LEFT?

It has often been argued that neoliberalism succeeded (and continues to succeed in spite of its failures) because it is supported by a series of overlapping and powerful interests – the transnational elite, the financiers, the major stockholders of the largest corporations. While these interests have certainly assisted the potency of the neoliberal ideology, such an explanation nevertheless leaves certain questions unanswered. If elite support was sufficient for ideological success, and if neoliberalism was clearly beneficial to elites, there would not have been a forty-year delay between the initial formulation of the ideas and their implementation. Instead, the embedded liberalism of Keynesianism remained ideologically dominant even as it constrained powerful interests. In particular, financial interests were sidelined for a long period after the 1929 crash and ensuing Great Depression. The power dynamics maintaining the Keynesian consensus needed to be taken apart piecemeal. Equally, an explanation of neoliberalism's success that relies solely on its compatibility with particular elite interests also leaves unexplained why other possible responses to the problems of the 1970s were never implemented. An important element of neoliberalism's eventual ideological success is that there was both a crisis and a readily available solution. The crisis (stagflation) was one that no government knew how to deal with at the time, while the solution was the preconceived neoliberal ideas that had been fermenting for decades in its ideological ecology. It was not that neoliberals presented a better argument for their position (the myth of rational political discourse); rather, an institutional infrastructure was constructed to project their ideas and establish them as the new common sense of the political elite.

In all of this there are important lessons to be learned, which have led some to call for a Mont Pelerin of the left.[66] On the broadest level, this history of neoliberalism serves to demonstrate that the greatest recent success of the right – installing a neoliberal hegemony on a global scale – was accomplished through non–folk-political means. This means, in the first place, that the neoliberals thought in long-term visions. This was a different temporality from both election cycles and the boom-and-bust of individual protests. Instead, what the left can learn from is how the MPS patiently set out explicit objectives and analysed the terrain of their historical conjunction, all in order to propose specific and effective means to alter that terrain. It set its sights on long-term change, waiting forty years for the crisis of Keynesianism and the emergence of Reagan and Thatcher. In taking this approach, the intellectuals of neoliberalism thought abstractly in terms of possibilities: what was impossible during their own time became possible later, partly through their actions and preparations. Secondly, they sought to build a counter-hegemonic project that would overturn the consensus around social democracy and Keynesian policies. They took a full-spectrum approach to changing hegemonic conditions and built up an entire ideological infrastructure that was capable of insinuating itself into every political issue and every fibre of political common sense. It overthrew the hegemonic ideas of its time. As Philip Mirowski writes, their strategic genius was

> to appreciate that it is not enough to dangle a utopian vision just beyond reach as eventual motivation for political action; the cadre that triumphs is the side that can simultaneously mount a full set of seemingly unrelated political proposals that deal with the short-, medium-, and long-term horizons of action, combining regimes of knowledge and interim outcomes, so that the end result is the inexorable movement of the polis ever closer to the eventual goal. The shrewd strategy of simultaneously conducting both a short game and a long game, superficially appearing to the uninformed to be in mutual conflict but united behind the scenes by overarching theoretical aims, is probably the single most significant explanation of the triumph of neoliberal policies during a conjuncture where their opponents had come to expect utter refutation.[67]

The third major lesson for the left to learn is that the loose collective of MPS also thought expansively in spatial terms – aiming to spread the network globally, through key nodes. In the think tank, they found an organisational form adapted to the task of global intellectual hegemony. They established networks between think tanks, politicians, journalists, the media and teachers – building a consistency between these disparate groups that did not require a unity of purpose or organisational form. This entailed an admirable flexibility in their project. While neoliberalism is often denounced as being too empirically disparate to make sense as a coherent project, it is in fact the willingness to modify its ideas in light of conditions on the ground that has made it particularly powerful as an ideology.

The call for a Mont Pelerin of the left should therefore not be taken as an argument to simply copy its mode of operation. The argument is rather that the left can learn from the long-term vision, the methods of global expansion, the pragmatic flexibility and the counter-hegemonic strategy that united an ecology of organisations with a diversity of interests. The demand for a Mont Pelerin of the left is ultimately a call to build anew the hegemony of the left.

Chapter 4

Left Modernity

In the present climate, around the world, almost everything that can be proposed as an alternative will appear to be either utopian or trivial. Thus our programmatic thinking is paralysed.

Roberto Mangabeira Unger

This chapter marks a turning point. From the negative task of diagnosing the strategic limitations of the contemporary left, this chapter begins the positive project of elaborating an escape route from our current condition. In the following chapters, we argue that the contemporary left should reclaim modernity, build a populist and hegemonic force, and mobilise towards a post-work future. Folk-political attempts at prefiguration, direct action and relentless horizontalism are unlikely to achieve this, partly because they misrecognise the nature of their opponent. Capitalism is an aggressively expansive universal, from which efforts to segregate a space of autonomy are bound to fail.[1] Withdrawal, resistance, localism and autonomous spaces represent a defensive game against an uncompromising and incessantly encroaching capitalism. Moreover, particularisms can easily coexist with capitalist universalism. The innumerable cultural and political variants of capitalism do little to stifle the expansion of commodification, the creation of proletariats, and the imperative of accumulation. The much-lamented capacity of capitalism to incorporate resistance more often than not simply reveals that particularisms are, in themselves, incapable of competing against a universalism.[2] Indeed, given neoliberalism's inherently expansionary nature, only an alternative expansionary and inclusive universal of some kind will be able to combat and supersede capitalism on a global scale.[3] With the dynamics of accumulation at the heart of capital, a non-expansionary capitalism is an oxymoron. An ambitious leftist politics therefore cannot be satisfied with measures to defend localities. It must seek instead to construct a new future-oriented politics capable of challenging capitalism at the largest scales. It must unmask the pseudo-universality of capitalist social relations and recapture the meaning of the future.

This chapter takes a step back from the empirical and historical focus of the earlier chapters, and seeks to elaborate a philosophical ground for the chapters that follow. We argue that a key element of any future-oriented left must be to contest the idea of 'modernity'. Whereas folk-political approaches lack an enticing vision of the future, struggles over modernity have always been struggles over what the future should look like: from the communist modernism of the early Soviet Union to the scientific socialism of postwar social democracy, and on to the sleek neoliberal efficiency of Thatcher and Reagan.[4] What it means to be modern is not pre-established, but is instead a highly 'contested field'.[5] Yet, in the face of capitalism's success at universalising itself, this term has been almost fully ceded to the right. 'Modernisation' has come to signify simply some dread combination of privatisation, heightened exploitation, rising inequality and inept managerialism.[6] Likewise, notions of the future tend to revolve around ideas of ecological apocalypse, the dismantling of the welfare state, or corporate-led dystopia, rather than anything bearing the mark of utopia or universal emancipation. For many, therefore, modernity is simply a cultural expression of capitalism.[7] From this accepted wisdom, the necessary conclusion follows: only the cancellation of modernity can bring about the end of capitalism. The result has been an anti-modern tendency within numerous social movements from the 1970s onward. Yet this mistaken conflation of modernity with the institutions of capitalism overlooks the alternative forms it can take, and the ways in which many anti-capitalist struggles rely upon its ideals.[8] Modernity presents both a narrative for popular mobilisation and a philosophical framework for understanding the arc of history. As the term that indexes the direction of society, it must be a key discursive battleground for any leftist politics invested in creating a better world.[9] This chapter sets out the broad philosophical stakes of such a project by examining three factors that would help to elaborate a left modernity: an image of historical progress, a universalist horizon and a commitment to emancipation.

In discussing 'modernity', we face the immediate problem of clarifying what it means. It can refer to a chronological period, typically filtered through European history with a variety of events having been posited as its origin: the Renaissance, the Enlightenment, the French Revolution, the Industrial Revolution.[10] For others, modernity is defined by a distinct set of practices and institutions: widespread bureaucratisation, a basic framework of liberal democracy, the differentiation of social functions, the colonisation of the non-European world, and the expansion of capitalist social relations. Yet modernity also refers to a repertoire of conceptual innovations revolving around universal ideals of progress, reason, freedom and democracy. This chapter emphasises these latter aspects: modernity names a set of concepts that have been independently developed in numerous cultures across the world, but which took on a particular resonance in Europe. These are the elements of modernity that cannot be renounced, and that form the wellspring from which more popular discourses around modernisation are generated. The conceptual ideals – such as freedom, democracy and secularism – are the source of both capitalist modernity and the struggles against it. Ideas associated with modernity animated the work of abolitionists, formed the basis of numerous African trade union struggles,[11] and continue today in 'those thousands of campaigns for wages, land rights, basic health, and security, dignity, self-determination, autonomy, and so forth'.[12] In broad terms, then, whether it is explicitly recognised or not, the political struggles of today are struggles *within* the space of modernity and its ideals. Modernity must be contested, not rejected.[13]

HYPERSTITIONAL PROGRESS

To invoke modernity is ultimately to raise the question of the future. What should the future look like? What courses should we set? What does it mean to be contemporary? And whose future is it? Since the emergence of the term, modernity has been concerned with unravelling a circular or retrospective notion of time and introducing a rupture between the present and the past. With this break, the future is projected as being potentially *different from* and *better than* the past.[14] Modernity is tantamount to 'the discovery of the future' and has therefore found itself intimately linked with notions such as 'progress, advance, development, emancipation, liberation, growth, accumulation, Enlightenment, embetterment, [and the] avant-garde'.[15] Suggesting that history can progress through deliberate human action, it is the nature of this progress that competing definitions of modernity have struggled over.[16] Historically, the left has found its natural home in being oriented towards the future. From early communist visions of technological progress, to Soviet space utopias, to the social democratic rhetoric of the 'white heat of technology', what set the left apart from the right was its unambiguous embrace of the future. The future was to be an improvement over the present in material, social and political terms. By contrast, the forces of the political right were, with a few notable exceptions, defined by their defence of tradition and their essentially reactionary nature.[17]

This situation was reversed during the rise of neoliberalism, with politicians like Thatcher commanding the rhetoric of modernisation and the future to great effect. Co-opting these terms and mobilising them into a new hegemonic common sense, neoliberalism's vision of modernity has held sway ever since. Consequently, discussions of the left in terms of the future now seem aberrant, even absurd. With the postmodern moment, the seemingly intrinsic links between the future, modernity and emancipation were prized apart. Philosophers like Simon Critchley can now confidently assert that 'we have to resist the idea and ideology of the future, which is always the ultimate trump card of capitalist ideas of progress'.[18] Such folk-political sentiments blindly accept the neoliberal common sense, preferring to shy away from grand visions and replace them with a posturing resistance. From the radical left's discomfort with technological modernity to the social democratic left's inability to envision an alternative world, everywhere today the future has largely been ceded to the right. A skill that the left once excelled at – building enticing visions for a better world – has deteriorated after years of neglect.

If the left is to recover a sense of progress, however, it cannot simply adopt the classic images of history headed towards a singular destination. Progress, for these approaches, was not only possible, but in fact woven as a necessity into the very fabric of history. Human societies were thought to travel along a pre-defined pathway towards a single outcome modelled after Europe. The

nations of Europe were deemed to have developed capitalist modernity independently, and their historical experiences of development were considered
to be both necessary and superior to those of other cultures.[19] Such ideas
dominated traditional European philosophy and continued on in the influential modernisation literature of the 1950s and 1960s, with their attempts to
naturalise capitalism against a Soviet opponent.[20] Partly endorsed by both
early Marxism and later Keynesian and neoliberal capitalisms, a one-size-fits-
all model of historical progress positioned non-Western societies as lacking
and in need of development – a position that served to justify colonial and
imperial practices.[21]

From the standpoint of their philosophical critics, these notions of progress
were disparaged precisely for their belief in preconceived destinations –
whether in the liberal progression towards capitalist democracy or in the
Marxist progression towards communism. The complex and often disastrous
record of the twentieth century demonstrated conclusively that history could
not be relied upon to follow any predetermined course.[22] Regression was as
likely as progress, genocide as possible as democratisation.[23] In other words,
there was nothing inherent in the nature of history, the development of
economic systems, or sequences of political struggle that could guarantee any
particular outcome. From a broadly left perspective, for example, even those
limited but not insignificant political gains that have been achieved – such as
welfare provision, women's rights and worker protections – can be rolled
back. Moreover, even in states where nominally communist governments
took power, it proved far more difficult than expected to transition from a
capitalist system of production to a fully communist one.[24] This series of
historical experiences fuelled an internal critique of European modernity by
way of psychoanalysis, critical theory and poststructuralism. For the thinkers
of postmodernism, modernity came to be associated with a credulous
naivety.[25] In Jean-François Lyotard's epochal definition, postmodernity was
identified as the era that has grown to be suspicious of the grand metanarra-
tive.[26] On this account, postmodernity is a cultural condition of disillusion-
ment with the kinds of grandiose narratives represented by capitalist, liberal
and communist accounts of progress.

To be sure, these critiques capture something important about the chronological texture of our time. And yet, the announcement of the end of grand
narratives has often been viewed by those outside Europe as being absolutely

of a piece with modernity.[27] Further, with the benefit of thirty years' hindsight, the broader impact of the cultural condition diagnosed by Lyotard has not been the decline of belief in metanarratives per se, but rather a broad disenchantment with those offered by the left. The association between capitalism and modernisation remains, while properly progressive notions of the future have wilted under postmodern critique and been quashed beneath the social wreckage of neoliberalism. Most significantly, with the collapse of the Soviet Union and the rise of globalisation, history does *appear* to have a grand narrative.[28] Throughout the world, markets, wage labour, commodities and productivity-enhancing technologies have all expanded under the systemic imperative to accumulate. Capitalism has become the destiny of contemporary societies, happily coexisting with national differences and paying little heed to clashes between civilisations. But we can draw a distinction here between the endpoint (capitalism) and the pathway towards it. Indeed, the mutual entanglement of countries means that the European pathway (heavily reliant on exploiting colonies and slavery) is barred for many of the newly developing countries. While there are broad paradigms of development, each country has had to find its own unique way to respond to the imperatives of global capitalism. The path of capitalist modernisation is therefore instantiated in different cultures, following different trajectories and with different rhythms of development.[29] Uneven and combined development is the order of the day.[30] Progress is therefore not bound to a single European path, but is instead filtered through a variety of political and cultural constellations, all directed towards instantiating capitalist relations. Today, modernisers simply fight over which variant of capitalism to install.

Recuperating the idea of progress under such circumstances means, first and foremost, contesting the dogma of this inevitable endpoint. Capitalist modernity was never a necessary outcome, but instead a successful project driven by various classes and a systemic imperative towards accumulation and expansion. Various modernities are possible, and new visions of the future are essential for the left. Such images are a necessary supplement to any transformative political project. They give a direction to political struggles and generate a set of criteria to adjudicate which struggles to support, which movements to resist, what to invent, and so on. In the absence of images of progress, there can only be reactivity, defensive battles, local resistance and a bunker mentality – what we have characterised as folk politics. Visions of the future are therefore indispensable for elaborating a movement against capitalism. Contra the earlier thinkers of modernity, there is no necessity to progress, nor a singular pathway from which to adjudicate the extent of development. Instead, progress must be understood as *hyperstitional*: as a kind of fiction, but one that aims to transform itself into a truth. Hyperstitions operate by catalysing dispersed sentiment into a historical force that brings the future into existence. They have the temporal form of 'will have been'. Such hyperstitions of progress form orienting narratives with which to navigate forward, rather than being an established or necessary property of the world. Progress is a matter of political struggle, following no pre-plotted trajectory or natural tendency, and with no guarantee of success. If the supplanting of capitalism is impossible from the standpoint of one or even many defensive stances, it is because any form of prospective politics must set out to construct *the new*. Pathways of progress must be cut and paved, not merely travelled along in some pre-ordained fashion; they are a matter of political achievement rather than divine or earthly providence.

SUBVERSIVE UNIVERSALS

Any elaboration of an alternative image of progress must inevitably face up to the problem of universalism – the idea that certain values, ideas and goals may hold across all cultures.[31] Capitalism, as we have argued, is an expansionary universal that weaves itself through multiple cultural fabrics, reworking them as it goes along. Anything less than a competing universal will end up being smothered by an all-embracing series of capitalist relations.[32] Various particularisms – localised, specific forms of politics and culture – cohabitate with ease in the world of capitalism. The list of possibilities continues to grow as capitalism differentiates into Chinese capitalism, American capitalism, Brazilian capitalism, Indian capitalism, Nigerian capitalism, and so on. If defending a particularism is insufficient, it is because history shows us that the global space of universalism is a space of conflict, with each contender requiring the relative provincialisation of its competitors.[33] If the left is to compete with global capitalism, it needs to rethink the project of universalism.

But to invoke such an idea is to call forth a number of fundamental critiques directed against universalism in recent decades. While a universal politics must move beyond any local struggles, generalising itself at the global scale and across cultural variations, it is for these very reasons that it has been criticised.[34] As a matter of historical record, European modernity was inseparable from its 'dark side' – a vast network of exploited colonial dominions, the genocide of indigenous peoples, the slave trade, and the plundering of colonised nations' resources.[35] In this conquest, Europe presented itself as embodying the universal way of life. All other peoples were simply residual particulars that would inevitably come to be subsumed under the European way – even if this required ruthless physical violence and cognitive assault to guarantee the outcome. Linked to this was a belief that the universal was equivalent to the homogeneous. Differences between cultures would therefore be erased in the process of particulars being subsumed under the universal, creating a culture modelled in the image of European civilisation. This was a universalism indistinguishable from pure chauvinism. Throughout this process, Europe dissimulated its own parochial position by deploying a series of mechanisms to efface the subjects who made these claims – white, heterosexual, property-owning males. Europe and its intellectuals abstracted away from their location and identity, presenting their claims as grounded in a 'view from nowhere'.[36] This perspective was taken to be untarnished by racial, sexual, national or any other particularities, providing the basis for both the alleged universality of Europe's claims and the illegitimacy of other perspectives. While Europeans could speak and embody the universal, other cultures could only be represented as particular and parochial. Universalism has therefore been central to the worst aspects of modernity's history.

Given this heritage, it might seem that the simplest response would be to rescind the universal from our conceptual arsenal. But, for all the difficulties with the idea, it nevertheless remains necessary. The problem is partly that one cannot simply reject the concept of the universal without generating other significant problems. Most notably, giving up on the category leaves us with nothing but a series of diverse particulars. There appears no way to build meaningful solidarity in the absence of some common factor. The universal also operates as a transcendent ideal – never satisfied with any particular embodiment, and always open to striving for better.[37] It contains the conceptual impulse to undo its own limits. Rejecting this category also risks Orientalising other cultures, transforming them into an exotic Other. If there are only particularisms, and provincial Europe is associated with reason, science, progress and freedom, then the unpleasant implication is that non-Western cultures must be devoid of these. The old Orientalist divides are inadvertently sustained in the name of a misguided anti-universalism. On the other hand, one risks licensing all sorts of oppressions as simply the inevitable consequence of plural cultural forms. All the problems of cultural relativism reappear if there are no criteria to discern *which* global knowledges, politics and practices support a politics of emancipation. Given all of this, it is unsurprising to see aspects of universalism pop up throughout history and across cultures,[38] to see even its critics begrudgingly accept its necessity,[39] and to see a variety of attempts to revise the category.[40]

To maintain this necessary conceptual tool, the universal must be identified not with an established set of principles and values, but rather with an empty placeholder that is impossible to fill definitively. Universals emerge when a particular comes to occupy this position through hegemonic struggle:[41] the particular ('Europe') comes to represent itself as the universal ('global'). It is not simply a false universal, though, as there is a mutual contamination: the universal becomes embodied in the particular, while the particular loses some of its specificities in functioning as the universal. Yet there can never be a fully achieved universalism, and universals are therefore always open to contestation from other universals. This is what we will later outline in politico-strategic terms as counter-hegemony – a project aimed at subverting an existing universalism in favour of a new order. This leads us to our second point – as counter-hegemonic, universals can have a subversive and liberating strategic function. On the one hand, a universal makes an unconditional demand – everything must be placed under its rule.[42] Yet, on the other hand, universalism is never an achieved project (even capitalism remains incomplete). This tension renders any established hegemonic structure open to contestation and enables universals to function as insurrectionary vectors against exclusions. For example, the concept of universal human rights, problematic as it may be, has been put to use by numerous movements, ranging from local housing struggles to international justice for war crimes. Its universal and unconditional demand has been mobilised in order to highlight those who are left out of its protections and rights. Similarly, feminists have criticised certain concepts as exclusionary of women and mobilised universal claims against their constraints, as in the use of the universal idea that 'all humans are equal'. In such cases, the particular ('woman') becomes a way to prosecute a critique against an existing universal ('humanity'). Meanwhile, the previously established universal ('humanity') becomes revealed as a particular ('man').[43] These examples show that universals can be revitalised by the struggles that both challenge and elucidate them. In this regard, 'to appeal to universalism as a way of asserting the superiority of Western culture is to betray universality, but to appeal to universalism as a way of dismantling the superiority of the West is to realize it'.[44] Universalism, on this account, is the product of politics, not a transcendent judge standing above the fray.

We can turn now to one final aspect of universalism, which is its heterogeneous nature.[45] As capitalism makes clear, universalism does not entail homogeneity – it does not necessarily involve converting diverse things into the same kind of thing. In fact, the power of capitalism is precisely its versatility in the face of changing conditions on the ground and its capacity to accommodate difference. A similar prospect must also hold for any leftist universal – it must be one that integrates difference rather than erasing it. What then does all of this mean for the project of modernity? It means that any particular image of modernity must be open to co-creation, and further transformation and alteration. And in a globalised world where different peoples necessarily co-exist, it means building systems to live in common despite the plurality of ways of life. Contrary to Eurocentric accounts and classic images of universalism, it must recognise the agency of those outside Europe, and the necessity of their voices in building truly planetary and universal futures. The universal, then, is an empty placeholder that hegemonic particulars (specific demands, ideals and collectives) come to occupy. It can operate as a subversive and emancipatory vector of change with respect to established universalisms, and it is heterogeneous and includes differences, rather than eliminating them.

SYNTHETIC FREEDOM

While the left has traditionally been associated with ideals of equality (manifested today in the focus on income and wealth inequalities), we believe that freedom is an equally essential principle of left modernity. This concept has been central to the political battles fought throughout the twentieth century, with the United States routinely posing as 'the free world' against a totalitarian enemy (in the figure of the USSR, and then the increasingly incoherent images of 'Islamofascism'). In these hegemonic battles, capitalism has repeatedly asserted its superiority by upholding an idea of *negative freedom*.[46] This is the freedom of individuals from arbitrary interference by other individuals, collectives and institutions (paradigmatically, the state). Negative freedom's insistence on the absence of interference has made it an ideal tool to wield against purportedly totalitarian opponents, yet it is a woefully emaciated concept of freedom. In practice, it translates into a modicum of political freedom from the state (ever less so in an age of digital spying and the war on terror) and the economic freedoms to sell our labour power and to choose between shiny new consumer goods.[47] Under negative freedom, the rich and the poor are considered equally free, despite the obvious differences in their capacities to act.[48] Negative freedom is entirely compatible with mass poverty, starvation, homelessness, unemployment and inequality. It is also entirely compatible with our desires being manufactured and designed by pervasive advertising. Against this limited concept of freedom, we argue for a much more substantial version.

Whereas negative freedom is concerned with assuring the formal right to avoid interference, 'synthetic freedom' recognises that a formal right without a material capacity is worthless.[49] Under a democracy, for example, we are all formally free to run for political leadership. But without the financial and social resources to run a campaign, this is a meaningless freedom. Equally, we are all formally free to not take a job, but most of us are nevertheless practically forced into accepting whatever is on offer.[50] In either case, various options may be theoretically available, but for all practical purposes are off the table. This reveals the significance of having the means to realise a formal right, and it is this emphasis on the means and capacities to act that is crucial for a leftist approach to freedom. As Marx and Engels wrote, 'it is possible to achieve real liberation only in the real world and by real means'.[51] Understood in this way, freedom and power become intertwined. If power is the basic capacity to produce intended effects in someone or something else,[52] then an increase in our ability to carry out our desires is simultaneously an increase in our freedom. The more capacity we have to act, the freer we are. One of the biggest indictments of capitalism is that it enables the freedom to act for only a vanishingly small few. A primary aim of a postcapitalist world would therefore be to maximise synthetic freedom, or in other words, to enable the flourishing of all of humanity and the expansion of our collective horizons.[53] Achieving this involves at least three different elements: the provision of the basic necessities of life, the expansion of social resources, and the development of technological capacities.[54] Taken together, these form a synthetic freedom that is constructed rather than natural, a collective historical achievement rather than the result of simply leaving people be. Emancipation is thus not about detaching from the world and liberating a free soul, but instead a matter of constructing and cultivating the right attachments.

In the first place, synthetic freedom entails the maximal provision of the basic resources needed for a meaningful life: things like income, time, health and education. Without these resources, most people are left *formally* but not *really* free. Understood in this way, rising global inequality is revealed as an equally massive disparity in freedom. One initial step in resolving this is the classic social democratic goal of providing the common goods of society, such as healthcare, housing, childcare, education, transport and internet access.[55] The liberal idea in which these basic necessities of life are supposedly enhanced by freedom of choice in the market ignores the actual (financial and cognitive) burdens involved in making such choices.[56] In a world of synthetic freedom, high-quality public goods would be provided for us, leaving us to get on with our lives rather than worrying about which healthcare provider to go with. Beyond the social democratic imagination, however, lie two further essentials of existence: time and money. Free time is the basic condition for self-determination and the development of our capacities.[57] Equally, synthetic freedom demands the provision of a basic income to all in order for them to be fully free.[58] Such a policy not only provides the monetary resources for living under capitalism, but also makes possible an increase in free time. It provides us with the capacity to choose our lives: we can experiment and build unconventional lives, choosing to foster our cultural, intellectual and physical sensibilities instead of blindly working to survive.[59] Time and money therefore represent key components of freedom in any substantive sense.

A full image of synthetic freedom must also seek to expand our capacities beyond what is currently possible. If it is to avoid the problem of manipulating people into contentment with the status quo, synthetic freedom must be open to whatever people might desire.[60] That is to say, freedom cannot simply be equated with making existing options viable, but instead must be open to the largest possible set of options. In this, collective resources are essential.[61] Processes of social reasoning, for instance, can enable common understandings of the world, creating a 'we' in the process that has much greater powers to act than individuals alone.[62] Equally, language is effectively cognitive scaffolding that enables us to leverage symbolic thought to expand our horizons.[63] The development, deepening and expansion of knowledge enable us to imagine and achieve capacities that are otherwise unattainable. As we acquire technical knowledge of our built environment and scientific knowledge of the natural world, and come to understand the fluid tendencies of the social world, we gain greater powers to act. As Louis Althusser put it,

> Just as knowledge of the laws of light has never prevented men from seeing . . . so knowledge of the laws that govern the development of societies does not prevent men from living, or take the place of labour, love and struggle. On the contrary: knowledge of the laws of light has produced the glasses which have transformed men's sight, just as knowledge of the laws of social development has given rise to endeavours which have transformed and enlarged the horizon of human existence.[64]

The anti-intellectualism that permeates the political right, and increasingly infects the critical left, is therefore a retrogression of the worst kind. Healthy scepticism is transformed into an abdication of our commitments to expand freedom. This retrogression in relation to knowledge also occurs in the fantasies of immediate and unbound freedoms in practice. The voluntaristic image that sees mediations, institutions and abstractions as opposed to freedom simply confuses the absence of artifice with the full expression of freedom. Needless to say, this is misguided. Collective action, with its expansion of synthetic freedom, is more often than not carried out through complex divisions of labour, mediated chains of engagement and abstract institutional structures. The social aspect of synthetic freedom is therefore not a return to some human desire for face-to-face sociality and simple cooperation, but instead a call for collective, complex and mediated self-determination.

Finally, if we are to expand our capacities to act, the development of technology must play a central role. As has always been the case, 'technology is the source of our options [and] options are the basis of a future that keeps us above the level of pawn'.[65] Our level of freedom is highly dependent upon the historical conditions of scientific and technological development.[66] The artifices that emerge from these fields both expand existing capacities for action and create entirely new ones in the process. The full development of synthetic freedom therefore requires a reconfiguration of the material world in accordance with the drive to expand our capacities for action. It demands experimentation with collective and technological augmentation, and a spirit that refuses to accept any barrier as natural and inevitable.[67] Cyborg augmentations, artificial life, synthetic biology and technologically mediated reproduction are all examples of this elaboration.[68] The overall aim must therefore be picked out as an unrelenting project to unbind the necessities of this world and transform them into materials for the further construction of freedom.[69] Such an image of emancipation can never be satisfied with or condensed into a static society, but will instead continually strain beyond any limitations. Freedom is a synthetic enterprise, not a natural gift.

Underlying this idea of emancipation is a vision of humanity as a transformative and constructible hypothesis: one that is built through theoretical and practical experimentation and elaboration.[70] There is no authentic human essence to be realised, no harmonious unity to be returned to, no unalienated humanity obscured by false mediations, no organic wholeness to be achieved. Alienation is a mode of enablement, and humanity is an incomplete vector of transformation. What we are and what we can become are open-ended projects to be constructed in the course of time. As Sadie Plant puts it,

> It's always been problematic to talk about the liberation of women because that presupposes that we know what women are. If both women and men have been organised into the forms we currently take, then we don't want to liberate what we are now, if you see what I mean . . . It's not a question of liberation so much as a question of evolution – or engineering. There's a gradual re-engineering of what it can be to be a woman and we don't yet know what it is. We have to find out.[71]

What must therefore be articulated is a humanism that is not defined in advance. This is a project of self-realisation, but one without a pre-established endpoint.[72] It is only through undergoing the process of revision and construction that humanity can come to know itself. This means revising the human both theoretically and practically, engaging in new modes of being and new forms of sociality as practical ramifications of making 'the human' explicit.[73] It is to undertake an interventionist approach to the human that is opposed to those humanisms that protect a parochial image of the human at all costs.[74] These interventions range from individual bodily experimentation to collective political mobilisations against restricted images of the human, and everything in between.[75] It means liberating ourselves from the decrepit economic image of humanity that capitalist modernity has installed, and inventing a new humanity. Emancipation, under this vision, would therefore mean increasing the capacity of humanity to act according to whatever its desires might become. And universal emancipation would be the insistent and maximal extension of this goal to the entirety of our species. It is in this sense that universal emancipation lies at the heart of a modern left.[76]

We have seen that, without a conception of the future, the left becomes bound to a defence of tradition, and to protecting bunkers of resistance. What, then, would a left modernity look like? It would be one that offered enticing and expansive visions of a better future. It would operate with a universal horizon, mobilise a substantial concept of freedom, and make use of the most advanced technologies in order to achieve its emancipatory goals. Rather than a Eurocentric view of the future, it would rely upon a global set of voices articulating and negotiating in practice what a common and plural future might be. Whether operating through slave revolts, workers' struggles, anti-colonial uprisings or women's movements, the critics of sedimented universalisms have always been essential agents in modernity's construction of the future; they are the ones who have continually revised, revolted and created a 'universalism from below'.[77] Yet to truly enable the liberation of futures in the plural, the current global order premised on waged labour and capitalist accumulation will need to be transcended first. A left modernity will, in other words, require building a postcapitalist and post-work platform upon which multiple ways of living could emerge and flourish. The next two chapters will set out both the necessity and desirability of this particular vision of the future.

Chapter 5

The Future Isn't Working

It is already contained in the concept of the free labourer, *that he is a* pauper: *a virtual pauper.*

Karl Marx

We have so far argued that the contemporary left tends towards a folk politics that is incapable of turning the tide against global capitalism. In its place, the left needs to reclaim the contested legacy of modernity and advance visions for a new future. It is imperative, however, that its vision of a new future be grounded upon actually existing tendencies. This chapter sets out a conjunctural analysis of contemporary capitalism, viewed through the lens of work. On the basis of this analysis, the next chapter will argue for the desirability of a future without work. What does it mean to call for the end of work? By 'work', we mean our jobs – or wage labour: the time and effort we sell to someone else in return for an income. This is time that is not under our control, but under our bosses', managers' and employers' control. A full one-third of our adult lives is spent in submission to them. Work can be framed in contrast to 'leisure', typically associated with the weekend and holidays. But leisure should not be confused with idleness, as many of the things we enjoy most involve immense amounts of effort. Learning a musical instrument, reading literature, socialising with friends and playing sports all involve varying degrees of effort – but these are things that we freely choose to do. A post-work world is therefore not a world of idleness; rather, it is a world in which people are no longer bound to their jobs, but free to create their own lives. Such a project draws upon a long line of thinkers – Marxists, Keynesians, feminists, black nationalists and anarchists alike – who have rejected the centrality of work.[1] These thinkers have, each in their own way, sought to liberate humanity from the drudgery of work, the dependence on wage labour, and the submission of our lives to a boss. They have struggled to open up the 'realm of freedom' from which humanity can continue its project of emancipation.[2]

While the broad aims of this project have a long series of precedents, recent developments in capitalism give renewed urgency to these issues. Rapid automation, expanding surplus populations and the continued imposition of austerity all heighten the need to rethink work and prepare for the new crises of capitalism. Just as the Mont Pelerin Society foreshadowed the crisis of Keynesianism and prepared a full-spectrum set of responses, so too should the left prepare for the coming crisis of work and surplus populations. While the effects of the 2008 crisis continue to reverberate throughout the world, it is too late to take advantage of that moment; all around us we can see that capital has recovered and consolidated itself in a renewed and sharpened form. The left must instead prepare for the next opportunity.[3]

This chapter explains why a post-work world is an increasingly pressing option. The first section outlines the emerging crisis of work – the breakdown of stable jobs in developed countries, the rise of unemployment and surplus populations, and the collapse of 'work' as a disciplinary measure holding society together. We then turn to the various symptoms of this crisis as it is manifested not only in unemployment figures, but also in increased precarity, jobless recoveries, growing slums and expanding urban marginality. All around us we can see the effects of this shift bubbling up in new social conflicts and problems. Finally, we look at the various ways in which capitalism's tendency to produce surplus populations has been managed by the state. Today, the crisis of work threatens to overrun these traditional tools of control, laying the social conditions for the shift to a post-work world.

VIRTUAL PAUPERS

While work is common to every society, under capitalism it takes on historically unique qualities. In pre-capitalist societies, work was necessary, but people had shared access to land, subsistence farming and the necessary means of survival. Peasants were poor but self-sufficient, and survival was not dependent on working for someone else. Capitalism changed all this. Through the process called primitive accumulation, pre-capitalist workers were uprooted from their land and dispossessed of their means of subsistence.[4] Peasants struggled against this and continued to survive on the margins of the emerging capitalist world,[5] and it eventually took violent force and harsh new legal systems to impose wage labour on the population. Peasants, in other words, had to be made into a *proletariat*. This new figure of the proletariat was defined by its lack of access to the means of production or subsistence, and its requirement for wage labour in order to survive.[6] This means that the 'proletariat' is not just the 'working class' nor is it defined by an income level, profession or culture. Rather, the proletariat is simply that group of people who must sell their labour power to live – whether they are employed or not.[7] And the history of capitalism is the history of the world's population being transformed into proletarian existence through the advancing dispossession of the peasantry. With the recent integration of post-communist countries and the rise of China and India, the global proletariat has seen a 'great doubling', with 1.5 billion more people now reliant upon waged work for survival.[8] But with the emergence of the proletariat, there also comes a new form of unemployment. In fact, unemployment as we understand it today was an invention of capitalism.[9] Having been torn away from their means of subsistence, for the first time in history a new 'surplus population' emerges that is unable to find waged work.[10] While capitalism may exploit the employed working class, as Joan Robinson once wrote, 'The misery of being exploited by capitalists is nothing compared to the misery of not being exploited at all.'[11]

For the most part, the size of this surplus expands and contracts in tandem with economic cycles. All things being equal, as economies grow, workers are drawn from the surplus and into waged labour, the unemployment level decreases, and the labour market tightens. At a certain point, however, economic demand stalls, wages begin to cut into profitability, or workers become too politically bold. For reasons of profitability, or inflation,[12] or simply to regain political power over the working class, workers are laid off.[13] The surplus subsequently expands, held in reserve for the next cycle of growth. Yet these cyclical mechanisms only partly explain our current situation, particularly given that wage pressures have been stagnant for decades, inflation has remained stable, and the labour movement has been devastated. The cyclical account based on economic demand certainly accounts for the depth of the 2008 crisis, but it does not explain longer-term changes in the labour market such as the rise in precarity, the emergence of jobless recoveries, and the growth of non-capitalist labour markets. To understand the current conjuncture fully, other tendencies therefore need to be taken into account. These are the mechanisms that produce a secular trend towards a larger and larger surplus population, independently of cyclical boom-and-bust patterns.[14] It is these that pose the biggest threat to the reproduction of capitalist social relations.

Today, the production of surplus populations through technological change has increasingly hypnotised the media's imagination. While this attention has been focused on fears of an imminent job apocalypse carried out by vast armies of robots,[15] technological developments can also make older processes more productive without automation (for example, advances in agriculture). In either case, productivity enhancements mean that capitalism needs less labour to produce the same output. Automation appears as the most imminent threat, however, with estimates suggesting that anything from 47 to 80 per cent of current jobs are likely to be automatable in the next two decades.[16] But estimates based solely on advances in technology are insufficient to predict growing unemployment. After all, despite continually rising productivity, employment has remained relatively stable throughout the history of capitalism. With some painful delays, new jobs have been created to replace those that were lost. Yet sanguinity based on past experiences overlooks the political and contingent basis of this historical record: government policies, workers' movements, the gendered division of the labour force, and simultaneous reductions in the work week have all played a role in sustaining employment in the past. As a result, additional qualifications are necessary to understand under what conditions technological change will lead to increased unemployment. A first qualification argues that because increased productivity lowers production prices, unemployment only increases when demand fails to grow enough in response to these lower prices.[17] If the cheaper prices spark more sales, the company may expand rather than cut workers. A similar argument suggests that technological developments often create new industries, and that this potentially creates replacement jobs.[18]

Since the introduction of the personal computer, for instance, over 1,500 new job types have emerged.[19] In either of these cases, consumers buy more goods (because they are cheaper or new) and others are kept employed. The same logic holds for services. The rollout of ATMs, for example, led to fewer bank tellers being employed in each branch – but banks responded to the cheaper costs by opening more branches and expanding their market share.[20] The result was that the number of bank tellers remained steady (though this may be changing today, as banks move their services online).[21] In all of these cases, the logic is that even if technology eliminates some jobs, demand grows sufficiently to create new jobs. In a second situation, technological change reaches such a speed that an increasingly large portion of the population becomes unable to keep up with the skills needed.[22] In this case, even if new demand can be created, there simply are not enough capable workers to take up these jobs – the supply of labour falters.[23] The speed of technological change and diffusion may render entire segments of the population as an obsolete surplus. In a third situation, labour-saving technologies can be of such general use that they diffuse across the entire economy, dampening the overall demand for labour.[24] In this circumstance, even if new industries are created, they will require increasingly less labour because these technologies have a wide range of applicability.[25] If any of the above conditions hold, then technological change can lead to increased unemployment. As we will see, there are good reasons to believe a number of these conditions do hold. But while technological unemployment is the most prominent reason today for swelling surplus populations, it is not the only one.

Another mechanism that actively changes the size of the surplus is one we have already noted: primitive accumulation.[26] This is not just an origin story of capitalism, but also an ongoing process that involves the transformation of pre-capitalist subsistence economies into capitalist economies. Through various means, a poor but self-sufficient peasantry is forced off its land and made to rely on wage labour to survive. As have seen, with globalisation this process has accelerated and led to a doubling of the proletariat. The supply of rural labour that China can draw upon is dwindling, but the integration of Africa and South Asia means the worldwide supply of labour continues to increase at a rapid pace.[27] The outcome of this is a vast new global labour force, dependent upon the creation of equally vast numbers of new jobs. Therefore, independently of any technological changes in capitalist production, surplus population have increased because of this new labour supply. In addition to this, a third mechanism involves the active exclusion of a particular population from capitalist wage labour. Both in the past and present, this has predominantly involved the exclusion of women and racial minorities from the job market.[28] While the problems of slavery, racism and sexism are not reducible to capitalist imperatives – indeed, they have separate logics of domination – these phenomena have also indirectly served capitalist goals.[29] Unfree labour in the form of slavery is well documented as a key element of capitalism's origins (and continues today),[30] and the unpaid labour of many women and racialised prison populations continues to act as a source of hyper-exploitation.[31] On a more modest level, unemployment continues to be distributed unevenly across distinctions of race, gender and geography (witness the devastation of post-industrial cities, for instance). Certain groups are more likely to be the last hired during a boom, and the first fired during a recession.[32] The vulnerabilities that surplus populations face are therefore differentiated between sexes and races; an economic logic of exploitation and expulsion intersecting with other logics of oppression. But in all of these cases, surplus populations are concentrated within a particular group as a result of political, legal and social structures. It is not, in other words, technological change or primitive accumulation that is responsible for their difficulties in finding waged labour. But these mechanisms often intersect with each other: some people are more likely to be affected by technological change,[33] and the incorporation of new surplus populations usually involves racial coding.[34] In a myriad of ways, these mechanisms – technological change, primitive accumulation and active exclusion – generate an expanding number of proletariat outside the formal workforce.

What, then, is the composition of the surplus population today? Broadly, we can divide it into four different strata: the capitalist segment, the non-capitalist segment, the latent segment and the inactive segment.[35] The first segment we are all familiar with: the unemployed and underemployed, situated within the normal capitalist labour market. This group has access to at least some minimal state welfare, is actively seeking a(nother) job, and therefore exerts pressure on the wages of the employed. Yet, for most of the world, being 'unemployed' is a relative luxury.[36] In the absence of any social safety net, most people must constantly work to survive, and are therefore forced into creating new subsistence economies alongside capitalism.[37] This is the non-capitalist segment of the surplus population, filled with people who have been dispossessed of their means of subsistence[38] but have few social safety nets (either community- or state-based) to allow them to go without work for long. These subsistence economies produce goods for the market – small trinkets, for example – but they are organised as non-capitalist forms of production in that they do not seek to accumulate.[39] These types of economies increasingly dominate the labour market of the developing world, ranging from 30 to 80 per cent of the working population in any given country.[40] A third latent group exists primarily in pre-capitalist economic formations that can be readily mobilised into the capitalist labour market. This includes the reservoir of proto-proletarians (including peasants), but this group also includes unwaged domestic labourers, as well as salaried professionals who are under threat of being returned to the proletariat, often through deskilling (for example, medical professionals, lawyers and academics).[41] The importance of this group is that it forms an additional reservoir of labour for capitalism when existing labour markets are tight.[42] Finally, in addition to the other strata, a vast number of people are considered economically inactive (including the discouraged, the disabled and students).[43] Overall, determining the precise size and nature of the global surplus population is difficult with existing data, and subject to fluctuations as individuals move in and out of categories, but a variety of measures converge to suggest it significantly outnumbers the active working class.[44]

This is the crisis of work that capitalism faces in the coming years and decades: a lack of formal or decent jobs for the growing numbers of the proletarian population. In an earlier generation, the identification of surplus populations as a problem was an idea that was often derided. During the 'golden age' of capitalism, low unemployment, stable jobs, rising wages and rising living standards meant the idea that capitalism produced a surplus humanity enjoyed little material support. Yet, while most leftist thinkers turned to the economic problems of growth for capitalism, an occluded intellectual tradition has instead emphasised the social reproduction problem of surplus populations. It is no surprise that it was often those outside the functioning capitalist order who saw the potential in this surplus class.[45] Writing from Algiers in the 1970s, Eldridge Cleaver presciently argued that 'When workers become permanently unemployed, displaced by the streamlining of production, they revert back to their basic [proletarian] condition' and that 'the real revolutionary element of our era is the [proletariat]'.[46] From the capitalist core, Paul Mattick called it 'the most important of all capitalistic contradictions'.[47] And more recently, communisation theorists have made important contributions to analysing the crisis of wage labour, and Fredric Jameson has argued that *Capital* 'is not a book about politics, and not even a book about labour: it is a book about unemployment'.[48] Indeed, it is often forgotten that Marx argued that the expulsion of surplus populations was part of 'the absolute general law of capitalist accumulation'.[49] In the wake of the 2008 crisis and continued sluggishness in the labour market, it is no surprise that the issue of surplus populations should emerge again. With technological change proceeding apace, the already large numbers of surplus humanity look set to swell. The very social basis of capitalism as an economic system – the relationship between the proletariat and employers, with waged work mediating between them – is crumbling.

THE MISERY OF NOT BEING EXPLOITED

As we have seen, very little of the global labour force is employed in formal wage labour, and this number has only decreased in the wake of the 2008 crisis. The most obvious symptoms of this rising surplus population are embodied in the long-term changes in unemployment statistics. In the immediate postwar era, unemployment as low as 1 to 2 per cent was once considered a viable goal of developed economies: during the 1950s and 1960s, the UK and the United States saw unemployment hover around 2 per cent, while Germany even saw unemployment dip below 1 per cent.[50] Each decade since has seen a ratcheting up of the acceptable level of unemployment, combined with decreases in employment growth.[51] Today, the Federal Reserve considers 5.5 per cent to be the optimal long-term unemployment rate – more than doubling the postwar levels.[52] In the United States the percentage of men not working has tripled since the late 1960s, and the percentage of women has also increased, despite starting at a much higher level.[53] The proportion of people employed has dropped precipitously, and the overall surplus population has been growing consistently in recent decades.[54] At a global level, the unemployment rate has continued to rise after the 2008 crisis, both in absolute and relative terms.[55] The global rate of job creation has remained significantly lower, has largely generated part-time jobs, and is forecast to continue its sluggish trend.[56] Meanwhile, labour force participation rates have been declining globally for decades, and are set to continue falling for decades more.[57] Yet these statistics are only the tip of the iceberg. The crisis of work and the effects of surplus populations are expressed not only in these direct measures, but also through a series of more subtle and indirect effects.

One of these – increased precarity – has come to exemplify the neoliberal labour market in developed economies.[58] Relative to the stable and well-paying careers of earlier generations, today's jobs typically involve more casual working hours, low and stagnant wages, decreasing job protections and widespread insecurity.[59] This trend towards precarity has a number of causes, but one of the primary functions of a surplus population is that it enables capitalists to place extra pressure on the lucky few who have found a job.[60] As the surplus grows and the labour market slackens, more workers seek after fewer jobs, and power passes over to the employers. The threat of moving a factory, for instance, is only possible with a global labour glut. The result is that employers gain strength over workers and the quality of jobs decreases (supplementing the quantity measured by unemployment statistics). This is exactly what we have seen in the past few decades. Throughout Europe the intensity of work, in terms of both speed and demands, has increased.[61] The shift to just-in-time supply chains has exacerbated the demands of work, while new surveillance technologies are being forced upon labourers (in some cases, even monitoring them outside of work hours).[62] The decline in the quality of jobs can also be seen in the cutting of work hours, rather than the outright elimination of jobs. We can see this in the small but growing number of part-time, flexible and freelance jobs over the past thirty years.[63] For instance, the relatively low unemployment levels of the UK after the 2008 crisis are largely a result of more self-employed people living off poverty wages.[64] In the United States, more than 6.5 million people are forced to work part-time despite desiring full-time work.[65] This casualisation also involves innovations such as crowd-sourced tasks, temporary staffing agencies and zero-hours contracts, along with the harsh working conditions and lack of benefits that accompany them. In the UK, for example, it is estimated that nearly 5 per cent of the working population is presently on zero-hours contracts.[66] Surplus populations have also put downward pressure on wages. Estimates suggest that every 1 per cent increase in labour market slack is associated with a 1.6 per cent increase in income inequality.[67] The stagnation of real wages and the declining share of income going to labour are both tied to an excess supply of labour,[68] and most economists believe automation and the globalisation of the proletariat are central reasons why wages have been stagnant in recent decades.[69] All of these trends have continued since the 2008 crisis as well, with slow real wage growth across the G20, and outright decline in the UK.[70] The slow growth of wages leads precarity to also be expressed in the anxiety over high levels of consumer debt and low levels of personal savings.[71] In the United States, for example, a full 34 per cent of full-time workers live paycheque-to-paycheque, while in the UK, 35 per cent of people could not live off their savings for more than a month.[72] And at its most vicious, precarity is indicated by a rise in depression, anxiety and suicides – an 'excess' that goes uncounted in traditional economic measures.[73] Indeed, unemployment is associated with a fifth of all global suicides, and this has only worsened in the wake of the financial crisis.[74]

In addition to precarity, surplus populations and technological automation help to make sense of a recent labour market phenomenon: the emergence of 'jobless recoveries', in which economic growth returns after a crisis but job growth remains anaemic.[75] Such recoveries have become standard for the US economy,[76] and since the 1990s the trend has been towards longer and longer jobless recoveries.[77] The current crisis is no exception, with more than a million full-time jobs yet to return, and forecasts suggesting that US unemployment will remain above pre-crisis levels until 2024.[78] This is a global phenomenon as well, with the world economy creating jobs so slowly that the number of jobs will remain significantly below pre-crisis levels for at least a decade.[79] While their cause is ultimately still a mystery, jobless recoveries appear to be closely related to automation.[80] In fact, the only occupations that have experienced jobless recoveries are those that have been under threat from automation in recent decades – semi-skilled, routine jobs.[81] Moreover, these job losses have occurred almost entirely during and in the wake of recessions.[82] In other words, crisis periods are when automatable jobs disappear, never to be heard from again. If automation accelerates over the coming decades, these problems are likely to intensify – with capital using periods of crisis to permanently eliminate such jobs.[83] The slow return of jobs also expresses itself as a rise in long-term unemployment, whereby entire groups of people become increasingly segregated from the normal labour market. Since the most recent crisis, the average length of unemployment has doubled and remained stubbornly high.[84] These extended periods of unemployment suggest that a structural problem is responsible – that is to say, a problem that takes longer for unemployed workers to adapt to, such as retraining for an entirely new skill set. Workers laid off from an area like retail will find it difficult to immediately step into a job in growth sectors like programming. Meanwhile, when the long-term unemployed do find a job, they are more likely to enter at the margins of the labour market, with lower pay and more temporary work.[85] Jobless recoveries, in other words, exacerbate the problems of precarity, and increasingly segregate out a portion of the population as permanently underemployed. Ultimately, unemployment and the threat of it are becoming the norms for the labour force.

In some urban areas, joblessness and segregation from the normal labour market have long been features of everyday existence. In the *banlieues* of Paris, the ghettos of the United States and the rising spaces of suburban poverty, entire communities have been economically separated from broader economic trends, stagnating even during periods of growth.[86] More often than not, these segregated spaces are also divided along racial lines, with deliberate neglect and outright exclusion transforming these communities into increasingly harsh areas of poor social cohesion, inadequate housing and high unemployment.[87] The historical origin of these spaces is well known: racism, slavery and the active exclusion carried out by policy choices, physical violence and white migration.[88] In early-twentieth-century America, for example, the mechanisation of agriculture led the rural black population to migrate and concentrate in urban areas. Yet jobs were hard to come by, as continued racism excluded them from working in textiles or manufacturing. (The racialisation of the surplus population also enabled owners to manipulate the white working class, keeping wages low and preventing unionisation.)[89] As capitalism grew in the postwar era, manufacturing jobs eventually opened up to the black population, and by the mid 1950s rates of black and white youth unemployment were broadly similar.[90] But then the globalisation of the labour supply wreaked havoc on low-skilled black workers. With manufacturing jobs shipped overseas or subject to automation, these workers were disproportionately affected by deindustrialisation.[91] Industrial jobs left the urban centres and were replaced by service work often located in distant suburban areas.[92] The urban ghettos were left to rot, becoming concentrated hubs of long-term joblessness.[93] They became poverty traps, devoid of jobs, with little community support and a proliferation of underground economies.[94] Entire communities were cast aside from the machinery of capitalism and left to fend for themselves with whatever means could be scraped together. People seeking an income were forced into off-the-books work, new businesses turned to loan sharks after being denied by white-owned banks, and increasing desperation led to outright illicit activities.[95]

Mirroring the concentration of joblessness in the urban margins, developing economies have had to deal with the expansion and concentration of surplus populations in slums, favelas and shantytowns. Globally, these have swelled to unprecedented levels as the urban workforce is tossed aside into the informal and marginal economies.[96] As one UN report puts it, 'the cities have become a dumping ground for a surplus population working in unskilled, unprotected and low-wage informal service industries and trade'.[97] The primary cause behind this expansion of slums has been primitive accumulation. Spurred on, first by colonialism and then by structural adjustment policies, the peasantry in many developing countries has been forced off their lands via global competition, rapid industrialisation and rampaging climate change. Like the earlier European experience of industrialisation, dispossessed rural workers have migrated to urban areas to find jobs. And in Europe, too, this process sometimes led to slum-dwelling and destitution for the new urban proletariat.[98] But this is where the similarities end, as in Europe the transition involved creating sufficient numbers of jobs, the emergence of a strong industrial working class, and the eventual provision of housing for migrants.[99] Under conditions of postcolonial development, this narrative has been broken. Rather than a scarcity of labour, recent industrialisation has occurred in the context of a large and global labour force.[100] The result has been little development of anything resembling a traditional working class, continually weak job prospects and a lack of adequate housing.[101] New urban migrants have been left in a permanent state of transition between peasantry and proletarianisation, and sometimes in seasonal circulation between rural existence and urban poverty.[102] Slums and other improvised housing therefore represent a dual expulsion from the land and from the formal economy.[103] This surplus humanity, having been deprived of its traditional means of subsistence yet left without employment, has been forced to create its own non-capitalist subsistence economies. Much of the labour performed here is informal: low-paid, insecure, irregular and without state support. In these economies, production is typically organised in non-capitalist forms but remains directed towards commodity production – to selling goods on the market, rather than for individual use. Mediation by the market distinguishes these postcolonial subsistence economies from pre-capitalist subsistence economies,[104] even though they both function as a desperate means of survival.[105]

But while primitive accumulation is responsible for the origins of these slums, it is 'premature deindustrialisation' that looks set to consolidate their existence. If previous periods of industrialisation at least had the benefit of providing enough factory jobs for the new proletariat, premature deindustrialisation threatens to eliminate this traditional pathway entirely. Technological and economic developments now enable countries to virtually leapfrog the industrialisation phase, which means that developing economies are now deindustrialising at much lower rates of per capita income and with much lower shares of manufacturing employment.[106] China is a good example of this, with manufacturing employment in decline,[107] labour struggles becoming more confident,[108] real wages surging[109] and demographic limits leading to a focus on 'technological upgrading [and] productivity enhancements' in order to maintain growth.[110] The automation of factories is at the leading edge of this deindustrialisation trend, with China already the biggest purchaser of industrial robots, and expected to soon have more industrial robots in operation than either Europe or North America.[111] The factory of the world is going robotic. Deindustrialisation can also be seen in 'reshoring', where manufacturing returns to developed economies in jobless, automated forms.[112] These deindustrialisation trends are taking hold across the developing economies of Latin America, sub-Saharan Africa and most of Asia.[113] Even in countries where manufacturing employment has increased in absolute terms, there have been significant decreases in the labour-intensity of the process.[114] The result of all of this is not only an incomplete transition to a significant working class, but also the stymying of the expected employment path for the workforce. Premature deindustrialisation is leaving most of the world's urban proletariat dispossessed of its agricultural livelihood and without the opportunity to be hired for manufacturing jobs. Some hold out the hope that an emerging service sector will absorb the surplus populations, yet this appears increasingly unlikely. Even in India, the centre of service and high-tech outsourcing, only a small portion of the labour force works in the information and communication technology sector.[115] More importantly, the potential of service jobs is constrained by the newest wave of automation, which is likely to eliminate the low-skilled, low-wage service jobs that have traditionally been outsourced – clerical work, call-centre work or data entry, for example.[116] As this non-routine cognitive labour is increasingly automated, what may occur is a premature shift away from a service-based economy – on top of premature deindustrialisation. What this means is that the maintenance of large portions of humanity within slums and informal, non-capitalist economies is likely to be consolidated by emerging technological trends. In the end, while unemployment measures give us some sense of the size of the surplus population problem, it is precarity, jobless recoveries and mass urban marginality that truly express the squeeze on the global labour market.

REVENGE OF THE SURPLUS

Larger surpluses of labour are, on the one hand, beneficial to capitalist interests. They serve as a disciplinary tool against the working class (particularly when filtered through racism, nationalism and sexism) and as a reserve to call upon in times of growth. They reduce wages, sow competition among workers and shackle the ambitions of the proletariat. These are among the reasons behind a gradual drive to incorporate the world's population into a global labour force, fostered by imperialism and globalisation.[117] On the other hand, capital requires a particular *type* of surplus population: cheap, docile and pliable.[118] Without these characteristics, this excess of humanity becomes a problem for capital. Not content to lie down and accept its disposability, it makes itself heard through riots, mass migration, criminality, and all sorts of actions that disrupt the existing order. Capitalism therefore has simultaneously to produce a disciplined surplus and deploy violence and coercion against those who resist.

One of the principal ways to manage the unruly surplus has been to champion the social democratic ideal of full employment, whereby every physically capable (male) worker has a job. In support of this ideal, economic policies aim to reincorporate the surplus into capitalism as disciplined and waged workers, secured by a hegemonic consensus between the representatives of labour and capital. The apogee of this approach was the postwar period, when working-class struggle and conservative concern with social order positioned full employment as a necessary economic goal.[119] In this brief 'golden age' of capitalism, unemployment was kept to a minimum, and capital had to seek out pre-capitalist populations around the world in order to expand and accumulate.[120] For the most part, job growth was achieved through healthy economic growth that increased the demand for labour.[121] Historically, growth of the national economy has often been important in warding off the effects of technological unemployment – either by increasing the output of existing industries or by inventing new industries to employ the displaced workers. For instance, during the latter half of the 1800s, the rise in capital goods output created jobs that offset the surplus population newly released from the agricultural sector.[122] In the prewar and postwar eras, growth in manufacturing jobs was sustained by the rise of mass consumerism and surges in government military spending.[123] Today, we can see similar attempts at creating new markets through accumulation by dispossession – turning public or common goods into privatised (and monetised) commodities. If increases in labour demand are to be successful, however, they require the right supply of labour – which means an increasingly high-skilled workforce. Education has been the primary way to achieve this, with, for example, secondary education having its origins in efforts to produce more skilled workers. The demand to educate workers for jobs held wide support during the high unemployment period of the Great Depression,[124] and early neoliberals went so far as to argue that education was necessary *only* to adapt human beings to the constant changes in the economy.[125] Today, the growth areas of the labour market tend to be in high-skilled, non-routine and cognitive jobs.[126] This means any attempt at full employment increasingly requires new skills from workers – a demand that helps explain the aggressive efforts to reduce higher education to glorified job training.[127] The overall societal aim becomes the production of competitive subjects undergoing constant self-improvement in an endless effort to be deemed 'employable'.[128] The demands that workers be constantly retraining and that policies support healthy economic growth are necessary components to the drive for full employment.[129]

But while calls for more jobs remain ideologically pervasive, the practical viability of full employment has largely disappeared. With tight labour markets in the postwar era, the ensuing strength of the working class increasingly became a problem for capitalism. The crisis of stagflation in the 1970s, in particular, presented an opportunity to reverse the priority given to employment. Class pressure and its effects – work stoppages, wage inflation, declining profits – were a major factor in central banks' decisions to raise interest rates, in the hope of reducing aggregate demand and increasing unemployment.[130] Indeed, Thatcher's chief economic advisor eventually admitted that the war against inflation was in fact a proxy war against the working class.[131] The tight monetary policy of the early 1980s was therefore precisely an effort to undermine the power of the working class, increase unemployment to a level acceptable for capital, and end the dream of full employment. Yet even if full employment had not been attacked, it requires strong economic growth – a condition that looks increasingly unlikely for the global economy. In recent years, global growth has remained significantly lower than during the pre-crisis period.[132] Across the political spectrum, economists are warning that fundamental changes to the economy mean growth may have settled into a permanently lower state.[133] Moreover, firms that are leading growth sectors – such as Facebook, Twitter and Instagram – simply do not create jobs on the scale of classic firms like Ford and GM.[134] In fact, new industries currently only employ 0.5 per cent of the American workforce – hardly an inspiring record of job creation.[135] And after a steady decline, the average new business creates 40 per cent fewer jobs than it did twenty years ago.[136] The old social democratic plan to encourage employment in new industries falters in the face of low labour-intensity firms and sputtering economic growth. Still, it might be imagined that, with the right political pressure and policies, a return to full employment could be an option.[137] But, given that the height of the social democratic era required the exclusion of women from the waged workforce, we should in fact wonder whether full employment has ever been possible.

If full employment remains operative only as an ideological mystification, its normalisation of work still extends to the unemployed. The transformation of welfare and the rise of workfare – forcing people to work in order to receive benefits – represent an increasingly insidious example of this. Mirroring the changing fortunes of full employment, unemployment has long been governed according to different ideas.[138] Initial approaches saw unemployment as an individual accident – something to be mitigated by insurance-like solutions. But the mass unemployment of the Great Depression overwhelmed this approach, and unemployment subsequently came to be seen as a structural (and male) problem. The labour movement became an employment movement, and governments adopted welfare and full employment policies partly in response. Today, many of the transformations that the welfare state is undergoing can be understood as an attempt to revive the disciplinary function of the unemployed. Their free labour, in the form of workfare, acts to repress wages and threaten the jobs of the employed; the figure of the 'jobseeker' imposes a norm of work on everyone; and attacks on disability benefits turn even those outside the labour force into a reserve army of potential workers.[139] The unemployed have to fulfil an increasingly long list of conditions in order to gain even minimal benefits: attending training, constantly applying for jobs, listening to advice, and even working for free. The increase in surveillance and control is designed to produce not only an obedient, skilled and flexible surplus population, but also one that exerts pressure on the employed. It therefore makes little difference whether these schemes actually reduce unemployment or not, since their purpose lies elsewhere.[140] Increasingly, the welfare state is becoming little more than an institution designed to deploy the surplus against the working class.

The management of surplus populations does not just revolve around the production of disciplined workers and pliable jobseekers. Increasingly, domination and punitive measures are becoming the norm in dealing with the excess to capital. For instance, the size and composition of this group is heavily regulated through immigration policies. For the surplus, migrating to countries with better job prospects is a common response to high unemployment and has been the historical norm. In the nineteenth century, as the mechanisation of agriculture transformed the countryside, the dominant outlet was mass emigration to the New World.[141] Yet today the option to migrate is increasingly closed off for the developing world. While there are a variety of reasons voiced to justify tighter immigration controls, reducing the potentially unruly excess labour supply has often been a dominant one.[142] Today, we see the militarisation of America's border with Mexico and the rise of Fortress Europe in response to mistaken fears about jobs being taken by foreigners. Yet the desperation of immigrants to find a decent job is such that, even when faced with the threat of death, they still make the perilous trip to a new country. The result is that the past fifteen years have seen over 22,000 migrants die trying to get into Europe, more than

6,000 die trying to cross the Mexico–US border, and over 1,500 die trying to get to Australia.[143] These lethal barriers to migration are one of the primary mechanisms used today to segregate and manage global surplus populations. And inextricable from this treatment of migrants is racialised coding: these immigrants are not simply other individuals, but other races. Whether 'foreign hordes' threatening the sanctity of the European border, or immigrant textile workers in Thailand being subject to hyper-exploitation and abuse, racial hierarchies are an essential component of the control of surplus populations.[144]

When the co-optation of the surplus into a disciplined excess workforce has failed, the state can always resort to simply locking up, excluding and brutalising large sections of the surplus population. Across the world, mass incarceration has been increasing as the size of prison populations rise in both absolute and relative terms.[145] Moreover, there is a significant racial component to this – most notably in the mass incarceration of the US black population, but also of Muslims in much of Europe, Aboriginals in Canada, and the detention and deportation of foreign migrants around the world.[146] These systems of mass incarceration must be understood to extend beyond prisons, as they encompass an entire network of laws, courts, policies, habits and rules that work to subjugate a group of people.[147] Mass incarceration is a system of social control aimed primarily at surplus populations rather than at crime. For example, increases in manufacturing unemployment are associated globally with increases in police employment.[148] As the reserve army grows, so too does the state's punitive apparatus. Likewise, the expansion of immigrant detention centres responds to the demise of subsistence economies and the formation of a mobile proletariat.[149] Those who are unwilling to be forced into slums seek better opportunities elsewhere, only to be locked up or left for dead on the Mediterranean. The American system is perhaps the clearest example of how surplus populations and police enforcement intertwine. The well-documented surge in mass incarceration over the past few decades was not a response to rising crime rates,[150] but rather to the proliferation of jobless ghettos and the advances made by the civil rights movement. The racialised nature of this system is well known, but the patterns of incarceration cannot be fully understood without reference to class and surplus populations. For instance, middle-class and upper-class black populations are largely left alone,[151] and the vast majority of the prison population consists of the 'working or workless poor'.[152] Likewise, the disparities in incarceration between races are outpaced by the disparities in terms of class,[153] and the rise of mass black incarceration coincides with the decline in employment for that same population.[154] In fact, the racial nature of mass incarceration in America stems 'exclusively' from the wildly disproportionate locking up of lower-class black populations.[155] Mass incarceration has therefore become a means to manage and control this surplus that has been excluded from the labour market and left in poverty. Spatially concentrated in inner-city ghettos, these groups became an easy target of state control. This intersects with race, of course, as the origins of jobless ghettos lie in the active exclusion of the black population of the United States. And in many ways, the carceral system perpetuates the legacy of slavery, Jim Crow, and the ghettos – replacing many of their functions with a new system of exclusion.[156] But class enables us to see a distinction: whereas those previous systems of social control exploited free labour and attempted to transform black populations into a disciplined workforce, the modern prison system is designed largely to exclude and control the surplus population.[157] Given the effects of having a criminal record, the carceral system brings about a triple exclusion: from cultural and educational capital, from political participation and from public aid.[158] The end result is that incarceration initiates a vicious circle with the urban poor left unemployed and unable to find a job, thereby endlessly reproducing these groups as outside of capital.[159] Rather than trying to reform, educate and reintegrate prisoners into capitalist society, convoluted systems are set up to keep them out and to prevent their re-entry into normal wage labour after prison. At its extreme, these populations become simply disposable, situated outside of normal society and subject to gratuitous violence. The end result is a system that produces and reproduces permanent exclusion from the formal economy. These populations are deemed dispensable, and subjected to all the police brutality and state violence that can be mustered against them. We have, therefore, an entire range of mechanisms that the state and capital use to manage surplus populations, ranging from disciplined integration to violent exclusion.

THE CRISIS OF WORK

As we have seen, there is a growing population of people that are situated outside formal, waged work, making do with minimal welfare benefits, informal subsistence work, or by illegal means. In all cases, the lives of these people are characterised by poverty, precarity and insecurity. Increasingly, there are simply not enough jobs to employ everyone. As the hegemonic order predicated upon decent and stable jobs breaks down, social control is likely to revert to increasingly coercive measures: harsher workfare, heightened antagonisms over immigration, stricter controls on the movement of peoples, and mass incarceration for those who resist being cast aside. This is the crisis of work facing neoliberalism and the surplus populations who make up most of the world's labour force.

With the potential for extensive automation of work – a topic that will be discussed further in the next chapter – it is likely that we will see the following trends in the years to come:

1. The precarity of the developed economies' working class will intensify due to the surplus global labour supply (resulting from both globalisation and automation).
2. Jobless recoveries will continue to deepen and lengthen, predominantly affecting those whose jobs can be automated at the time.
3. Slum populations will continue to grow due to the automation of low-skilled service work, and will be exacerbated by premature deindustrialisation.
4. Urban marginality in the developed economies will grow in size as low-skilled, low-wage jobs are automated.
5. The transformation of higher education into job training will be hastened in a desperate attempt to increase the supply of high-skilled workers.
6. Growth will remain slow and make the expansion of replacement jobs unlikely.
7. The changes to workfare, immigration controls and mass incarceration will deepen as those without jobs are increasingly subjected to coercive controls and survival economies.

Of course, none of these outcomes is inevitable. But this analysis is based on the current tendencies of capitalism, and on the problems that are likely to arise as surplus populations continue to grow. These trends portend a crisis of work, and a crisis of any society based upon the institution of wage labour.

Under capitalism, jobs have been pivotal to our social lives and sense of who we are, as well as being the sole source of income for most people. What the next two decades portend is a future in which the global economy is increasingly unable to produce enough jobs (let alone good jobs), yet where we remain dependent upon jobs for our living. Political parties and trade unions appear ignorant of this crisis, struggling to manage its symptoms even as automation promises to toss more and more workers aside. In the face of these tensions, the political project for the twenty-first-century left must be to build an economy in which people are no longer dependent upon wage labour for survival.

As we will argue in the next few chapters, this struggle can and should span an array of different approaches: it means creating hegemonic ideas about the obsolescence of drudgery, shifting the goals of trade unions from resisting automation to job-sharing and reduced working weeks,[160] government subsidies for automation investment, and raising the cost of labour for capital,[161] along with many other options.[162] It means opposing the expulsion of surplus populations and attacking the mechanisms of control over them. Mass incarceration and the racialised system of domination associated with it must be abolished,[163] and the spatial mechanisms of control – ranging from ghettos to border controls – must be taken apart to ensure the free movement of peoples. And the welfare state must be defended, not as an end in itself, but as a necessary component of a broader post-work society. The future remains open, and which direction the crisis of work takes is precisely the political struggle before us.

Chapter 6

Post-Work Imaginaries

The goal of the future is full unemployment.

Arthur C. Clarke

Whereas the previous chapter analysed the changing social conditions that are making a post-work world increasingly necessary, this chapter will outline what a post-work world might mean in practice.[1] To that end, we advance some broad demands to start building a platform for a post-work society. In asserting the centrality of demands, we are breaking with a widespread tendency of today's radical left that believes making no demands is the height of radicalism.[2] These critics often claim that making a demand means giving into the existing order of things by asking, and therefore legitimating, an authority. But these accounts miss the antagonism at the heart of making demands, and the ways in which they are essential for constituting an active agent of change.[3] In this light, the rejection of demands is a symptom of theoretical confusion, not practical progress. A politics without demands is simply a collection of aimless bodies. Any meaningful vision of the future will set out proposals and goals, and this chapter is a contribution to that potential discussion. None of the proposals presented will be radically new, but this is part of their strength: it is not a free-floating project, since frameworks and movements already exist and have traction in the world.

Today, revolutionary demands appear naive, while reformist demands appear futile. Too often that is where the debate ends, with each side denouncing the other and the strategic imperative to change our conditions forgotten. The demands we propose are therefore intended as *non-reformist reforms*. By this we mean three things. First, they have a utopian edge that strains at the limits of what capitalism can concede. This transforms them from polite requests into insistent demands charged with belligerence and antagonism. Such demands combine the futural orientation of utopias with the immediate intervention of the demand, invoking a 'utopianism without apology'.[4] Second, these non-reformist proposals are grounded in real tendencies of the world today, giving them a viability that revolutionary dreams lack. Third, and most importantly, such demands shift the current political equilibrium and construct a platform for further development. They project an open-ended escape from the present, rather than a mechanical transition to the next, predetermined stage of history.[5] The proposals in this chapter will not break us out of capitalism, but they do promise to break us out of neoliberalism, and to establish a new equilibrium of political, economic and social forces. From the social democratic consensus to the neoliberal consensus, our argument is that the left should mobilise around a post-work consensus. With a post-work society, we would have even more potential to launch forward to greater goals. But this is a project that must be carried out over the long term: decades rather than years, cultural shifts rather than electoral cycles. Given the reality of the weakened left today, there is only one way forward: to patiently rebuild its power – a topic that will be covered in the chapters to follow. There simply is no other way to bring about a post-work world. We must therefore attend to these longer-term strategic goals, and rebuild the collective agencies that might eventually bring them about. By directing the left towards a post-work future, not only will significant gains be aimed for – such as the reduction of drudgery and poverty – but political power will be built in the process. In the end, we believe a post-work society is not only achievable, given the material conditions, but also viable and desirable.[6] This chapter charts a way forward: building a post-work society on the basis of fully automating the economy, reducing the working week, implementing a universal basic income, and achieving a cultural shift in the understanding of work.

FULL AUTOMATION

Our first demand is for a fully automated economy. Using the latest technological developments, such an economy would aim to liberate humanity from the drudgery of work while *simultaneously* producing increasing amounts of wealth. Without full automation, postcapitalist futures must necessarily choose between abundance at the expense of freedom (echoing the work-centricity of Soviet Russia) or freedom at the expense of abundance, represented by primitivist dystopias.[7] With automation, by contrast, machines can increasingly produce all necessary goods and services, while also releasing humanity from the effort of producing them.[8] For this reason, we argue that the tendencies towards automation and the replacement of human labour should be enthusiastically accelerated and targeted as a political project of the left.[9] This is a project that takes an existing capitalist tendency and seeks to push it beyond the acceptable parameters of capitalist social relations.

Capitalism has long been synonymous with rapid changes in technology: driven by the imperative to accumulate, the means of production are continually transformed.[10] In the nineteenth century, agriculture began to be mechanised, and small plots of land became increasingly centralised under larger and larger industrial farms. Craftwork was transformed too, with machinery appearing as an alien intervention into the production process. Work that had traditionally been undertaken by a skilled labourer was now broken down into its deskilled constituent tasks, and often carried out using machinery.[11] Workers became assigned to partial tasks, and tools that had once been governed by workers became machines that rhythmically conducted the labourers.[12] Work became increasingly repetitive, deskilled and ruled by machinery – with greater demand for cheap unskilled labourers (particularly women and children).[13] In the early twentieth century, this tendency began to shift with the introduction of technologies that eliminated the most routine and mundane of manual tasks (such as hauling and conveying goods). Skilled workers became increasingly necessary in overseeing the new machines, carrying out expanding service work, and managing the increasingly large firms that were emerging.[14] The need for skilled labour was further amplified in the early twentieth century by the rise of office technologies – typewriters, photocopiers, and so on – that required relatively well-educated operators. In other words, technology is not uniformly deskilling, and the increased demand for skilled labour over the past century testifies to that.[15] Over this period, manufacturing employment continued to decline, due to its susceptibility to productivity-enhancing technology.[16] The automation of mass-production manufacturing in the early twentieth century was eventually extended, with the automation of small-batch manufacturing.[17] While the industrial sector employed 1,000 robots in 1970, today it uses over 1.6 million robots.[18] In terms of employment, manufacturing has reached a global saturation point. Even in developing countries, the trend is towards deindustrialisation, with employment growth now confined predominantly to the service sector.[19] Concurrent with the decline of manufacturing, the latter half of the twentieth century oversaw another shift. While earlier office technologies had *supplemented* workers and increased demand for them, the development of the microprocessor and computing technologies began to *replace* semi-skilled service workers in many areas – for example, telephone operators and secretaries.[20] The roboticisation of services is now gathering steam, with over 150,000 professional service robots sold in the past fifteen years.[21] Under particular threat have been 'routine' jobs – jobs that can be codified into a series of steps. These are tasks that computers are perfectly suited to accomplish once a programmer has created the appropriate software, leading to a drastic reduction in the numbers of routine manual and cognitive jobs over the past four decades.[22] The result has been a polarisation of the labour market, since many middle-wage, mid-skilled jobs are routine, and therefore subject to automation.[23] Across both North America and Western Europe, the labour market is now characterised by a predominance of workers in low-skilled, low-wage manual and service jobs (for example, fast-food, retail, transport, hospitality and warehouse workers), along with a smaller number of workers in high-skilled, high-wage, non-routine cognitive jobs.[24]

The most recent wave of automation is poised to change this distribution of the labour market drastically, as it comes to encompass every aspect of the economy: data collection (radio-frequency identification, big data); new kinds of production (the flexible production of robots,[25] additive manufacturing,[26] automated fast food); services (AI customer assistance, care for the elderly); decision-making (computational models, software agents); financial allocation (algorithmic trading); and especially distribution (the logistics revolution, self-driving cars,[27] drone container ships and automated warehouses).[28] In every single function of the economy – from production to distribution to management to retail – we see large-scale tendencies towards automation.[29] This latest wave of automation is predicated upon algorithmic enhancements (particularly in machine learning and deep learning), rapid developments in robotics and exponential growth in computing power (the source of big data) that are coalescing into a 'second machine age' that is transforming the range of tasks that machines can fulfil.[30] It is creating an era that is historically unique in a number of ways. New pattern-recognition technologies are rendering both routine *and* non-routine tasks subject to automation: complex communication technologies are making computers better than humans at certain skilled-knowledge tasks, and advances in robotics are rapidly making technology better at a wide variety of manual-labour tasks.[31] For instance, self-driving cars involve the automation of non-routine manual tasks, and non-routine cognitive tasks such as writing news stories or researching legal precedents are now being accomplished by robots.[32] The scope of these developments means that everyone from stock analysts to construction workers to chefs to journalists is vulnerable to being replaced by machines.[33] Workers who move symbols on a screen are as at risk as those moving goods around a warehouse. One report forecasts a 'depopulation of trading floors' as robots continue infiltrating the financial world;[34] retail jobs – long a bastion of post-industrial employment – are set to be taken over by machines;[35] and over 140 million cognitive jobs worldwide are forecast to be eliminated.[36] While the last wave of automation led to a polarisation of the labour market, this newest wave looks set to decimate the low-skilled, low-wage end of the labour market.[37] And as robots substitute for human labour, workers are likely to face lower wages and increasing immiseration.[38] At the very least then, the emerging wave of automation will drastically change the composition of the labour market, and potentially lead to a significant reduction in demand for workers.

A number of economists have pointed out, however, that productivity has not increased to the degree that would be expected by a revolution in automation.[39] If a machine is replacing half of the workers in a factory, productivity should double if the factory produces the same number of goods. In fact, however, there has been a broad global slowdown in productivity growth over the past decade, particularly following the crisis.[40] Leaving aside the fact that productivity is a notoriously difficult thing to measure, we believe a few phenomena can help explain this anomaly. First, it is highly likely that low wages are repressing investment in productivity-enhancing technologies. Access to a large reserve of cheap labour means that companies have less incentive to focus on capital investment. Why purchase new machines when cheaper workers will do the same for less? This means that in the effort to bring about full automation, fighting for higher global wages is a crucial complementary task. Second, there is likely a delay factor at work. In the 1990s, the IT revolution took some time to become expressed in productivity figures, as companies had to invest and then adapt to the new capacities of these technologies. Organisations have to be changed, new skills have to be learned, and processes have to be reworked in order to make effective use of these new technologies. In general, it appears that investments in digital technologies face productivity lags of five to fifteen years.[41] Today, many of the technologies under discussion are incredibly new and were unimaginable even a decade ago. This novelty means that we should expect a delay in the response of productivity figures, as the technologies are adopted and then adapted into the way businesses run.[42] Finally, and most importantly, our argument here relies largely on a normative claim rather than a descriptive one. Full automation is something that can and should be achieved, regardless of whether it is yet being carried out. For instance, out of the US companies that could benefit from incorporating industrial robots, less than 10 per cent have done so.[43] This is but one area for full automation to take hold in, and this reiterates the importance of making full automation a *political demand*, rather than assuming it will come about from *economic necessity*. A variety of policies can help in this project: more state investment, higher minimum wages and research devoted to technologies that replace rather than augment workers. In the most detailed estimates of the labour market, it is suggested that between 47 and 80 per cent of today's jobs are capable of being automated.[44] Let us take this estimate not as a deterministic prediction, but instead as the outer limit of a political project against work. We should take these numbers as a standard against which to measure our success.

While full automation of the economy is presented here as an ideal and a demand, in practice it is unlikely to be fully achieved.[45] In certain spheres, human labour is likely to continue for technical, economic and ethical reasons. On a technical level, machines today remain worse than humans at jobs involving creative work, highly flexible work, affective work and most tasks relying on tacit rather than explicit knowledge.[46] The engineering problems involved in automating these tasks appear insurmountable for the next two decades (though similar claims were made about self-driving cars ten years ago), and a programme of full automation would aim to invest research money into overcoming these limits. A second barrier to full automation occurs for economic reasons: certain tasks can already be completed by machines, but the cost of the machines exceeds the cost of the equivalent labour.[47] Despite the efficiency, accuracy and productivity of machine labour, capitalism prefers to make profits, and therefore uses human labour whenever it is cheaper than capital investment. A programme of full automation would aim to overcome this as well, through measures as simple as raising the minimum wage, supporting labour movements and using state subsidies to incentivise the replacement of human labour.

A final limit of full automation is the moral status we give to certain jobs, such as care work.[48] These tasks, including the raising of children, are ones that many would argue must be carried out by human beings. We can outline two broad approaches to these sorts of labours. A first approach would agree that such labour has moral value and should be carried out by humans rather than machines. In a post-work society, however, care labour could be given greater value, turning society away from the privileged status bestowed upon profitable labour. The free time that accrues from full automation could also facilitate experimentation with alternative domestic arrangements. There is a long history of utopian experiments that can be drawn upon to rethink how our societies organise domestic, reproductive and care labour.[49] All of this, it must be stressed, would still require a political movement to achieve; a post-work world may facilitate change, but it cannot guarantee it. A more radical approach, however, argues that automating much of this labour should be a goal for the future.[50] Indeed, the stereotype that women are naturally nurturing and desiring of this affective labour is often a pernicious cover for their continued exploitation. But what if much of this labour could be eliminated? Traditionally, the household has been a space that featured little technological change: its unpaid nature and lack of productivity norms have given capitalism few incentives to invest in the reduction of household labour.[51] Yet increasingly, domestic tasks like cleaning the house and folding clothes, for example, can be delegated to machines.[52] Assistive technologies and affective computing are also making inroads in automating some of the highly personal and embarrassing care work that might be better suited to impersonal robots.[53] More speculatively, some have argued that the pain and suffering involved in pregnancy is something that should be relegated to the past, rather than mystified as natural and beautiful.[54] In this vision, synthetic forms of biological reproduction would enable a newfound equality between the sexes. We will not adjudicate on these paths here, but simply set them out as options opened up by a post-work world. Whatever approach is taken, though, the point is that labour will not be immediately or entirely eliminated, but instead progressively reduced. Full automation is a utopian demand that aims to reduce necessary labour *as much as possible*.

IT'S NOT MONDAYS YOU HATE, IT'S YOUR JOB

A second major demand for building a post-work platform involves a return to classic ideas about reducing the length of the working week with no cut in pay. From the beginning of capitalism, workers have struggled against the imposition of fixed working hours, and the demand for shorter hours was a key component of the early labour movement.[55] Initial battles saw high levels of resistance in the form of individual absenteeism, numerous holidays and irregular work habits.[56] This resistance to normal working hours continues today in widespread slacking off, with workers often surfing the internet rather than doing their job.[57] At every step of the way, then, workers have struggled to escape normal working hours, and many of the labour movement's earliest successes had to do with reducing work time. The two-day weekend, for example, emerged spontaneously from workers' predilection for drinking and spending an extra day recovering rather than working.[58] The weekend's eventual consolidation as a recognised and bounded period of time off was the product of sustained political struggles (a process that was not completed in the Western world until the 1970s).[59] Likewise, workers achieved significant success in reducing the working week from sixty hours in 1900 to just below thirty-five hours during the Great Depression.[60] Such was the speed of success that, over a period of five years in the 1930s, the working week declined by eighteen hours.[61] During the earlier years of the Depression, the idea of a shorter working week enjoyed bipartisan support in the United States, and legislation for a thirty-hour working week was thought to be imminent.[62] Simultaneously, intellectuals prophesied even further reductions in work time – imagining worlds where work was reduced to a bare minimum. In a classic statement, Paul Lafargue argued for limiting work to just three hours a day.[63] Keynes famously argued for the same outcome, calculating that by 2030 we would all be working fifteen-hour working weeks – though it is less well known that he was simply verbalising what were the broadly held beliefs of the time.[64] And Marx made the shortening of the working week central to his entire postcapitalist vision, arguing that it represented a 'basic prerequisite' to reaching 'the realm of freedom'.[65]

But such visions of a three-hour work day have disappeared. The near century-long push for shorter working hours ended abruptly during the Great Depression, when business opinion and government policy decided to use make-work programmes in response to unemployment.[66] Soon after World War II, the working week stabilised at forty hours across much of the Western world, and there has since been little serious consideration of changing this.[67] Instead there has been a general expansion of work in the ensuing decades. First, there has been an increase in time spent at jobs throughout society.[68] As women entered the workforce, the working week remained the same, and the overall amount of time devoted to jobs therefore increased.[69] Secondly, there has been a progressive elimination of the work–life distinction, with work coming to permeate every aspect of our waking lives. Many of us are now tied to work all the time, with emails, phone calls, texts and job anxieties imping-ing upon us constantly.[70] Salaried workers are often compelled to work unrec-ognised overtime, while many workers feel the social pressure to be seen working long hours. These demands mean that the average full-time US worker in fact logs closer to forty-seven hours a week.[71] On top of this, a vast amount of work is unpaid and therefore uncounted in official data (there is also an ongoing gender divide within this unpaid labour force).[72] While waged work remains difficult for many to find, unpaid work is proliferating – an entire sphere of 'shadow work' is emerging with automation at the point of sale, with work being delegated to users (think self-checkouts and ATMs).[73] Moreover, there is the hidden labour required to retain a job: financial management, job searching if unemployed, constant skills training, commuting time, and the all-important (gendered) sphere of the labour involved in caring for children, family members and other dependents.[74]

If work has extended itself into so many areas of our lives, a return to a shorter working week would bring with it a number of benefits. Beyond the most obvious – that it increases free time – it would bring with it a series of more subtle benefits.[75] In the first place, reducing the working week constitutes a key response to rising automation. In fact, the role of this policy in previous periods of automation is often forgotten. Many commentators have rightly pointed to the history of technological change to show that it need not lead to mass unemployment. However, the primary periods of automation coincided with significant reductions in the working week; employment was often sustained by redistributing the work. A second benefit of this policy is its various environmental advantages. For instance, reductions in the working week would lead to significant reductions in energy consumption and our overall carbon footprint.[76] Increased free time would also mean a reduction in all the convenience goods bought to fit into our hectic work schedules. More broadly, using productivity improvements for less work, rather than more output, would mean that energy efficiency improvements would go towards reducing environmental impacts.[77] A reduction in working hours is therefore an essential plank in any response to climate change. Other research suggests that a shorter working week would bring a general reduction in the stress, anxiety and mental health problems fostered by neoliberalism.[78] But one of the most important reasons for reducing work time is that it is a demand that both consolidates and generates class power. In the first place, reducing work time can be deployed as a temporary tactic in political struggle – working to contract, strikes and other ways of removing labour time are means to exert pressure on capitalists. But secondly – and most importantly – the reduction of the working week also makes the labour movement stronger. By withdrawing labour hours from the market, the total supply of labour goes down and worker power increases. As two commentators recently noted, 'No other bargaining demand simultaneously enhances bargaining position. Furthermore, no other strategic logic initiates a continuous virtuous cycle in which each victory establishes the conditions for strength in the next struggle.'[79] For these reasons, the goal of reducing the working week should be an immediate and prominent demand of the twenty-first-century left.

Our preference is for the establishment of a three-day weekend, rather than a reduction in the working day, in order to cut down on commuting and to build upon the long holiday weekends already in existence. This demand can be achieved in a number of ways – through trade union struggles, pressure from social movements, and legislative change by political parties. Trade unions building a strategy for the future, rather than accepting the capitalist demand for jobs at all costs, could use collective bargaining to accept automation in return for a shorter working week. Indeed, the historical record suggests that trade unions are often reactive in the face of technological change, and that wage concessions only delay automation, rather than preventing it.[80] An alternative approach that focused on the reduction and diffusion of work could reduce work without leaving workers out on the streets.[81] Efforts can also be made to gain recognition for unofficial, unpaid labour as part of the working week, reducing it simply by bringing attention to it.[82] A focus on a shorter working week also requires that unions build links with part-time and precarious workers. But while unions are necessary in this struggle, they are not sufficient, for the simple reason that each sector has different potentials for automation and productivity increases.[83] A broader struggle is necessary if there is to be a break with the current logic of neoliberalism. Social movements and ideological institutions must contribute to this struggle by shaping the space of possibility. A number of think tanks, including the New Economics Foundation and the Jimmy Reid Foundation, have started to call openly for a reduction of the working week.[84] Groups in the UK such as the Precarious Workers Brigade and Plan C are highlighting unpaid work and mobilising around issues concerning the status of work in society today.[85] But, most significantly, there is already a high level of public desire for the reduction of the working week, with public opinion polls showing a majority of the population support the idea.[86] There are also a variety of policy approaches to shorten the working week. Interventions can alter labour costs from a per-person basis to a per-hour basis, making it less cost-effective for businesses to enforce long hours.[87] Countries like Belgium and the Netherlands have given workers the right to demand reduced hours without being discriminated against by employers. The Netherlands has also begun to shorten the working week at each end of the age spectrum. The young and the old are now transitioned into and out of the workforce, respectively, through gradual changes in their work hours.[88] All of these options can and should be mobilised in pursuit of a project to reduce the working week.

THE WAGE DON'T FIT

These first two proposals equate to the reduction of labour demand through full automation, and the reduction of labour supply through the shortening of the working week.[89] The combined outcome of these measures would be the liberation of a significant amount of free time without a reduction in economic output or a significant increase in unemployment. Yet this free time will be of little value if people continue struggling to make ends meet. As Paul Mattick puts it, 'the leisure of the starving, or the needy, is no leisure at all but a relentless activity aimed at staying alive or improving their situation'.[90] The underemployed, for instance, have plenty of free time but lack the means to enjoy it. Underemployed, it turns out, is really just a euphemism for under-waged. This is why an essential demand in a post-work society is for a universal basic income (UBI), giving every citizen a liveable amount of money without any means-testing.[91] It is an idea that has periodically popped up throughout history.[92] In the early 1940s, a version of it was advanced as an alternative to the Beveridge Report that eventually shaped the UK welfare state.[93] In a now largely forgotten period during the 1960s and 1970s, the basic income was central to proposals for US welfare reform. Economists, NGOs and policymakers explored the idea in detail,[94] and a number of small-scale experiments were set up in Canada and the United States.[95] Such was the influence of UBI that over 1,300 economists signed a petition pushing the US Congress to enact a 'national system of income guarantees'.[96] Three separate administrations gave serious consideration to the proposal, and two presidents – Nixon and Carter – attempted to pass legislation to achieve it.[97] In other words, UBI very nearly became a reality in the 1970s.[98] While Alaska eventually implemented a basic income funded by its oil wealth, the idea largely disappeared from debate in the wake of neoliberal hegemony.[99] But recent years have seen the idea undergo a resurgence in popularity. In both mainstream and critical media, it has gained traction, being taken up by Paul Krugman, Martin Wolf, the *New York Times*, the *Financial Times* and the *Economist*.[100] The Swiss are holding a referendum on UBI in 2016, the proposal has been recommended by parliamentary committees in other countries, various political parties have adopted it in their manifestos, and there have been new experiments with it in Namibia and India.[101] The idea has global scope, having been promoted forcefully by groups in Brazil, South Africa, Italy and Germany, and by an international network involving over twenty countries.[102] The movement for a UBI is thus once again resurgent in the wake of the 2008 crisis and the austerity regimes put in place after it.

The demand for a UBI, however, is subject to competing hegemonic forces. It is just as open to being mobilised for a libertarian dystopia as for a post-work society – an ambiguity that has led many to mistakenly conflate the two poles. In demanding a UBI, therefore, three key factors must be articulated in order to make it meaningful: it must provide a *sufficient* amount of income to live on; it must be *universal*, provided to everyone unconditionally; and it must be a *supplement* to the welfare state rather than a replacement of it. The first point is obvious enough: a UBI must provide a materially adequate income. The exact amount will vary between countries and regions, but it can be relatively easily arrived at with existing data. The risk is that, if set too low, UBI becomes just a government subsidy to businesses. In addition, UBI must be universal and given to everyone unconditionally. As there would be no means-testing or other measures required to receive the UBI, it would break free of the disciplinary nature of welfare capitalism.[103] Moreover, a universal grant avoids the stigmatisation of welfare, since everyone receives it. As we argued in Chapter 4, the invocation of 'universalism' also obliges the continual subversion of any restricted application of a basic income (in terms of individuals' status as citizens, immigrants or prisoners). The demand for universality provides the basis for a continued struggle to expand the scope and scale of the basic income. Lastly, the UBI must be a supplement to the welfare state. The conservative argument for a basic income – which must be avoided at all costs – is that it should simply replace the welfare state by providing a lump sum of money to every individual. In this scenario, the UBI would just become a vector of increased marketisation, transforming social services into private markets. Rather than being some aberration of neoliberalism, it would simply extend its essential gesture by creating new markets. By contrast, the demand made here is for UBI as a supplement to a revived welfare state.[104]

Drawing upon moral arguments and empirical research, there are a vast number of reasons to support a UBI: reduced poverty, better public health and reduced health costs, fewer high school dropouts, reductions in petty crime, more time with family and friends, and less state bureaucracy.[105] Depending on how UBI is presented, it is capable of generating support from across the political spectrum – from libertarians, conservatives, anarchists, Marxists and feminists, among others. The potency of the demand lies partly in this ambiguity, making it capable of mobilising broad popular support.[106]

However, for our purposes the significance of UBI as a demand lies in four key interrelated factors.

The first point to emphasise is that the demand for UBI is a demand for a political transformation, not just an economic one. It is often thought that UBI is simply a form of redistribution from the rich to the poor, or that it is just a measure to maintain economic growth by stimulating consumer demand. From this perspective, UBI would have impeccable reformist credentials and be little more than a glorified progressive tax system. Yet the real significance of UBI lies in the way it overturns the asymmetry of power that currently exists between labour and capital. As we saw in the discussion of surplus populations, the proletariat is defined by its separation from the means of production and subsistence. The proletariat is thereby forced to sell itself in the job market in order to gain the income necessary to survive. The most fortunate among us have the leisure to choose *which* job to take, but few of us have the capacity to choose *no* job. A basic income changes this condition, by giving the proletariat a means of subsistence without dependency on a job.[107] Workers, in other words, have the option to choose whether to take a job or not (in many ways, taking neoclassical economics at its word, and making work truly voluntary). A UBI therefore unbinds the coercive aspects of wage labour, partially decommodifies labour, and thus transforms the political relationship between labour and capital.

This transformation – making work voluntary rather than coerced – has a number of significant consequences. In the first place, it increases class power by reducing slack in the labour market. Surplus populations show what happens when there are large amounts of slack in the labour market: wages fall, and employers are free to debase workers.[108] By contrast, when the labour market is tight, labour gains the political edge. The economist Michał Kalecki recognised this long ago when he argued that it explained why full employment would be resisted at every step.[109] If every worker were employed, the threat of being fired would lose its disciplinary character – there would be more than enough jobs waiting just outside. Workers would gain the upper hand, and capital would lose its political power. The same dynamic holds for a basic income: by eliminating the reliance on wage labour, workers gain control over how much labour to supply, giving them significant power in the labour market. Class power is also increased in a variety of other ways. Strikes are easier to mobilise, since workers no longer have to worry about pay being docked or dwindling strike funds. The amount of time spent working for a wage can be modified to one's own desire, with free time spent building communities and engaging with politics. One can slow down and reflect, safely protected from the constant pressures of neoliberalism. The anxieties that surround work and unemployment are reduced with the safety net of a UBI.[110] Moreover, the demand for UBI combines the needs of the employed, the unemployed, the underemployed, migrant labour, temporary workers, students and the disabled.[111] It articulates a common interest between these groups and provides a populist orientation for them to mobilise towards.

The second related feature of UBI is that it transforms precarity and unemployment from a state of insecurity to a state of voluntary flexibility. It is often forgotten that the initial push for flexible labour came from workers, as a way of demolishing the constraining permanency of traditional Fordist labour.[112] The repetitiveness of a nine-to-five job, combined with the tediousness of most work, is hardly an appealing prospect for a life-long career. The demands of care labour often require a flexible approach as well, further undermining the appeal of traditional jobs. Marx himself invokes the liberating aspects of flexible labour in his famous claim that communism 'makes it possible for me to do one thing today and another tomorrow, to hunt in the morning, fish in the afternoon, rear cattle in the evening, criticise after dinner, just as I have a mind, without ever becoming hunter, fisherman, herdsman or critic'.[113] In the face of these desires for flexibility, capital adapted and co-opted them into a new form of exploitation. Today, flexible labour simply presents itself as precarity and insecurity, rather than freedom. The UBI responds to this generalisation of precarity and transforms it from a state to be feared back into a state of liberation.

Third, a basic income would necessitate a rethinking of the values attributed to different types of work. Given that workers would no longer be forced to take a job, they could instead simply reject jobs that paid too little, required too much work, offered too few benefits, or were demeaning and undignified. Low-waged work is often crass and disempowering, and under a programme of UBI it is unlikely that many would want to undertake it. The result would be that hazardous, boring and unattractive work would have to be better paid, while more rewarding, invigorating and attractive work would be less well paid. In other words, the *nature* of work would become a measure of its value, not merely its *profitability*.[114] The outcome of this revaluation would also mean that, as wages for the worst jobs rose, there would be new incentives to automate them. UBI therefore forms a positive-feedback loop with the demand for full automation. On the other hand, a basic income would not only transform the value of the worst jobs, but also go some way towards recognising the unpaid labour of most care work. In the same way that the demand for wages for housework recognised and politicised the domestic labour of women, so too does UBI recognise and politicise the generalised way in which we are all responsible for reproducing society: from informal to formal work, from domestic to public work, from individual to collective work. What is central is not productive labour, defined in either traditional Marxist or neoclassical terms, but rather the more general category of reproductive labour.[115] Given that we all contribute to the production and reproduction of capitalism, our activity deserves to be remunerated as well.[116] In recognising this, the UBI indicates a shift from remuneration based upon ability to remuneration based upon basic need.[117] All the genetic, historical and social variations that make effort a poor measure of a person's worth are rejected here, and instead people are valued simply for being people.

Finally, a basic income is a fundamentally feminist proposal. Its disregard for the gendered division of labour overcomes some of the biases of the traditional welfare state predicated upon a male breadwinner.[118] Equally, it recognises the contributions of unwaged domestic labourers to the reproduction of society and provides them with an income accordingly. The financial independence that comes with a basic income is also crucial to developing the synthetic freedom of women. It enables experimentation with different forms of family and community structure that are no longer bound to the model of the privatised nuclear family.[119] And financial independence can reconfigure intimate relationships as well: one of the more unexpected findings of experiments with UBI has been that the divorce rate tended to rise.[120] Conservative commentators jumped on this as proof of the demand's immorality, but higher divorce rates are easily explained as women gaining the financial means to leave dysfunctional relationships.[121] A basic income can therefore enable easier experimentation with the family structure, more possibilities for the provision of childcare and an easier transformation of the gendered division of labour. Moreover, unlike the demand for 'wages for housework' in the 1970s, the demand for UBI promises to break out of the wage relation rather than reinforce it.

While a universal basic income may appear economically reformist, its political implications are therefore significant. It transforms precarity, it recognises social labour, it makes class power easier to mobilise, and it extends the space in which to experiment with how we organise communities and families. It is a redistribution mechanism that transforms production relations. It is an economic mechanism that changes the politics of work. And in terms of class struggle, there is little to distinguish full employment from full unemployment: both tighten the labour market, give power to labour, and make it more difficult to exploit workers. Full unemployment has the added advantages of not being reliant upon the gendered division of labour between the household and the formal economy, of not keeping workers chained to the wage relation, and of allowing workers autonomy over their lives. For all of these reasons, the classic social democratic demand for full employment should be replaced with the future-orientated demand for full unemployment.

THE RIGHT TO BE LAZY

What are the impediments to implementing a basic income? While the problem of funding UBI appears immense, most research in fact suggests that it would be relatively easy to finance through some combination of reducing duplicate programmes, raising taxes on the rich, inheritance taxes, consumption taxes, carbon taxes, cutting spending on the military, cutting industry and agriculture subsidies, and cracking down on tax evasion.[122] The most difficult hurdles for UBI – and for a post-work society – are not economic, but political and cultural: political, because the forces that will mobilise against it are immense; and cultural, because work is so deeply ingrained into our very identity. We will examine the political obstacles in the next two chapters, but turn to the cultural ones here.

One of the most difficult problems in implementing a UBI and building a post-work society will be overcoming the pervasive pressure to submit to the work ethic.[123] Indeed, the failure of the United States' earlier attempt to implement a basic income was primarily because it challenged accepted notions about the work ethic of the poor and unemployed.[124] Rather than seeing unemployment as the result of a deficient individual work ethic, the UBI proposal recognised it as a structural problem. Yet the language that framed the proposal maintained strict divisions between those who were working and those who were on welfare, despite the plan effacing such a distinction. The working poor ended up rejecting the plan out of a fear of being stigmatised as a welfare recipient. Racial biases reinforced this resistance, since welfare was seen as a black issue, and whites were loath to be associated with it. And the lack of a class identification between the working poor and unemployed – the surplus population – meant there was no social basis for a meaningful movement in favour of a basic income.[125] Overcoming the work ethic will be equally central to any future attempts at building a post-work world. As we saw in Chapter 3, neoliberalism has established a set of incentives that compel us to act and identify ourselves as competitive subjects. Orbiting around this subject is a constellation of images related to self-reliance and independence that necessarily conflict with the programme of a post-work society. Our lives have become increasingly structured around competitive self-realisation, and work has become the primary avenue for achieving this.[126] Work, no matter how degrading or low-paid or inconvenient, is deemed an ultimate good. This is the mantra of both mainstream political parties and most trade unions, associated with rhetoric about getting people back into work, the importance of working families, and cutting welfare so that 'it always pays to work'. This is matched by a parallel cultural effort demonising those without jobs. Newspapers blare headlines about the worthlessness of welfare recipients, TV shows sensationalise and mock the poor, and the ever looming figure of the welfare cheat is continually evoked. Work has become central to our very self-conception – so much so that when presented with the idea of doing less work, many people ask, 'But what would I do?' The fact that so many people find it impossible to imagine a meaningful life outside of work demonstrates the extent to which the work ethic has infected our minds.

While typically associated with the protestant work ethic, the submission to work is in fact implicit in many religions.[127] These ethics demand dedication to one's work regardless of the nature of the job, instilling a moral imperative that drudgery should be valued.[128] While originating in religious ideas about ensuring a better afterlife, the goal of the work ethic was eventually replaced with a secular devotion to improvement in this life. More contemporary forms of this imperative have taken on a liberal-humanist character, portraying work as the central means of self-expression.[129] Work has come to be driven into our identity, portrayed as the only means for true self-fulfilment.[130] In a job interview, for instance, everyone knows the worst answer to 'Why do you want this job?' is to say 'Money', even as it remains the repressed truth. Contemporary service work heightens this phenomenon. In the absence of clear metrics for productivity, workers instead put on performances of productivity – pretending to enjoy their job or smiling while being yelled at by a customer. Working long hours has become a sign of devotion to the job, even as it perpetuates the gender pay gap.[131] With work tied so tightly into our identities, overcoming the work ethic will require us overcoming ourselves.

The central ideological support for the work ethic is that remuneration be tied to suffering. Everywhere one looks, there is a drive to make people suffer before they can receive a reward. The epithets thrown at homeless beggars, the demonization of those on the dole, the labyrinthine system of bureaucracy set up to receive benefits, the unpaid 'job experience' imposed upon the unemployed, the sadistic penalisation of those who are seen as getting something for free – all reveal the truth that for our societies, remuneration requires work and suffering. Whether for a religious or secular goal, suffering is thought to constitute a necessary rite of passage. People must endure through work before they can receive wages, they must prove their worthiness before the eyes of capital. This thinking has an obvious theological basis – where suffering is thought to be not only meaningful, but in fact the very condition of meaning. A life without suffering is seen as frivolous and meaningless. This position must be rejected as a holdover from a now-transcended stage of human history. The drive to make suffering meaningful may have had some functional logic in times when poverty, illness and starvation were necessary features of existence. But we should reject this logic today and recognise that we have moved beyond the need to ground meaning in suffering. Work, and the suffering that accompanies it, should not be glorified.

What is needed, therefore, is a counter-hegemonic approach to work: a project that would overturn existing ideas about the necessity and desirability of work, and the imposition of suffering as a basis for remuneration. The media is already changing the conditions of possibility – positioning UBI as not only a possible solution, but increasingly as a necessary solution to problems of technological unemployment. These hegemonic trends should be amplified. The dominance of the work ethic also runs up against the changing material basis of the economy. Capitalism demands that people work in order to make a living, yet it is increasingly unable to generate enough jobs. The tensions between the value accorded to the work ethic and these material changes will only heighten the potential for transformation of the system. Actions to make precarity and joblessness an increasingly visible political problem would go some way to generating the support for a post-work society. (In the same way that Occupy raised awareness of inequality, and UK Uncut highlighted tax evasion.)[132] Perhaps most importantly, there is already a widespread hatred for jobs that can be tapped into. Much as neoliberal hegemony co-opted real desires and garnered active consent, so too must any post-work hegemony find its active force in the real desires of people. The widespread demand that others adopt the work ethic is matched only by the disdain we feel for our own jobs. Today, across the world, only 13 per cent of people say they find their jobs engaging.[133] Physically degraded, mentally drained and socially exhausted, most workers find themselves under immense amounts of stress in their jobs. For the vast majority of people, work offers no meaning, fulfilment or redemption – it is simply something to pay the bills. Those already excluded from jobs should not be fighting for inclusion in a society of work and labour, but rather be building the conditions to reproduce their lives outside of work. Changing the cultural consensus about the work ethic will mean taking actions at an everyday level, translating these medium-term goals into slogans, memes and chants. It will require undertaking the difficult and essential work of workplace organizing and campaigning – of mobilising people's passions in order to topple the dominance of the work ethic. The success of these efforts will be clear when media discussions about automation shift from fear-mongering over lost jobs to celebrations of the freedom from drudgery.[134]

THE REALM OF FREEDOM

A twenty-first-century left must seek to combat the centrality of work to contemporary life. In the end, our choice is between glorifying work and the working class or abolishing them both.[135] The former position finds its expression in the folk-political tendency to place value upon work, concrete labour and craftwork. Yet the latter is the only true postcapitalist position. Work must be refused and reduced, building our synthetic freedom in the process.[136] As we have set out in this chapter, achieving this will require the realisation of four minimal demands:

1. Full automation
2. The reduction of the working week
3. The provision of a basic income
4. The diminishment of the work ethic

While each of these proposals can be taken as an individual goal in itself, their real power is expressed when they are advanced as an integrated programme. This is not a simple, marginal reform, but an entirely new hegemonic formation to compete against the neoliberal and social democratic options. The demand for full automation amplifies the possibility of reducing the working week and heightens the need for a universal basic income. A reduction in the working week helps produce a sustainable economy and leverage class power. And a universal basic income amplifies the potential to reduce the working week and expand class power. It would also accelerate the project of full automation: as worker power rose and as the labour market tightened, the marginal cost of labour would increase as companies turned towards machinery in order to expand.[137] These goals resonate with each other, magnifying their combined power. And a new post-work hegemony would be resistant to reversion, having created a mass constituency benefiting from its continuation.[138] The ambition here is to take back the future from capitalism and build ourselves the twenty-first-century world we want. It is to provide the time and money that are central to any meaningful conception of freedom. The traditional battle cry of the left, demanding full employment, should therefore be replaced with a battle cry demanding full unemployment. But let us be clear: there is no technocratic solution, and there is no necessary progression into a post-work world. The struggles for full automation, a shorter working week, the end of the work ethic and a universal basic income are primarily political struggles. The post-work imaginary generates a hyperstitional image of progress – one that aims to make the future an active historical force in the present. The struggles that such a project will face require that the left move past its folk-political horizon, rebuild its power and adopt an expansive strategy for change. It is to these issues that we now turn.

Chapter 7

A New Common Sense

The key is to succeed in making 'common sense' go in a direction of change.

Pablo Iglesias

A post-work society holds a potentially broad appeal and would materially improve the lives of most – but this is no guarantee of it coming about. Media discussions of basic income and automation today often seem to assume the benevolence of elites, the political neutrality of technology and the inevitability of a post-work society. Yet an array of powerful forces is invested in the continuation of the status quo, and the left has been devastated over the past few decades. Misery remains more likely than luxury. Under current conditions, automation is likely to cause more unemployment, with the benefits of new technologies going to their wealthy owners. Any free time we get will be eliminated with the production of dreary new jobs or the extension of precarious existence. And if a basic income were achieved tomorrow, it would almost certainly be set below poverty levels and simply act as a handout to companies. To achieve a meaningful post-work society therefore requires changing the present political conditions. In turn, this requires the left to face squarely up to the dismal situation before it: trade unions lying in ruin, political parties rendered into neoliberal puppets, and a waning intellectual and cultural hegemony. State and corporate repression of the left has significantly intensified in recent decades, legal changes have made it more difficult to organise, generalised precarity has made us more insecure, and the militarisation of policing has rapidly gathered speed.[1] And beyond this lies the fact that our inner lives, our social world and our built environment are organised around work and its continuation. The shift to a post-work society, much like the shift to a decarbonised economy, is not just a matter of overcoming a few elite interests. More fundamentally, it is a matter of transforming society from the ground up. An engagement with the totality of power and capital is inevitable, and we should be under no illusions about the difficulties facing such a project. If full transformational change is not immediately possible, our efforts must be directed towards cracking open those spaces of possibility that do exist and fostering better political conditions over time. We must first reach a space within which more radical demands can be meaningfully articulated, and must therefore prepare for the long term if we wish to alter the terrain of politics substantially.

This ought not to be entirely unexpected. Capitalism did not emerge all at once, but instead percolated to a position of dominance over the course of centuries.[2] A large number of components had to be put in place: landless labourers, widespread commodity production, private property, technical sophistication, centralisation of wealth, a bourgeois class, a work ethic, and so on. These historical conditions are the components that enabled the systemic logic of capitalism eventually to gain traction in the world. The lesson here is that, just as capitalism relied upon the accumulation of a particular set of components, so too will postcapitalism. It will neither emerge all at once nor in the wake of some revolutionary moment. The task of the left must be to work out the conditions for postcapitalism and to struggle to build them on a continually expanding scale.

This chapter therefore begins from the premise that the contemporary left is in a dire situation and that any transformative project will take time. We limit our analysis here largely to Western capitalist democracies, with their peculiar apparatuses of political and economic power. We will mostly leave aside the immense (and immensely important) regions of the rest of the world.[3] However, it is worth reiterating that the problems of automation and surplus populations are global in nature, and the grounds for post-work are flourishing around the world – as demonstrated by recent experiments with basic incomes in India and Namibia, the surge in industrial automation across the most populous regions of the world, and the spontaneous emergence of movements against work in numerous countries. Though these dynamics are global, any political project to transform this situation will necessarily need to respond to particular conditions on the ground. While certain core principles will be translatable between contexts, they will need to be realised differently under different circumstances. With these qualifications in mind, how can a better future be built? The classic Leninist strategy of building dual power with a revolutionary party and overthrowing the state is obsolete.[4] Proponents of the Bolshevik Revolution model appear more useful as historical re-enactors than as guides for contemporary politics. Likewise, the recent history of revolutions – from the Iranian Revolution to the Arab Spring – has simply led to some combination of theocratic authoritarianism, military dictatorship and civil war. The electoral reformist approach is equally a failure. The idea of voting in a new world mutated into a convivial elite consensus during the postwar era and became ensconced within neoliberal ideology in recent decades. At its best, such reformism is doomed simply to ameliorate capitalism and act as a type of politically mediated homeostatic system. And as the latest cycle of struggles has shown, the folk-political approach of prioritising various forms of immediacy has failed to transform society. Piecemeal efforts, defensive struggles, withdrawals and prefigurative pockets of activity have been largely incapable of stemming the tide, let alone gaining ground on global capitalism. Equally, it remains insufficient simply to posit that progress will be worked out in practice or that the masses will spontaneously create a better world.[5] While there are undoubtedly elements of luck and unpredictability in any struggle, the difficulty of building a new world demands that strategic thought be carried out in advance. Our efforts must be organised strategically along broad lines, rather than dissipating into a series of partial and disconnected achievements. As modernity asserts, progress towards a better future comes on the back of deliberate reflection and conscious action.

Given the limits of these other approaches, we argue that the best way forward is a counter-hegemonic strategy. This is a strategy that is adaptable from positions of weakness, is scalable from the local to the global, and recognises the hold that capitalism has over every aspect of our lives, from our most intimate desires to the most abstract financial flows. A counter-hegemonic strategy entails a project to overturn the dominant neoliberal common sense and rejuvenate the collective imagination. Fundamentally, it is an attempt to install a new common sense – one organised around the crisis of work and its effects on the proletariat. In this, it involves preparatory work for moments when full-scale struggle erupts, transforming our social imagination and reconfiguring our sense of what is possible. It builds up support and a common language for a new world, seeking to alter the balance of power in preparation for when a crisis upsets the legitimacy of society. Unlike forms of folk politics, such a strategy is expansive, long-term, comfortable with abstraction and complexity, and aimed at overthrowing capitalist universalism.[6] In this chapter, we examine three possible sites of struggle – over the intellectual, cultural and technological mediums of neoliberal hegemony. The next section will examine hegemony at a theoretical level, while the rest of the chapter will explore illustrations of how a counter-hegemonic project might be put into practice – through utopian narratives, pluralist economics and the repurposing of technologies.

ENGINEERING CONSENT

The idea of 'hegemony' initially emerged as a way of explaining why ordinary people were not revolting against capitalism.[7] According to the traditional Marxist narrative, workers would become increasingly aware of the exploitative nature of capitalism and eventually organise to transcend it. Capitalism, it was believed, ought to be producing an ever more polarised world of capitalists versus the working class, in a process that underpinned a political strategy in which the organised working class would win control over the state through revolutionary means. But by the 1920s it was clear that this was not about to happen in western European democratic societies. How was it, then, that capitalism and the interests of the ruling classes were secured in democratic societies largely devoid of overt force? The Italian Marxist Antonio Gramsci answered that capitalist power was dependent on what he termed hegemony – the engineering of consent according to the dictates of one particular group. A hegemonic project builds a 'common sense' that installs the particular worldview of one group as the universal horizon of an entire society. By this means, hegemony enables a group to lead and rule over a society primarily through consent (both active and passive) rather than coercion.[8] This consent can be achieved in a variety of ways: the formation of explicit political alliances with other social groups, the dissemination of cultural values supporting a particular way of organising society (for example, the work ethic instilled by the media and through education), the alignment of interests between classes (for example, workers are better off when a capitalist economy is growing, even if this means mass inequality and environmental devastation) and through building technologies and infrastructures in such a way that they silently constrain social conflict (for example, by widening streets to prevent the erection of barricades during insurrections). In a broad and diffuse sense, hegemony enables relatively small groups of capitalists to 'lead' society as a whole, even when their material interests are at odds with those of the majority. Finally, as well as securing active and passive consent, hegemonic projects also deploy coercive means, such as imprisonment, police violence and intimidation, to neutralise those groups that cannot otherwise be led.[9] Taken together, these measures enable small groups to influence the general direction of a society, sometimes through the achievement and deployment of state power, but also outside the confines of the state.

The latter point is particularly important, because hegemony is not just a strategy of governance for those in power, but also a strategy for the marginal to transform society. A counter-hegemonic project enables marginal and oppressed groups to transform the balance of power in a society and bring about a new common sense. To abjure hegemony therefore implies an abandonment of the basic idea of winning and exercising power, and is to effectively give up on the primary terrain of political struggle.[10] While there are some on the left who explicitly endorse such a position,[11] to the degree that horizontalist movements have been successful they have tended to operate as a counter-hegemonic force. Occupy's major success – transforming the public discourse around inequality – is a prime example of this. A counter-hegemonic project will therefore seek to overturn an existing set of alliances, common sense, and rule by consent in order to install a new hegemony.[12] Such a project will seek to build the social conditions from which a new post-work world can emerge and will require an expansive approach that goes beyond the temporary and local measures of folk politics. It requires mobilisation across different social groups,[13] which means linking together a diversity of individual interests into a common desire for a post-work society. The neoliberal hegemony in the United States, for instance, came about by linking together the interests of economic liberals with those of social conservatives. This is a fractious (sometimes even contradictory) alliance, but it is one that finds common interests in the broad neoliberal framework by emphasising individual freedoms.[14] In addition, counter-hegemonic projects operate across diverse fields – from the state, to civil society, to the material infrastructure. This means an entire battery of actions are needed, such as seeking to spread media influence, attempting to win state power, controlling key sectors of the economy and designing important infrastructures. This project requires empirical and experimental work to identify the parts of these various fields that are operating to reinforce the present general direction of society. The Mont Pelerin Society is a good example of this. Painstakingly aware of the ways in which Keynesianism was the hegemonic common sense of its time, the MPS undertook the long-term task of taking apart the elements that sustained it. This was a project that took decades to come to full fruition, and during that time the MPS had to undertake counter-hegemonic actions in order to install it. Such long-term thinking is an important corrective to the tendency today to focus on immediate resistance and new daily outrages. However, hegemony is not just an immaterial contestation of ideas and values. Neoliberalism's ideological hegemony, for example, depends upon a series of material instantiations – paradigmatically in the nexus of government power, media framing and the network of neoliberal think tanks. As we observed in our examination of the rise of neoliberalism, the MPS was particularly adept at creating an intellectual infrastructure, consisting of the institutions and material paths necessary to inculcate, embody and spread their worldview.

The combination of social alliances, strategic thinking, ideological work and institutions builds a capacity to alter public discourse. Crucial here is the idea of the 'Overton window' – this is the bandwidth of ideas and options that can be 'realistically' discussed by politicians, public intellectuals and news media, and thus accepted by the public.[15] The general window of realistic options emerges out of a complex nexus of causes – who controls key nodes in the press and broadcast media, the relative impact of popular culture, the relative balance of power between organised labour and capitalists, who holds executive political power, and so on. Though emerging from the inter-section of different elements, the Overton window has a power of its own to shape which future paths are taken by societies and governments. If something is not deemed 'realistic', then it will not even be tabled for discussion and its proponents will be silenced as 'unserious'. We can evaluate the success of neoliberal ideas in terms of this by the degree to which they have framed what is possible over a period of more than thirty years.[16] While it has never been possible to convince the majority of the population of the positive merits of key neoliberal policies, active assent is unnecessary. A sequence of neoliberal administrations throughout the world, in conjunction with a network of think tanks and a largely right-leaning media, have been able to transform the range of possible options to exclude even the most moderate of socialist measures.[17] Through this, the hegemony of neoliberal ideas has enabled the exercise of power without always requiring executive state power. Providing that the window of possible options can be stretched further to the right, it matters little whether right-wing governments hold power – a reality that the US Republican Party has consistently exploited over the last two decades, often to the surprise of those on the liberal left. Ideological hegemony as we present it here is therefore not about maintaining a strict party line on what can be discussed. Simply bringing leftist issues and categories into positions of prominence would already be a major step forward.

While often understood as something that pertains to ideas, values and other immaterial aspects of society, there is in fact also a material sense to hegemony. The physical infrastructures of our world exert a significant hegemonic force upon societies – imposing a way of life without overt coercion. For instance, with regard to urban infrastructure, David Harvey writes that 'projects concerning what we want our cities to be are ... projects concerning human possibilities, who we want, or perhaps even more pertinently, who we do not want to become'.[18] Infrastructure such as suburbs in the United States was built with the explicit intention of isolating and individualising existing solidarity networks, and installing a gendered division between the private and the public in the form of single-family households.[19] Economic infrastructures also serve to modify and sculpt human behaviours. Indeed, technical infrastructures are often developed for political as well as economic purposes. If we think of global just-in-time supply chains, for example, these are economically efficient under capitalism, but also exceptionally effective in breaking the power of unions. In other words, hegemony, or rule by the engineering of consent, is as much a material force as it is a social one. It is something embedded in human minds, social and political organisations, individual technologies and the built environment that constitutes our world.[20] And, whereas the social forces of hegemony must be continually maintained, the materialised aspects of hegemony exert a force of momentum that lasts long past their initial creation.[21] Once in place, infrastructures are difficult to dislodge or alter, despite changing political conditions. We are facing up to this problem now, for example, with the infrastructure built up around fossil fuels. Our economies are organised around the production, distribution and consumption of coal, oil and gas, making it immensely difficult to decarbonise the economy. The flipside of that problem, though, is that once a postcapitalist infrastructure is in place, it would be just as difficult to shift away from it, regardless of any reactionary forces. Technology and technological infrastructures therefore pose both significant hurdles for overcoming the capitalist mode of production, as well as significant potentials for securing the longevity of an alternative. This is why, for example, it is insufficient even to have a massive populist movement against the current forms of capitalism. Without a new approach to things like production and distribution technologies, every social movement will find itself forced back into capitalistic practices.

The left must therefore develop a sociotechnical hegemony: both in the sphere of ideas and ideology, and in the sphere of material infrastructures. The objective of such a strategy, in a very broad sense, is to navigate the present technical, economic, social, political and productive hegemony towards a new point of equilibrium beyond the imposition of wage labour. This will require long-term and experimental praxis on multiple fronts. A hegemonic project therefore implies and responds to society as a complex emergent order, the result of diverse interacting practices.[22] Some combinations of social practices will lead to instability, but others will tend towards more stable (if not literally static) outcomes. In this context, hegemonic politics is the work that goes into retaining or navigating towards a new point of relative stability across a variety of societal subsystems, from the national-level politics of the state, to the economic domain, from the battle of ideas and ideologies to different regimes of technology. The order which emerges as a result of the interactions of these different domains is hegemony, which works to constrain certain kinds of action and enable others. In the rest of this chapter, we examine three possible channels through which to undertake this struggle: pluralising economics, creating utopian narratives and repurposing technology. These certainly do not exhaust the points of possible attack, but they do identify potentially productive areas to focus resources on.

REMEMBERING THE FUTURE

Today, one of the most pervasive and subtle aspects of hegemony is the limitations it imposes upon our collective imagination. The mantra 'there is no alternative' continues to ring true, even as more and more people strive against it. This marks a significant change from the long twentieth century, when utopian imaginaries and grandiose plans for the future flourished. Images of space flight, for instance, were constant ciphers for humanity's desire to control its destiny.[23] In pre-Soviet Russia, there was remarkably widespread fascination with space exploration. Though aviation was still a novelty, the dreams of space flight promised 'total liberation from the signifiers of the past: social injustice, imperfection, gravity, and ultimately, the Earth'.[24] The utopian inclinations of the time made sense of the rapidly changing world, gave credence to the belief that humanity could channel history in a rational direction and cultivated anticipations for a future society. In the more mystical formulations, cosmists argued with admirable ambition that geoengineering and space exploration were only partial steps towards the real goal: resurrecting the entirety of the dead.[25] Meanwhile, more secular approaches outlined detailed plans for fully automated economies, mass economic democracy, the end of class society and the flourishing of humanity.[26] Such was the level of enthusiasm and belief in imminent space travel that in 1924 a riot nearly erupted when rumours circulated about a possible rocket flight to the moon.[27] Popular culture was saturated with these images and with stories in which technological and social revolution intertwined. But these were not simply matters of extraterrestrial fantasy, as they had concrete effects on people's ways of living. In the post-revolutionary period, this culture of ambition fostered a series of social experiments with new ways of communal living, domestic arrangements and political formations.[28] These experiments gave credence to the idea that anything was achievable in a time of rapid modernisation, lending support to the Bolsheviks and the people. While utopian ambitions were largely forced underground during the Stalinist era, they re-emerged in the 1950s with the growth of newfound economic confidence and the resources to make good on some of the earlier dreams.[29] The greatest moments of the Soviet experiment – the launch of Sputnik and the economic dominance that it appeared on the verge of attaining in the 1950s – were ultimately inseparable from a popular culture imbued with utopian desires.[30] A similar period of utopian ambition also held sway in the early years of the United States. Fuelled by a widespread belief that the new industrial capitalism was temporary and that a better world would soon emerge, workers militantly struggled for this new world. In a climate far more hostile than our own, labour was able to create an array of strong organisations and exert significant pressure.[31] The successes of this time were inseparable from a broader utopian culture.

By contrast, today's world remains firmly confined within the parameters of capitalist realism.[32] The future has been cancelled. We are more prone to believing that ecological collapse is imminent, increased militarisation inevitable, and rising inequality unstoppable. Contemporary science fiction is dominated by a dystopian mindset, more intent on charting the decline of the world than the possibilities for a better one.[33] Utopias, when they are proposed, have to be rigorously justified in instrumental terms, rather than allowed to exist in excess of any calculation. Meanwhile, in the halls of academia the utopian impulse has been castigated as naive and futile. Browbeaten by decades of failure, the left has consistently retreated from its traditionally grand ambitions. To give but one example: whereas the 1970s saw radical feminism and queer manifestos calling for a fundamentally new society, by the 1990s these had been reduced to a more moderate identity politics; and by the 2000s discussions were dominated by even milder demands to have same-sex marriage recognised and for women to have equal opportunities to become CEOs.[34] Today, the space of radical hope has come to be occupied by a supposedly sceptical maturity and a widespread cynical reason.[35] And the goals of an ambitious left, which once aimed at the total transformation of society, have been reduced down to minor tinkering at the edges of society.

We believe that an ambitious left is essential to a post-work programme, and that to achieve this, the future must be remembered and rebuilt.[36] Utopias are the embodiment of the hyperstitions of progress. They demand that the future be realised, they form an impossible but necessary object of desire, and they give us a language of hope and aspiration for a better world. The denunciations of utopia's fantasies overlook the fact that it is precisely the element of imagination that makes utopias essential to any process of political change. If we want to escape from the present, we must first dismiss the settled parameters of the future and wrench open a new horizon of possibility. Without the belief in a different future, radical political thinking will be excluded from the beginning.[37] Indeed, utopian ideas have been central to every major moment of liberation – from early liberalism, to socialisms of all stripes, to feminism and anti-colonial nationalism. Cosmism, afro-futurism, dreams of immortality, and space exploration – all of these signal a universal impulse towards utopian thinking. Even the neoliberal revolution cultivated the desire for an alternative liberal utopia in the face of a dominant Keynesian consensus. But any competing left utopias have gone sorely under-resourced since the collapse of the Soviet Union. We therefore argue that the left must release the utopian impulse from its neoliberal shackles in order to expand the space of the possible, mobilise a critical perspective on the present moment and cultivate new desires.

First, utopian thought rigorously analyses the current conjuncture and projects its tendencies out into the future.[38] Whereas scientific approaches attempt to reduce discussions of the future to fit within a probabilistic framework, utopian thought recognises that the future is radically open. What may appear impossible today might become eminently possible. At their best, utopias include tensions and dynamism within themselves, rather than presenting a static image of a perfected society. While irreducible to instrumental concerns, utopias also foster the imagination of ideas that might be implemented when conditions change. For example, the nineteenth-century Russian cosmists were among the first to think seriously about the social implications and potentials of space flight. Initially considered ineffectual dreamers, they ended up heavily influencing the future science of rocketry.[39] Likewise, early science fiction dealing with space exploration and cosmist utopias went on to influence state policy towards science and technology in the wake of the Russian Revolution.[40] The creation of alternatives also makes it possible to recognise that another world is possible in the first place.[41] As the flawed but significant global alternative posed by the USSR disappears from living memory, such images of a different world become increasingly important, widening the Overton window and experimenting with ideas about what might be achieved under different conditions.

In elaborating an image of the future, utopian thought also generates a viewpoint from which the present becomes open to critique.[42] It suspends the appearance of the present as inevitable and brings to light aspects of the world that would otherwise go unnoticed, raising questions that must be constitutively excluded.[43] Recent US science fiction, for instance, has often been written in response to contemporary issues of race, gender and class, while early Russian utopias imagined worlds that overcame the problems posed by rapid urbanisation and conflicting ethnicities.[44] These worlds not only model solutions, but illuminate problems. As Slavoj Žižek notes in his discussion of Thomas Piketty, the seemingly modest demand to implement a global tax actually implies a radical reorganisation of the entire global political structure.[45] Implicit within this small claim is a utopian impulse, since the conditions for making it possible require such a fundamental reconfiguration of existing circumstances. Likewise, the demand for a universal basic income provides a perspective from which the social nature of work, its invisible domestic aspect and its extension to every area of our lives become more readily apparent. The ways we organise our work lives, families and communities are given a fresh appearance when viewed from the perspective of a post-work world. Why do we devote one-third of our lives in submission to someone else? Why do we insist that domestic work (performed primarily by women) go unpaid? Why are our cities organised around lengthy, dreary commutes from the suburbs? The utopian demand from the future therefore implores us to question the givens of our world. In these ways, utopias can be both a negation of the present and an affirmation of a possible future.[46]

Finally, in affirming the future, utopia functions as an affective modulator: it manipulates and modifies our desires and feelings, at both conscious and pre-conscious levels. In all its variations, utopia ultimately concerns the 'education of desire'.[47] It provides a frame for us, telling us both how and what to desire, while unleashing these libidinal elements from the bounds of the reasonable. Utopias give us something to aim for – something beyond the stale repetition of the same offered by the eternal present of capitalism. In cracking open the present and providing an image of a better future, the space between the present and the future becomes the space for hope and the desire for *more*.[48] By generating and channelling these affects, utopian thinking can become a spur to action, a catalyst for change; it disrupts habits and breaks down consent to the existing order.[49] Futural thinking, extended by communications mechanisms,[50] generates collective affects of hope that mobilise people to act on behalf of a better future – affects that are necessary to any political project.[51] While utopian thinking rejects the melancholy and transcendental miserabilism found in some parts of the contemporary left, it also invokes its own negative affect.[52] The obverse of hope is disappointment (an affect that is today embodied in figures like the young 'graduate with no future').[53] Whereas anger has traditionally been the dominant affect of the militant left, disappointment invokes a more productive relation – not merely a willed transformation of the status quo, but also a desire for what-might-be. Disappointment indexes a yearning for a lost future.

If the left is to counter the common sense of neoliberalism ('there's not enough money', 'everyone must work', 'government is inefficient'), utopian thinking will be essential. We need to think big. The natural habitat of the left has always been the future, and this terrain must be reclaimed. In our neoliberal era, the drive for a better world has largely been whittled away under the pressures and demands of everyday existence. In this repression, what has been lost is that ambition to produce 'a world that exceeds – existentially, aesthetically, as well as politically – the miserable confines of bourgeois culture'.[54] But as an apparently universal and irrepressible characteristic of human cultures, utopian thinking can surge forth under even the most repressive conditions.[55] Utopian inclinations play out across the human spectrum of feelings and affects – embodied in popular culture, high culture, fashion, city planning, and even quotidian daydreaming.[56] The popular desire for space exploration, for instance, points to a curiosity and ambition that lies beyond the profit motive.[57] The like-minded trend of afro-futurism offers not only a highly stylised image of a better future, but also ties it to a radical critique of existing structures of oppression and a remembrance of past struggles. The post-work imaginary also contains numerous historical precedents in utopian writing, pointing to a constant striving to move beyond the constraints of wage labour. Cultural movements and aesthetic production have essential roles to play in reigniting the desire for utopia and inspiring visions of a different world.

NAVIGATING NEOLIBERALISM

While utopias seek to transform the cultural hegemony of neoliberalism, education forms a key institution for transforming intellectual hegemony. It is the educational apparatus that indoctrinates new generations in the dominant values of a particular society, reproducing its ideology through the decades. In the education system, children learn the basic ideas of a society, respect for (in fact, submission to) the existing order, and the skills necessary to distribute them along different segments of the labour market.[58] Transforming the educational system of intellectuals is therefore a key task in building a new hegemony.[59] It is not for nothing that the Nobel Prize–winning economist Paul Samuelson wrote that: 'I don't care who writes a nation's laws, or crafts its advanced treatises, if I can write its economics textbooks.' Projects focused on changing this institutional element of society could focus on three broad goals: pluralising the teaching of economics, reinvigorating the study of leftist economics and expanding popular economic literacy.

It is often forgotten, so deeply are we embedded in neoliberalism, that economics was once a relatively pluralist discipline. The interwar period was a time of healthy competition between a variety of formalist and non-formalist approaches.[60] In academic journals, it was not unusual to see discussions of economic planning, the tendency for the rate of profit to fall, and other standard categories of Marxist economics. In the 1960s, the Cambridge capital controversy brought together heterodox and mainstream thinkers in a seminal debate about the foundations of the discipline – one that everyone admits the heterodox thinkers won.[61] As late as the 1970s, one of the founders of modern economics was discussing exploitation, the labour theory of value and the transformation problem in a leading economics journal.[62] Such an event is difficult to imagine today. While neoclassical economics is a large tent that contains a variety of approaches, it is nevertheless a fundamentally limited perspective on what counts as real economic knowledge. This problem is compounded by the particular methodological demands of the most preeminent journals, with formal modelling taking precedence over more sociological analyses and qualitative understandings.

If the broad cultural and academic ideas of how to run economies are to change, at a minimum it will require more pluralism in the education of students. Here, there are glimmers of hope for a pluralist revival. Work is being done across the world to bring alternative economics to mainstream universities, and groups of students and professionals alike are beginning to mobilise around this issue. Since 2000, numerous universities have seen students vocally demand pluralism in their economics education.[63] More recent years have seen students openly protesting the defenders of mainstream economics, and the emergence of groups like the Post-Crash Economic Society and Rethinking Economics that are making concerted efforts to change the curriculum.[64] Essential to a project of pluralising economics, however, is the development of a research programme and textbooks. Part of the reason for the rise of formalist approaches is precisely their fit with institutional requirements of higher education: they provided theories for researchers to spend time testing, textbooks and PhDs to continue a lineage of thought, and clear and transmissible principles.[65] Today, the field has come to be dominated by neoclassical textbooks, and the result is that, even if professors want to pluralise the discipline, they do not have many accessible resources to hand.[66] Indications that this might be changing include the creation of a heterodox textbook by two proponents of modern monetary theory.[67] But more work needs to be done on this front in order to broaden the parochial horizons of mainstream economics.

To support this process, there should be a movement to rejuvenate leftist economics. The dearth of economic analysis on the left could be seen in the wake of the 2008 crisis, when the most prominent critical response was a makeshift Keynesianism. The left was largely without a meaningful and desirable economic programme, having focused primarily on the critique of capitalism rather than the elaboration of alternatives. This is a crisis of utopian imagination, but also of cognitive limits. A series of emerging contemporary phenomena must be thought through carefully: for instance, the causes and effects of secular stagnation; the transformations invoked by the shift to an informational, post-scarcity economy; the changes wrought by the introduction of full automation and a universal basic income; the possible approaches to collectivising automated manufacturing and services; the progressive potentials of alternative approaches to quantitative easing; the most effective ways to decarbonise the means of production; the implications of dark pools for financial instability – and so on. Equally, research should be revived on what postcapitalism might look like in practice. Beyond a few outdated classics, very little research has been done to think through an alternative economic system – even less so in the wake of emerging technologies like additive manufacturing, self-driving vehicles and soft AI.[68] What role, for instance, could non-state cryptocurrencies have? How does one measure value if not by abstract or concrete labour? How can ecological concerns be fully accounted for in a postcapitalist economic framework? What mechanism can replace the market and overcome the socialist calculation problem?[69] And what are the likely effects of the possible tendency for the rate of profit to fall?[70] Building a postcapitalist world is as much a technical task as a political one, and in order to begin thinking about it, the left needs to overcome its general aversion to formal modelling and mathematics. There is no small amount of irony in the fact that the same people who criticise the abstraction of mathematical modelling often adhere to the most abstract dialectical readings of capitalism. This recognition of the uses of quantitative methods does not mean simply adopting neoclassical models or slavishly following the dictates of numbers, but the rigour and computational elaboration that can come with formal modelling are essential for grappling with the complexity of the economy.[71] However, from modern monetary theory to complexity economics, from ecological to participatory economics, trajectories of innovative thought are being launched – even if they remain marginal for now. Equally, organisations like the New Economics Foundation are leading the way in creating models of the economy that can inform leftist political goals, as well as fostering public literacy in economic matters.

The latter point is particularly important, as increasing economic literacy means not only transforming the practice of academic economists, but also making the economy intelligible to non-specialists. Sophisticated analyses of economic trends need to be connected to the intuitive insights of everyday lives. While, for the near future, the revival of leftist economics is likely to be centred in academia, the aim should be to spread such economics education far beyond the confines of universities. Unions could use their resources to educate their members about the changing nature of the contemporary economy. Through internal education programmes, rank-and-file workers can begin to situate the problems of their workplaces and communities within a larger economic context. Similar approaches can be – and in many cases already are – achieved through the training of activists. Open schools provide another medium for education, giving the public a chance to learn about ideas that are too often made impenetrable by academic jargon, and from which they are excluded by exorbitant tuition and publisher fees. There is a long tradition in the UK of working-class education, which can be drawn upon to learn from. For example, the Workers' Educational Association already provides low-cost adult education to local communities.[72] Such institutions provide ways in which abstract economic understandings can be linked up with the on-the-ground knowledge of workers, activists and community members, each mutually shaping the other. Working systematically to develop pluralism, economic research and public education will play a significant role in strengthening the utopian narratives outlined in the previous section, and providing the necessary navigational tools to chart a course out of capitalism.

REPURPOSING TECHNOLOGY

As we argued above, hegemony is embedded not only in the ideas of a society, but also in the built environment and technologies that surround us. These objects carry a politics within them: they facilitate particular uses and actions, while simultaneously constraining others. For instance, our current infrastructure tends to shape our societies into individualistic, carbon-based, competitive forms, regardless of what individuals or collectives may want. The significance of these politicised infrastructures is only increasing as technology expands into the smallest nano-scales and out to the largest postplanetary formations. No aspect of our lives remains untouched by technology, and indeed, many would argue that humanity is intrinsically technological.[73] In response to this materialised hegemony – one thoroughly constructed by and implicated in capitalism – a few different options present themselves. A first position argues we must destroy this built environment in order to ever liberate ourselves.[74] While this argument reaches its zenith in primitivism and its demand to be done with civilisation, similar inclinations permeate the left today. Given the devastation such a project would bring about, and the theoretical ineptitude behind these claims, we consider this position little more than an academic curiosity. A second position instead argues that technology is the basis for a postcapitalist order, but that any meaningful focus on changing our technology should wait until after the political project of postcapitalism is achieved.[75] This would undoubtedly make our task simpler, but, given the pervasive entanglement of technology with politics, and given the latent potentials in current technology, we believe the far more prudent option is to look at how developments can be redirected today, and existing technology repurposed immediately. A third approach therefore focuses on invention and emphasises that the choice of which technologies to develop and how they are designed is primarily a political matter.[76] The direction of technological development is determined not only by technical and economic considerations, but also by political intentions. More than just seizing the means of production, this approach declares the need to invent new means of production. A final approach focuses on how existing technology contains occluded potentials that strain at our current horizon and how they might be repurposed.[77] Under capitalism, technology's potential is drastically constrained – reduced to a mere vehicle for generating profit and controlling workers. Yet potentials continue to exist in excess of these current uses.[78] The task before us is to uncover the hidden potentials and link them up to scalable processes of change. This is ultimately a utopian intervention, insofar as repurposing aims to ignite collective imagination about what can be done with the resources to hand.[79]

We have, therefore, two effective strategies in approaching the question of technological hegemony. In the first approach, the focus is on the invention and adoption of new technologies, emphasising that we can create tools of change. In this vein, some have called for greater democratic control over the design and implementation of infrastructures and technologies.[80] In the workplace, this means struggling over which technologies are brought in and how they are used. Given that technologies are rarely, if ever, introduced all at once, there is a lengthy period of time in which to leverage power to gain control over how technologies are being developed and implemented. The rejection of surveillance measures is one of the most obvious goals, but workplace struggle also means resisting technologies which simply intensify, speed up and worsen working conditions.[81] At the level of the state, there is an equally strong case to be made for democratic control over technology development, given that most significant innovations come from public-sector financing rather than the private sector. It is the state that leads significant technological revolutions – from the internet to green technology, nanotechnology, the algorithm at the heart of Google's search engine, and all of the major components of Apple's iPhone and iPad.[82] The microprocessor, the touchscreen, the GPS, the batteries, the hard drive and SIRI are just a few of the components that emerged from government investment.[83] The fact of the matter is that capitalist markets tend towards short-term views and low-risk investments. It is governments that provide the long-term resources that enable major innovative changes to develop and flourish, whereas contemporary venture capital increasingly tends towards the generation of short-term profit.[84] It is governments that make investments in high-risk developments that are likely to fail – but for that reason are also likely to lead to major changes. Given government's role in technological development and consumer product innovation, public funding should be under democratic control. This would mean that governments have a role to play not only in the *rate* of technological development, but more importantly in its *direction*.[85] Particularly significant here are what have been called 'mission-oriented' projects.[86] These do not aim at product differentiation and marginal improvements to existing goods, but are instead concerned with large-scale inventive projects such as space travel and the internet. This is revolutionary development, aimed at creating entirely new paths of technology and open to the possibility of unexpected innovations emerging in the process. Under democratic control, it could respond to the biggest social problems of the day and foster large-scale thinking by, for instance, using state investment banks to shape the social value of projects through funding decisions.[87] A forward-thinking government could support mission-oriented projects such as decarbonising the economy, fully automating work, expanding cheap renewable energy,[88] exploring synthetic biology, developing cheap medicine, supporting space exploration and building artificial intelligence. The challenge is to develop institutional mechanisms that will enable popular control over the direction of technological creation.

Public control over how government funds are spent for development was also at the heart of a series of worker-based struggles in the 1970s. In now largely forgotten experiments, workers in the UK and Japan (and later across Brazil, India and Argentina) sought to channel technological development towards the production of 'socially useful goods'.[89] These were goods that responded to social needs and were produced in such a way as to minimise waste, be ecologically sustainable, and respect workers and their skills.[90] The most influential of these projects occurred at Lucas Aerospace in the UK – a company that focused on producing high-tech components, predominantly for the military, and received significant government funding.[91] Faced with rising structural unemployment and impending redundancies, workers at Lucas Aerospace came together to develop an alternative proposal for how to run the company and maintain jobs. Their basic argument was that, given the public funds being channelled into the corporation, society should have a say in, and benefit from, how these resources were being used. This was an argument that entailed channelling resources away from military armaments and into useful products. In order to develop the proposal for socially useful goods, the workers compiled a list of the skills and equipment available to them, took on the perspective of planners, sought product suggestions from workers and their communities, and collectively decided how these technologies and skills could be repurposed to different ends.[92] Rather than high-tech military equipment, the existing capacities were to be repurposed to design and produce medical technologies, renewable energy, safety improvements, and heating technology for social housing.[93] The final plan ran to over 1,200 pages and included detailed proposals for 150 products.[94] In order for it to achieve its political goals against an intransigent management, the strategy undertaken was in many ways a counter-hegemonic project, with workers explicitly aiming to 'inflame the imaginations of others' and revise what people thought production was for.[95]

Notably, the Lucas Plan refused to remain a temporary space of prefigurative politics, and instead aimed to mobilise the resources of unions and governments in an effort to create a new hegemonic order. In this endeavour, the plan resonated with peace activists, environmentalists, feminists and other labour movements, leading to the building of international connections and a wave of worker-led action.[96] Ultimately, however, the stagnation of the Labour Party and national trade unions, combined with the rising turn to neoliberalism, meant that the Lucas Plan fell short of its goals. But the successes it had – slowing job losses – were largely the result of moving beyond defensive approaches and towards creating an alternative.[97] Despite these failures, the Lucas Plan demonstrates a clear example of how repurposing the productive forces of society might be used to transform the technological direction of society. This was not an attempt simply to build a worker-controlled factory in the middle of a profit-orientated economy; more radically, it was an attempt to reorganise technological development away from marginal weapon improvements and towards socially useful goods.[98] It is an ideal model of how technical knowledge, political awareness and collective power can be combined to achieve a radical repurposing of the material world.

An even more ambitious project of repurposing occurred in Chile in the early 1970s. The newly elected government of Salvador Allende sought to transform Chile into a socialist nation through gradualist change, implemented through the existing economic and political institutions. A crucial part of this process was the development of Cybersyn, an innovative attempt at decentralised economic planning that sought to connect firms throughout the country to government and bureaucratic functions. The project involved transforming cybernetics from what has often been excoriated as a system of control[99] into an infrastructure of democratic socialism. The Cybersyn system was designed not for an omnipotent and external central government, but as a partial and internal modulator of ongoing economic flows.[100] It was intended to give workers a say in the planning process and enable factories to self-manage, all while giving a rational orientation to the national economy. To achieve these goals, Cybersyn was to include a proto-internet connecting factories, an economic simulator to test out policies, a statistical forecaster to predict problems, and an operations room taken straight from science fiction. But US hostility to the country made it virtually impossible to purchase new computers, and attempted deals with France only came to fruition after Allende had been overthrown.[101] The result was that Chile's effort to build a cybernetic socialism largely had to repurpose existing technologies in order to stand any chance at being successful. It was a sort of bricolage approach, using what was available and cobbling together something new. At the time, Chile possessed only four mainframe computers (only one of which was available to Cybersyn)[102] and fifty computers around the nation – so the proto-internet was pared down, and based instead on more widely available telex machines. The ambition for a system of democratic, worker-managed enterprises was ultimately cut short by the US-backed coup that ended Allende's regime in 1973. But while the project was never fully realised, parts of Cybersyn nevertheless demonstrated their potential in one notable experience. Faced with rising opposition from the economic elite, in 1972 the government had to deal with a strike by over 40,000 truck owners.[103] The petite bourgeoisie sought to undermine the government by preventing shipping of essential materials for factory production. But workers took over factories and continued to drive trucks wherever possible, while the national government deployed the telex network of Cybersyn in order to coordinate around the blockades and the strike. Effectively, as the preeminent historian of Cybersyn writes, 'the network offered a communications infrastructure to link the revolution from above, led by Allende, to the revolution from below, led by Chilean workers and members of grassroots organisations'.[104] In other words, the strike showed the potential of Cybersyn for repurposing the infrastructure of society towards democratic and socialist ends. It enabled a historically unique and promising vision of what an alternative future might have looked like. In the end, therefore, the experiment provides an imaginative and utopian example of the repurposing of cybernetic principles, existing Chilean technology and cutting-edge software.[105]

While the previous examples suggest how repurposing could be the focus of immediate political projects, more speculative propositions can also be imagined for a postcapitalist future. As a central source of productivity and the expansion of our capacities to act, technological innovations form an essential part of any mode of production beyond capitalism. A new world will have to be built, not on the ruins of the old, but on the most advanced elements of the present. Today we see the occluded potentials of this approach everywhere, in the fact that the technologies for achieving classic leftist goals (reduced work, increased abundance, greater democratic control) are more available than ever before. The problem is that they remain encased within social relations that obscure these potentials and render them impotent. In this context, the demand to reflect upon and repurpose technologies operates to reignite a utopian imagination in the heart of a stale capitalism. An entire array of possibilities already exists. The last chapter examined automation technologies as a key hinge between capitalism and postcapitalism, but repurposing extends much further than just the automation of the productive forces. Similar arguments have been mobilised around logistics networks, around repurposing cities for ecological reasons and around deploying the latest computing technology for postcapitalist ends.[106] Pinpointing these sorts of technologies can help to focus energy on political struggles over their development and use. Logistics provides a particularly significant example, insofar as it simultaneously exploits wage differentials, enables global production and is at the leading edge of automation. Without denying the significance of logistics to the project of exploiting cheap labour across the world, it is possible to see that logistics would be useful to postcapitalism in a variety of ways.[107] Its uses, in other words, go far beyond just capitalist ones. First, any postcapitalist economy will require flexibility in both production (for example, additive manufacturing) and distribution (for example, just-in-time logistics). This enables an economy to be responsive to changes in individual consumption, unlike the grand and inflexible planning efforts of the Soviet era. Without these technologies, postcapitalism would risk repeating all the economic problems already seen in the first communist experiment.[108] Second, global logistics makes possible the use of a wide array of comparative advantages – not simply wage differentials. To cite one example: research has found that it is more environmentally friendly for certain agricultural goods to be produced in New Zealand and shipped to the UK, as opposed to being produced and consumed in the UK.[109] Even after being shipped across the world, they still have a smaller carbon footprint. The simple reason for this is that reproducing the appropriate climate in the UK would involve intense energy consumption. Such environmental comparative advantages only exist where there is an efficient and global logistics network. Finally, logistics is at the forefront of the automation of work, and therefore represents a prime example of what a postcapitalist world might look like: machines humming along and handling the difficult labour that humans would otherwise be forced to do. It is worth recalling that before the logistics revolution, transporting goods was a physically demolishing task for the bodies of workers. The automation of this labour is something to be applauded, not held back for parochial reasons. For all these reasons, logistics therefore presents an important transition technology between capitalism and postcapitalism.

But there are important limits to repurposing. The Soviets, for example, believed that capitalist technologies and techniques could simply be taken over and turned towards communist ends,[110] but these technologies were biased towards maximal efficiency and rigorous control by management.[111] Given their wholesale adoption of capitalist machinery and management techniques, it was no surprise that the system tended towards capitalist modes of operation. Workers became – once again – mere cogs in the machine, deprived of autonomy and coerced into working harder. The ambitious plan to conquer the capitalist means of production ran aground on the reality that power relationships are embedded within technologies, which cannot therefore be infinitely bent towards purposes that oppose their very functioning.[112] Numerical control technologies, for example, have been used to set the pace of production, forcing workers to keep up with a machine – rendering the power of management more indirect and invisible.[113] In this way, machines can conceal power relations by making them appear as simple mechanical processes. Yet repurposing remains possible in spite of these limits because there is often a significant untapped reservoir of potentials lying dormant within a technology. The difficult point to understand is that, in the words of one historian, 'Technology is neither good nor bad; nor is it neutral.'[114] Any given technology is political but flexible, as it always exists in excess of the purposes for which it may have been designed.[115] Rather, the design, meaning and impact of a technology are constantly shifting, altering as users transform it and as its environment changes.[116] Paraphrasing Spinoza, we can say that we know not what a sociotechnical body can do. Who among us fully recognises what untapped potentials await discovery in the technologies that have already been developed? What sorts of postcapitalist communities could be built upon the material we already have? Our wager is that the true transformative potentials of much of our technological and scientific research remain unexplored.

How, then, can we distinguish between technologies that are bound by their limits and technologies whose properties offer potential affordances for a postcapitalist future? There is no a priori way to determine the potentials of a technology, but we can still establish broad parameters to adjudicate on the potentials of a technology, and to apply these in thinking through the specific aspects of individual technologies.[117] In terms of criteria, one approach is to determine what functions constitute necessary and/or exhaustive aspects of a technology. For example, if a technology's only role is that of exploiting workers, or if such a role is absolutely necessary to its deployment, then it can have no place in a postcapitalist future. Taylorism, based necessarily on the control and heightened exploitation of workers, would be rejected according to these criteria. Nuclear weapons, requiring the capacity to inflict mass destruction, would likewise have no place in a postcapitalist world.[118] For the most part, however, technologies will be more ambiguous than that. If technology designed to reduce skilled labour permits domination by a managerial class, it also opens up spaces for job-sharing and the reduction of work. If technology that reduces production costs reduces the percentage of people employed, it also reduces the need for people to work. If a technology that centralises decision-making over infrastructures facilitates private control, it also provides a nodal point for collective decision-making. These technologies embody both potentials at the same time, and the task of repurposing is simply one of how to alter the balance between them. One goal of any future-orientated left could be to outline these broad parameters of adjudication, and to pursue further research and analysis in determining how specific technologies can be repurposed and mobilised towards a postcapitalist project. This is particularly crucial for workers involved in the technology sector who are, through their design choices, building the terrain of future politics.[119] Let us be clear, though: without a simultaneous shift in the hegemonic ideas of society, new technologies will continue to be developed along capitalist lines, and old technologies will remain beholden to capitalist values.

This hegemonic strategy is therefore necessary to any project to transform society and the economy. And in many senses, hegemonic politics is the antithesis to folk politics. It seeks to persuade and influence, rather than presuming spontaneous politicisation; it works on multiple scales, rather than just the tangible and local; it sets out to achieve forms of social power that are long-lasting, rather than temporary; and it operates in domains that are often not superficially 'political' at all, rather than focusing on the most spectacular political mediums, such as street protests. A counter-hegemonic strategy would include efforts to transform the common sense of society, revive a utopian social imagination, rethink the possibilities of economics, and eventually repurpose technological and economic infrastructures. None of these steps are sufficient, but they are examples in which concrete action can be taken to build the social and material conditions for a post-work world. They prepare the ground for a moment when transformative change can occur, backed by a mass movement. However, the strategy of counter-hegemony as it has been outlined so far remains abstract. What is needed is some sense of exactly how a counter-hegemonic strategy might gain traction in the real world. Hegemony needs to be constructed, and power needs to be built. We turn next to how such power can be constructed, and who will be building it.

Chapter 8

Building Power

Constructing a people is the main task of radical politics.

Ernesto Laclau

A strategy may indicate the broad direction to take, but it still leaves open the question of what forces exist to carry it out. Any strategy requires an active social force, mobilised into a collective formation, acting upon the world. But while putting a counter-hegemonic strategy into practice will require the use of power, the left has been both overwhelmed by and systematically rendered averse to the use of power.[1] The traditional agents of leftist power (the working class and its associated institutional forms) have wilted under attacks from the right and from their own stagnation. Meanwhile, chastened by the failures of previous attempts at social transformation, many have mobilised behind marginal and defensive folk-political actions.[2] Yet building a post-work world will involve large-scale social transformation and require building capacity for the use of power. This chapter argues that, in order to install a new hegemonic order, at least three things will be required: a mass populist movement, a healthy ecosystem of organisations and an analysis of points of leverage.[3] The questions of class unity and organisational form are subjects of perennial debate among the left. Class unity is thought to generate networks of solidarity, strength in numbers, confidence and an awareness of common interests. Likewise, organisational strength provides leadership, coordination, stability over time and the concentration of resources. Leverage points are less often discussed, but no less important. These are points of political or economic power that can be used to compel others to adapt to the interests of a particular group.[4] The classic tactic of the strike, for instance, aims to disrupt production in order to force the owners to accede to workers' demands. Without such leverage points, change can only come about when it is in the interests of the powerful. This chapter examines these three elements for building power and outlines some ways forward. What follows is not intended as an exhaustive or sufficient prescription for what should be done, but offers reflections on the limits of historical precedents, and an argument for the significance of the factors listed above for rebuilding the power of the left. Reconstructing this power is probably the most difficult task facing the left today, yet it is an essential task if a post-work world is to emerge from the devastation wrought by neoliberalism.

A POPULIST LEFT

Perhaps the most important question for building power is the question of who will be the active agent of a post-work project. What social positions will find a post-work society in their interest? The most obvious answer is one we have already seen: the expanding surplus population. Indeed, as workers in developed countries fall back into precarity, and as more and more of the global population is incorporated as 'free' labourers under capitalism, the basic proletarian condition is coming to characterise a wider swathe of people. We are all, as Marx argued, virtual paupers. At first glance, these trends therefore seem to support a traditional Marxist narrative, whereby the working class was supposed to achieve a dominant position by incorporating ever greater numbers of people and simplifying its economic position.[5] Condensed into increasingly large industrial factories, the working class was forecast to unite in physical terms (sharing space), in terms of its interests (reduced labour, higher wages), and eventually in terms of consciousness (becoming aware of its position as a proletariat). The deskilling of labour would eliminate hierarchies between skilled and unskilled labour, while high demand for labour would mean capital cared little about identity-based divisions (over race, gender, nationality).[6] This did occur in some places and at some times. For instance, while the early twentieth century saw the US black working class violently excluded from white unions, after World War II these racial divisions began to break down in many areas.[7]

Distinctions based on age, sex, skill, nation and income were likewise supposed to fall aside as capitalism progressed.[8] Perhaps most importantly, this emerging working class had strategic importance because of its access to a set of leverage points centred on production. Strikes, factory takeovers, slow-downs and similar tactics were all designed to disrupt the production process and force management and capitalists to acquiesce to working-class demands.[9] This class – paradigmatically comprised of white, male factory workers – was therefore predicted to become large, homogeneous and powerful, making it the vanguard of a post-capitalist revolution. But this did not happen. The working class fragmented, its organisational structures fell apart, and today 'there is no longer a class fraction that can hegemonise the class'.[10]

Under the combined pressures of deindustrialisation, the globalisation of production, the rise of service economies, the expansion of precarity, the demise of classic Fordist footholds and the proliferation of diverse identities, the industrial working class has become severely fractured. Across the world, the traditional working class is predominantly marginal in terms of its strength (with a few exceptions in countries such as South Africa and Brazil).[11] The Chinese labour movement has some strength, but even here the outsourcing of production to peripheral countries is already working to undermine its power.[12] The power of the global working class is today severely compromised, and a return to past strength seems unlikely. As it stands today, the classical revolutionary subject therefore no longer exists; there is only a diverse array of partly overlapping interests and divergent experiences. However, we might question the idea that the industrial working class was ever in a position to transform the world – today's situation is not so different from the early years of the labour movement. First, the image of worker unity has always been more of an aspirational vision than an achieved reality. From its origins, the proletariat was riven by divisions – between the waged male worker and the unwaged female labourer, between the 'free' worker and the unfree slave, between skilled craftsmen and unskilled labourers, between the core and periphery, and between nation-states.[13] The tendency to unify was always a limited phenomenon, and these differences persist today, exacerbated under conditions of a globalised division of labour. Perhaps more fundamentally, if deindustrialisation (the automation of manufacturing) is a necessary stage along the path towards a postcapitalist society, then the industrial working class could never have been the agent of change. Its existence was predicated upon economic conditions that would have to be eliminated in the transition to postcapitalism. If deindustrialisation is required for the transition to postcapitalism, then the industrial working class was inevitably going to lose its power in the process – fragmenting and falling apart, just as we have seen in recent decades.

Who, then, can be the transformative subject today? Despite the growing size of the surplus population and common immiseration of the proletariat, we must accept that no answer readily presents itself. The breakdown of lines between employed and unemployed, formal and informal, coincides with the decline in a coherent transformative agent. The fragmentation of traditional groups of resistance and revolt and the generalised decomposition of the working class means that the task today must be to knit together a new collective 'we'. There is no pre-existing group that would embody universal interests or constitute the necessary vanguard of this transformative project – not the industrial worker, not the intellectual labourer and not the lumpenproletariat. How, then, to compose a people in light of the fragmentation of the proletariat?[14] In practice, there are a variety of ways to organise such a convergence. As we saw, the classic Marxist approach presupposed that the tendencies of capitalism would heighten the division between classes and lead to the unity of the proletariat. Others have argued for a unity on the basis of generic common interests – biological need, for instance – but minimal commonalities tend to lead to minimal demands.[15] By contrast, in the Occupy movements, unity often emerged out of physical proximity – bodies working and living together in camps. Yet such unity often papered over real differences, making it nothing more than a fragile façade. When the physical proximity was destroyed in the dismantling of occupied spaces, unity rapidly collapsed. With the Arab Spring, meanwhile, unity was forged through opposition to shared tyrannical opponents, bringing together a disparate series of groups.[16] However, these recent experiences demonstrate that a unity built solely upon opposition tends to break down when the opponent falls.

The problem for a post-work project is that, despite the underlying commonality of proletarian existence, this provides only a minimal cohesion, which can support a vast range of divergent experiences and interests.[17] The challenge facing a transformative politics is to articulate this series of differences into a common project – without simply asserting that class struggle is the only *real* struggle. Under these conditions, it is no surprise to see that many of the most promising political struggles in recent years have identified themselves as populist movements rather than class movements.[18] By 'populism', we do not mean a sort of mindless mass movement, or a lowest-common-denominator revolt, or a movement with any particular political content.[19] Populism is instead a type of political *logic* by which a collection of different identities are knitted together against a common opponent and in search of a new world.[20] From the anti-globalisation movements, to Syriza in Greece, Podemos in Spain, numerous Latin American movements, and Occupy across the Western world, these movements have mobilised large cross-sections of society rather than just particular class identities.[21]

These populist movements have originated out of the frustration of unmet demands. Under normal democratic circumstances, demands are dealt with separately and within existing institutions – for instance, minimum wage increases, unemployment benefits and healthcare provision. Small changes are granted, but institutional arrangements, including society as a whole, are never questioned. In this fashion, existing hegemonies can be reinforced and threats generally modulated effectively. By contrast, a populist movement begins to emerge when these demands – for fair pay, social housing, childcare, and so on – are increasingly blocked. As the leading thinker on political populism, Ernesto Laclau, explains:

> Once we move beyond a certain point, what were requests *within* institutions became claims addressed *to* institutions, and at some stage they became claims *against* the institutional order. When this process has overflown the institutional apparatuses beyond a certain limit, we start having the people of populism.[22]

Particular interests become increasingly general in this process, and populism emerges, set resolutely against the existing order. The 'people', unlike traditional class groupings, are held together by a *nominal* unity even in the absence of any *conceptual* unity. The people is a complex, contested and constructed actor. They name themselves as a coherent group, rather than having any necessary unity of material interests. This helps to explain why, for instance, it was so difficult to pin down the politics of the Occupy movement. The 99 per cent was held together more by a name than by any common politics. This nominal unity is complemented by populism naming the fracture in society and the opposition against which they set themselves.[23] In naming an enemy, it becomes possible for a wide range of people to see their interests and demands expressed by the movement. Occupy, for example, named the 1 per cent, Podemos named 'the caste', and Syriza named the Troika. As with the naming of the people, the naming of the antagonism has some attachment to empirical facts, but need not be bound by them. The division that Occupy posited between the 1 per cent and the 99 per cent, for instance, is an antagonism that mobilised people despite its lack of empirical accuracy.[24] The naming of the people and their opposition is a political act, not a scientific statement. Both the people and the antagonism in society are therefore constituted through an act of nomination. This represents a response to the impossibility of simply reading off the antagonism of society from brute historical necessity, in an era where class identities have fragmented and differences proliferated.

In order for the 'people' of populism to emerge, however, additional elements are necessary. First, one particular demand or struggle must come to stand in for the rest. The Occupy movement, for example, mobilised a range of local, regional and national grievances that became knotted together under the struggle against inequality. In such cases, it is not a particular group which seeks recognition from society, but rather a particular group which comes to speak universally for society. In order to do so, however, it must be seen to embody multiple interests. It must stand not only for its own self-interest but come to actually reflect a broad array of interests.[25] For a traditional working-class movement, common interests would be sufficient to secure the allegiance of all. But in a populist movement, the absence of an immediate unity based on material interests means its coherence is perpetually plagued by a tension between the struggle that has come to stand in for the rest and those other struggles. Populism thus involves a continual negotiation of differences and particularisms, seeking to establish a common language and programme in spite of any centrifugal forces. The difference between a populist movement and folk-political approaches lies in this stance towards differences: whereas the former seeks to build a common language and project, the latter prefers differences to express themselves as differences and to avoid any universalising function. The mobilisation of a populist movement around anti-work politics would require articulating a populism in such a way that a variety of struggles for social justice and human emancipation could see their interests being expressed in the movement. Importantly, anti-work politics provides such resources: for example, it is perhaps the best option for a red-green coalition, insofar as it overcomes the tensions between an economic programme of jobs and growth and an environmental programme of decreased carbon emissions. The post-work project is also an inherently feminist one, recognising the invisible labour carried out predominantly by women, as well as the feminisation of the labour market, and the necessity of providing financial independence for women's full liberation. Equally, it links up with anti-racist struggles, insofar as black and other minority populations are disproportionately affected by high unemployment and the mass incarceration and police brutality associated with jobless communities. Finally, the post-work project builds upon postcolonial and indigenous struggles with the aim of providing a means of subsistence for the massive informal labour force, as well as mobilising against barriers to immigration.[26]

Articulating the character of a movement that can bring together such differences helps to emphasise the importance of demands to any proper populism. Demands form a key medium for building unity, and must therefore connect in multiple ways with different people.[27] Such demands do not presume to know in advance who will be called into action by them, but they allow people to see their own particular interests within them while nevertheless maintaining their differences from each other.[28] For example, the demands of an anti-work politics have different meanings for a university student, a single mother, an industrial worker, and those outside the labour force; but in spite of these differences, each of them can find their own interests represented in the call for a post-work society. Mobilising these people together and under the name of a demand then becomes the work of on-the-ground politics. A movement predicated on a populist logic can therefore give consistency to a series of diffuse grievances and requests, without necessarily negating differences.[29] Particular demands are inscribed into a coherent narrative articulating how various demands share a common antagonist. This is why a vision of the future is essential to a proper populism, and it is what many recent populist movements have lacked. Occupy, for instance, never translated the negative moment of insubordination into a positive political project around which the people could be organised. It never combined diverse interests into a project for a better future, remaining at the negative level of rejection and never providing an 'autonomous focus of subjectivation'.[30]

In the end, while the post-work project demands that centrality be given to class, it is not sufficient to mobilise only on the basis of class interests. A broad spectrum of society needs to be brought together as an active and transformative force. It is to this need that populism responds. Yet the negotiation of commonality at the level of slogans, demands, signs, symbols and identities cannot remain the primary level on which such politics is conducted. A populist movement also needs to act in and through a series of organisations, as well as aiming to achieve the overturning of neoliberal common sense and create a new one in its place. It must seek to build hegemonic forms of power, in all their diverse forms, both inside and outside the state.

ORGANISATIONAL ECOLOGY

Organisation is a key mediator between discontent and effective action – it transforms a certain quantity of people into a qualitatively different form of power. As the Occupy movement, the anti-war movement and the anti-globalisation movement have made clear, the problem with the left is not necessarily one of raw numbers. On a purely quantitative level, the left is not noticeably 'weaker' than the right – in terms of its ability to achieve popular mobilisation, the reverse seems to be true. Particularly in times of crisis, the left seems eminently capable of mobilising a populist movement. The problem lies in the next step: how that force is organised and deployed. For folk politics, organisation has meant a fetishistic attachment to localist and horizontalist approaches that often undermine the construction of an expansive counter-hegemonic project.[31] Yet this organisational fetishism is one of the most detrimental aspects of recent leftist thought: the belief that if only the proper form of organisation is developed, political success will follow.[32] Folk politics is guilty of this, but the same holds for many orthodox positions as well – the range of miracle cures advanced for the decline of the left's power have included trade unions, vanguards, affinity groups and political parties. In most cases, these organisational forms are advocated without regard for the different strategic terrains they face. Folk politics, for example, takes a particular organisational form built under specific conditions and attempts to transpose it across the entire social and political field. Rather than a decontextualized approach to the problem of organisation, we need to think in terms of a healthy and diverse ecosystem of organisations.

The simple point to make against organisational fetishism is that a political project requires a division of labour. There are a variety of essential tasks to be carried out in a successful political movement: awareness raising, legal

support, media hegemony, power analysis, policy proposals, the consolidation of class memory, and leadership, to name just a few.[33] No single type of
organisation is sufficient for performing all of these roles and bringing about
large-scale political change. We therefore do not seek to promote any single
organisational form as the ideal means of embodying transformational
vectors. Every successful movement has been the result, not of a single organisational type, but of a broad ecology of organisations. These have operated,
in a more or less coordinated way, to carry out the division of labour necessary
for political change. In the process of transformation leaders will arise, but
there is no vanguard party – only mobile vanguard functions.[34] An ecology of
organisations means a pluralism of forces, able to positively feedback on their
comparative strengths.[35] It requires mobilisation under a common vision of
an alternative world, rather than loose and pragmatic alliances.[36] And it
entails developing an array of broadly compatible organisations:

> The point is to create something more than mere alliance building (where
> the parts, understood as constituted groupings of people, are supposed to
> stay the same, only co-operating punctually) and less than a one-size-fits-all
> solution (e.g. the idea of the party). This is about strategic interventions
> that can attract both constituted groups and the 'long tail' that does not
> belong to any groups, pitched not as exclusive but as complementary,
> whose effects can reinforce each other.[37]

This means that the overarching architecture of such an ecology is a relatively
decentralised and networked form – but, unlike in the standard horizontalist
vision, this ecology should also include hierarchical and closed groups as
elements of the broader network.[38] There is ultimately no privileged organisational form. Not all organisations need to aim for participation, openness and
horizontality as their regulative ideals. The divisions between spontaneous
uprisings and organisational longevity, short-term desires and long-term strategy,
have split what should be a broadly consistent project for building a post-work
world. Organisational diversity should be combined with broad populist unity.

A quick overview of how such an ecology might operate will offer some sense
of how these proposals might work together. This can only be highly schematic,
given the particularities of any given struggle and the complexity of the issues at
hand. Inevitably, an ecosystem of organisations is forged in specific circumstances,

with different decisions being made in the face of different political contexts. That said, a broad social movement would be essential to any anti-work politics, affording a wide range of different organisational and tactical compositions. At one end of the spectrum, there are transient bursts of political energy, in the form of riots and spontaneous protests. Urban unrest in America, for instance, was a key motivating factor behind elite support for a basic income in the 1960s.[39] Such eruptions may not make intricate demands, but they demand a response. In slightly more organised modes, social movements take on the folk-political approaches seen in recent decades. Operating under principles of direct democracy can be conducive to certain objectives, such as giving people a voice, creating a powerful sense of collective agency and enabling different perspectives to be articulated.[40] It can foster the creation of a populist identity and empower people to start to see themselves as a collective. But what these folk-political organisations lacked was the strategic perspective to transform spectacular scenes of protest and broad populist movements into effective long-term action.[41] It is often the ability of other, more long-term institutionalised organisations to hegemonise around the demands, tactics and strategies of relatively ephemeral movements that determines the ultimate effect of their protests. The most successful occupation movements in recent years have been those that have fostered ties to labour movements (in Egypt, for example) and/or to political parties. In Iceland, for instance, the greatest protest successes were achieved when a red-green coalition was voted in after forcing the conservative administration out;[42] as we write, Spain is showing the potential that arises when social movements engage in a dual strategy both within and outside the party system. If a major social transformation such as the post-work project is to occur, it will come on the back of a mass movement rather than simply decreed from on high. Populist movements on the street will be one of its essential elements.

It has already been hinted at in earlier chapters, but media organisations are an essential part of any emergent political ecology aimed at building a new hegemony. The tasks involved in such a strategy demand a healthy media presence – creating a new common language, giving voice to the people, naming the antagonism, raising expectations, generating narratives that resonate with people and articulating in clear language the grievances we feel. It is these elements that provide the anchors for media narratives to be changed over time. Foundations and journalists are particularly well placed to make efforts at changing media narratives.[43] It was no accident that the Mont Pelerin Society included numerous journalists among its members. This communication also has to be achieved in a way that resonates with everyday conversation. The jargon of academics is rightly deemed useless by most people. Leftist media organisations should not shy away from being approachable and entertaining, gleaning insights from the success of popular websites. At the same time, the left has typically focused on creating media spaces *outside* the mainstream, rather than trying to co-opt existing institutions and leaking more radical ideas *into* the mainstream. Too often, these news organisations end up simply preaching to the choir, pushing narratives that never escape their own insular echo-chamber. The internet has enabled everyone to have a voice, but it has not enabled everyone to have an audience. Mainstream media sources remain indispensable for this and will continue to do so in the future. Their ability to influence and alter public opinion through framing what is and is not 'realistic' remains surprisingly strong. If a counter-hegemonic project is to be successful, it will require an injection of radical ideas into the mainstream, and not just the building of increasingly fragmented audiences outside it. Indeed, one of the key lessons from the US experience with a basic income policy is that the framing of such issues in the media is central to its prospects of success.[44] It is for these reasons that existing media organisations constitute a key battleground in the project set out here.

Alongside the media, intellectual organisations are indispensable components of any political ecology. These extend from bodies like think tanks, to captive university departments and other educational institutions, through to more loosely organised training and consciousness-raising bodies. But building hegemony does not necessarily mean sending down decrees from vanguard intellectual organisations. It is no accident that it is Gramsci, the key thinker of hegemony, who also struck upon the idea of the 'organic intellectual' – the intellectual closely linked to and emerging from key material and economic forces within society.[45] Organic intellectuals are participants in practical life, organisers and constructors.[46] A properly functioning leftist intellectual infrastructure would operate to support those institutions identified as broadly in line with their own worldviews by participating in them, spreading their work and, where possible, providing resources. In a world of complexity, no one has a privileged view of the totality, and thus a healthy intellectual sphere will involve intellectuals with multiple perspectives. This will combine with on-the-ground inquiries carried out by workers – examining, for instance, the way in which retail logistics function and the potentials for their disruption,[47] or the detailed analysis of local power networks as a means to bring about change.[48] In addition to that of organic intellectuals, certain kinds of valuable work can only be carried out in specialist bodies that are able to retain a certain distance from the hurly-burly of everyday politics. As the Mont Pelerin Society understood, some intellectual efforts need to be devoted less to immediate and pressing concerns, and more to the development of long-term proposals. These would include such vital endeavours as the development of new ways of organising and understanding the economy, which requires highly technical knowledge and long-term research. But such work always needs to be fed back into the networks of political actors and social narratives to gain its full effect.

Labour organisations have traditionally been significant forces of social transformation, but today they find themselves on the back foot. At the same time, deeply entrenched habits and inflexible – if not outright corrupt – union leaderships have made the revitalisation of these organisations an uphill battle. Yet they remain indispensable to the transformation of capitalism, and any effort to imagine a new union structure must learn lessons from both the failures of older models and the changing economic conditions facing them today. These include basic things such as enriching the connection between leadership and members, building support across traditional sectoral boundaries (academics supporting cleaners in a university, for example), learning from innovative and often worker-led unions (those around immigrant labourers, for example), radicalising existing unions and building new unions in areas devoid of this organisational lever. In broad terms, the adequacy of a union depends on the alignment of its political form with economic and infrastructural conditions. As we saw in earlier chapters, these conditions are currently defined by the emerging crisis of work. The rise of surplus populations, the return of precarity, the stagnation of wages and the painfully slow recovery of employment all present key challenges for the traditional model of trade unionism. As the work–life distinction breaks down, job security dwindles and rising personal debt lurks in the background, issues around work have effects far beyond the workplace. These shifting social conditions alter the relationship between the union, its members and the wider community. This requires, first of all, a recognition of the social nature of struggle, and the bridging of the gap between the workplace and the community.[49] Problems at work spill over into the home and the community, and vice versa. At the same time, crucial support for union action comes from the community, and unions would be best served by recognising their indebtedness to the invisible labour of those outside the workplace.[50] These include not only domestic labourers, who reproduce the living conditions of waged workers, but also immigrant workers, precarious workers and the broad array of those in surplus populations who share in the miseries of capitalism. The focus of unions therefore needs to expand beyond supporting only dues-paying members. To be sure, there is a history of worker organisations establishing such connections with the broader community, but today this needs to be made an increasingly explicit goal of union organising. This process can work both ways. For instance, France has seen 'proxy strikes' in which workers declare themselves not to be on strike (and therefore continue to get paid), yet allow people to blockade or occupy their workplace.[51] In addition, workers' movements have always relied upon the local community for moral and logistical support, and if solidarity is built up, communities will come out to defend workers against state repression.[52] Unions can involve themselves in community issues like housing, demonstrating the value of organised labour in the process.[53] Rather than being built solely around workplaces, unions would therefore be more adequate to today's conditions if they organised around regional spaces and communities.[54]

In expanding the spatial focus of union organising, local workplace demands open up into a broader range of social demands. As we argued in Chapter 7, this involves questioning the Fordist infatuation with permanent jobs and social democracy, and the traditional union focus on wages and job preservation. An assessment must be made of the viability of these classic demands in the face of automation, rising precarity and expanding unemployment. We believe many unions will be better served by refocusing towards a post-work society and the liberating aspects of a reduced working week, job sharing and a basic income.[55] The West Coast longshoremen in the United States represent one successful example of allowing automation in exchange for guaranteeing higher wages and less job cuts (though they also occupy a key point of leverage in the capitalist infrastructure).[56] The Chicago Teachers' Union offers another example of a union going far beyond collective bargaining, and instead mobilising a broad social movement around the state of education in general. Moreover, shifting in a post-work direction overcomes some of the key impasses between ecological movements and organised labour. The deployment of productivity increases for more free time, rather than increased jobs and output, can bring these groups together. Changing the aims of unions and organising community-wide will help to turn unions away from classic – and now failing – social democratic goals, and will be essential to any successful renewal of the labour movement.

Lastly, the state remains a site of struggle, and political parties will have a role in any ecology of organisations – particularly if the traditional social democratic parties continue to collapse and enable a new generation of parties to emerge. Ensuring a post-work society for all will require more than just individual workplaces; it demands success at the level of the state as well.[57] While parties are frequently denounced for their cynical consent to electoralism and the limits posed by international capital, this changes within an ecology of organisations. Rather than making them the impossible vehicle of revolutionary desires – associated with the hopeless prospect of 'voting in' postcapitalism – they can instead take on the more realistic task of forming the 'tip of the iceberg' in terms of political pressure, as well as developing the ability to bring together a widely varied constituency.[58] The state can complement politics on the street and in the workplace, just as the latter two can broaden the options for parties. The avoidance of the state – common to so many folk-political approaches – is a mistake. Mass movements and parties should be seen as tools of the same populist movement, each capable of achieving different things. At their most general level, parties can integrate various tendencies within a social movement – from reformist to revolutionary – into a common project. While international capital and the inter-state system make radical change virtually impossible from within the state, there are still basic and important policy choices to be made about austerity, housing support, climate change, childcare, demilitarisation of the police and abortion rights. Simply to reject parliamentary politics is to ignore the real advances these policies can make. It takes quite a privileged position to not care about minimum wage regulations, immigration laws, changes to legal support or rulings on abortion. At their best, electoral entities can act as a disruptive force (stalling, publicising controversies, articulating popular outrage), and even act as a progressive force in some situations. This does not imply that social movements should simply be turned into the vote-mobilising wings of political parties. The relationship between parties and social movements should extend far beyond this, into a process of two-way communication. On the one hand, financial support can be given from the party to community initiatives, and various policies – such as laws on public protest – can be amended to facilitate the activities of social movements.

In Venezuela, for instance, the state supported the creation of neighbourhood communes as a way to embed socialism in everyday practices.[59] On the other hand, resources for new parties can be mobilised collectively – Podemos, for example, got started through crowd-funding €150,000 – and the vitality of the party can be maintained through constant institutionalised negotiations between local movements, party members and central party structures.[60]

Podemos, for instance, has aimed to build mechanisms for popular governance while also seeking a way into established institutions.[61] It is a multi-pronged approach to social change and offers greater potential for real transformation than either option on its own.[62] Meanwhile, Brazil's Partido dos Trabalhadores has maintained openness to multiple groups (liberation theology groups, peasant movements) while still organising around an essentially union-based core. In the words of one researcher, 'this combination of grassroots and vanguard constituted a Leninism that was not very Leninist'.[63] What all these experiences show, however, is the mass mobilisation of the people is necessary in order to transform the state into a meaningful tool of their interests, and to overcome the blunt division between the power of movements and the power of the state. The aim must be to avoid both 'the tendency to fetishise the state, official power, and its institutions and the opposing tendency to fetishise antipower'.[64] In a context of widespread discontent with the political system, this remains possible – though, again, the importance of having a discursive framework in place to channel this discontent is obvious. In the end, parties still hold significant political power, and the struggle over their future should certainly not be abandoned to reactionary forces.

It should be clear how far away we now are from the folk-political fetishism of localism, horizontalism and direct democracy. An ecology of organisations does not deny that such organisational forms may have a role, but it rejects the idea that they are sufficient. This is doubly true for a counter-hegemonic project that requires the toppling of neoliberal common sense. What we are calling for, therefore, is a functional complementarity between organisations, rather than the fetishising of specific organisations or organisational forms.

POINTS OF LEVERAGE

If a populist movement successfully built a counter-hegemonic ecosystem of organisations, in order to become effective it would still require the capacity to disrupt. Even with a healthy organisational ecology and a mass unified movement, change is impossible without opportunities to leverage the movement's power. Historically speaking, many of the most significant advances made by the labour movement were achieved by workers in key strategic locations. Regardless of whether they had widespread solidarity, high levels of class consciousness or an optimal organisational form, they achieved success by being able to insert themselves into and against the flow of capitalist accumulation. In fact, the best predictor of worker militancy and successful class struggle may be the workers' structural position in the economy.

For example, within the early logistics infrastructure, dockworkers found themselves occupying a key point in the circulation of capital. Intermodal transport – the transferring of goods between ships, trains and trucks – was labour-intensive and costly.[65] Lodged in a key passage through which goods had to circulate, the longshoremen who carried out the work controlled a major point of leverage. The result was that dockworkers were incredibly militant and lost more work days to labour disputes than almost any other industry.[66] The famed strength of unions like the United Automobile Workers also arose from their structural position in the production process and the importance of the car industry to the national economy. Their power emerged, moreover, in a time of high unemployment and low levels of organisation – it turned out that neither a supportive labour market nor organisational strength was necessary for success.[67] A similar point of leverage was held by coalminers. Working in mines lent itself to greater autonomy from management in an environment where work stoppages were particularly potent. The consequence was that 'their position and concentration gave them opportunities, at certain moments, to forge a new kind of political power'.[68] The same holds for mining today, which is resistant to the threat of capital flight, since the resource supply is itself immobile. The mining areas of South Africa present a contemporary example, revealing both the potency of the unions and the violence of capital. When miners went on a wildcat strike in 2012, the state was called in and over thirty workers were killed in the Marikana massacre. Less violent, but no less significant, is the monopoly position of certain suppliers. Strikes at these points, such as in the Pou Chen Group in China, pose a real threat to capitalist interests by blocking off an entire supply chain.[69] At the other end of that chain, retail distribution is also primed for significant militant action, providing rich opportunities for the disruption of contemporary capitalism's reliance on just-in-time logistics.[70] The significance of such points of leverage can hardly be overestimated.

But the past century has seen the conscious and unconscious winnowing away of these points of leverage. The development of shipping containers enabled the automation of intermodal transport;[71] the globalisation of logistics facilitated capital's ability to move factories in response to strikes; and the shift to oil as the primary energy source drastically reduced the number of choke-points available for political action. Today, the classic points of leverage have largely disappeared, necessitating a new round of experimentation and strategic reflection. Experimentation is necessary precisely because politics is a set of dynamic systems, driven by conflict, and by adaptations and counter-adaptations, leading to tactical arms races. This means that any one type of political action is highly likely to become ineffective over time, as its opponents learn and adapt. Thus, no given mode of political action is historically inviolable. Indeed, over time, there has been an increasing need to discard familiar tactics as the forces they are marshalled against learn to defend against and counter-attack them more effectively. Secrecy is met by undercover infiltrators; the use of masks is met by new legislation against it; kettling is met by apps that track police movements; the recording of police violence is met by its criminalisation; mass protest is met by heavy regulation that renders it boring and sterile; non-violent civil disobedience is met by violent police brutality. Political tactics are a dynamic field of forces, and experimentation is essential in working around new state and corporate impediments to change.

The history of the labour movement provides an exemplary picture of such an approach. One of its primary tactics has been to limit the supply of labour, thereby making it more powerful and valuable.[72] Early efforts towards this end often operated by withholding the training for particular jobs by discriminating on the basis of skills, gender and race.[73] Early typesetters, for example, organised to protect a male-centred skilled workforce against the threatened introduction of relatively unskilled female labourers.[74] However, deskilling by capital and the industrialisation of production made it possible to undermine many of the skilled labour unions and opened up the labour supply to a much wider extent. The result was the breakdown of many traditional craft unions that were based around particular skill sets, with the emergence instead of industrial unions organising both skilled and unskilled workers along industry lines.[75] Another possible tactic for reducing the labour supply is one that we examined earlier:

moving towards the reduction of working hours. This produces a reduction of the labour supply, as was achieved by the exclusionary unions above, but with an important difference. Rather than relying on excluding particular groups from skilled trades, the tactic of reducing working hours relies on withdrawing a portion of everyone's labour time.[76] For various reasons, though – not least because of the postwar consensus between capital and labour – this tactic fell out of favour, and the labour movement's attention instead turned towards collective bargaining over pay. As we argued earlier, however, this tactic has the potential to be revived in the effort to transform our socioeconomic system. Another key tactic has been strikes, whose logic is to inflict costs on capital and force its hand in negotiations. But this approach was limited by the fact that unskilled labour could be easily replaced with new (and more docile) scab workers. Strikes also allow employers to use the downtime to bring in new machinery – precisely the changes which workers may be struggling against. As a response, a new tactic of sit-down strikes and factory occupations emerged in the early twentieth century – making it impossible for replacement workers to operate and threatening to demonstrate that management was superfluous.[77] What we see here is a dynamic arms race occurring between opponents as each seeks to leverage new tactics and technologies for its own purposes.

Today, the terrain of these struggles is again changing, indicated by at least two broad and emerging problems with classic workplace disruption. In the first place, there is the tendency towards automation. Just as the automation of logistics took away some of the leverage points occupied by dockworkers, so too does the automation of factories, transportation, and eventually service work portend a significant decline in the potential for workplace struggles. The emergence of self-driving vehicles, for instance, will rapidly diminish the points of leverage contained within transportation systems. The National Union of Rail, Maritime and Transport Workers in the UK will have to face this problem directly in the near future, with self-driving trains already in operation and further expansion planned. The mayor of London, Boris Johnson, has explicitly stated that automation should be used to destroy one of the few remaining militant British unions.[78] Crucially, however, leverage points remain, and new ones will emerge in the wake of restructuring and automation. For instance, as one author pointed out – in 1957! – 'a strike by a very small number of workers is liable to hold up an entire automated factory'.[79] A decline in the number of workers overseeing a process also means a concentration of potential power within a smaller group of individuals. Likewise, while an automated transport system may not be subject to driver strikes, it may be open to strikes by programmers and IT technicians, as well as being more susceptible to blockades, because of the technical limitations of self-driving cars. These vehicles function by reducing environmental variation, making them 'more akin to a train running on invisible tracks'.[80] The intentional manipulation of the environment is therefore likely to be particularly disruptive. Equally, the use of pattern recognition algorithms in various tasks (e.g., diagnostics, emotion- and face-detection, surveillance) is highly susceptible to disruption.[81] A technical understanding of machines like these is essential to understanding how to interrupt them, and any future left must be as technically fluent as it is politically fluent. In the end, what is required is an analysis of the automation trends that are restructuring production and circulation, and a strategic understanding of where new points of leverage might develop.

The second related limitation of classic disruptive tactics is that they might falter in the face of mass unemployment and struggles organised around surplus populations rather than the working class. If there is no workplace to disrupt, what can be done? Again, the repertoires of contention were transformed in response to changing social, political, technological and economic conditions. As precarity, zero-hour contracts, temporary work and internships spread throughout society, movements of the unemployed and movements based around social reproduction offer important and instructive examples of resistance. These struggles have never had a workplace to disrupt, so they have always had to invent new means of leveraging power. It is one of the myopias of many on the left to only see workers' power coming from disrupting production, when in fact contesting the existing order has taken numerous forms outside the workplace. In Argentina, for instance, unemployed workers' movements blockaded major streets in order to make themselves heard and were central to the overthrow of the government.[82] Expelled from the wage, shorn of a workplace, blockading urban arteries becomes a primary means of exerting political power.[83] The surge in freeway blockades in the wake of the August 2014 police killing of Michael Brown in Ferguson, Missouri, demonstrates the increasing prevalence of this type of struggle.[84] Similar tactics take on other aspects of capitalist reproduction with the same basic objective, including rent strikes and debt strikes. Port blockades also have potential as a tactic, and computer modelling can offer insights into how to avoid scattershot and ineffective political action.[85] These new tactics must, of course, be situated within a larger strategic plan, or risk becoming so many temporary movements that erupt only to disappear without a trace.

The classic basis of power for the labour movement, then, has been diffused and weakened. Yet this need not herald the death-knell of class struggle. Automation and precarity may spell the decline of interruptions at points of production, but they do not mean the end of disruption in total. Just as traditional points of leverage have been effaced in the context of a flexible, global infrastructure, this shift has also increased the vulnerability of that infrastructure in other ways. Well-positioned local struggles can immediately become global.[86] The task before us must be to have a sober reckoning with changed material realities and to strategise over new spaces for action. There are precedents and lessons to be learned in existing practices like the 'power structure analysis' undertaken by unions and community organisers, which maps local social networks and key actors, determining their weaknesses, strengths, allies and enemies.[87] The argument we are making here is for the construction of a complement to this process, emphasising the material conditions of struggle rather than just its social networks. In either approach, though, on-the-ground knowledge must be linked up with more abstract knowledge of changing economic conditions.

A post-work world will not emerge out of the benevolence of capitalists, the inevitable tendencies of the economy or the necessity of crisis. As this and the previous chapter have argued, the power of the left – broadly construed – needs to be rebuilt before a post-work society can become a meaningful strategic option. This will involve a broad counter-hegemonic project that seeks to overturn neoliberal common sense and to rearticulate new understandings of 'modernisation', 'work' and 'freedom'. This will necessarily be a populist project that mobilises a broad swathe of society and that, while being anchored in class interests, nevertheless remains irreducible to them. It will involve a full-spectrum approach to organisations that seeks to use different organisational advantages in combination – not according to a pragmatism of loose alliances, but under the aegis of a vision for a better world. And these organisations and masses will have to identify and secure new points of leverage in the circuits of capitalism, with its increasingly barren workplaces. In the face of a globalised capitalism that is always on the move, opposition to it must pre-empt the transformations of tomorrow in a supple politics of anticipation.

Conclusion

You live the surprise results of old plans.

Jenny Holzer

Where, then, do we stand? The latest cycle of struggles has been exhausted, undone by their tendencies towards folk politics, and everywhere today mass outrage combines with mass impotence. We have argued that the most promising way forward lies in reclaiming modernity and attacking the neoliberal common sense that conditions everything from the most esoteric policy discussions to the most vivid emotional states. This counter-hegemonic project can only be achieved by imagining better worlds – and in moving beyond defensive struggles. We have outlined one possible project, in the form of a post-work politics that frees us to create our own lives and communities. Triumph in the political battles to achieve it will require organising a broadly populist left, building the organisational ecosystem necessary for a full-spectrum politics on multiple fronts, and leveraging key points of power wherever possible.

Yet the end of work would not be the end of history. Building a platform for a post-work society would be an immense accomplishment, but it would still only be a beginning.[1] This is why conceiving of left politics as a politics of modernity is so crucial: because it requires that we not confuse a post-work society – or indeed any society – with the end of history. Universalism always undoes itself, possessing its own resources for an immanent critique that insists and expands upon its ideals. No particular social formation is sufficient to satisfy its conceptual and political demands. Equally, synthetic freedom compels us to reject contentment with the existing horizon of possibilities. To be satisfied with post-work would risk leaving intact the racial, gendered, colonial and ecological divisions that continue to structure our world.[2] While such asymmetries of power would hopefully be unsettled by a post-work world, the efforts to eliminate them would undoubtedly need to continue. Further, we would still be seeking a systemic replacement for markets and facing the task of building new political institutions. We would still not know what a sociotechnical body can do, and we would still have to unfetter technological development and unleash new freedoms. Transcending our reliance on waged labour is important, but we would still be faced with the immense tasks of undoing other political, economic, social, physical and biological constraints. A project towards a post-work world is necessary but insufficient.

Yet a post-work platform does provide us with a new equilibrium to aim at, completing the shift from social democracy to neoliberalism to a new post-work hegemony. We believe it focuses the tasks of the present and provides a stable point from which to seek out further emancipatory gains. As with any platform, those who create it cannot fully predict how it will be used. While certain constraints and opportunities are built into a platform, they do not exhaustively determine the ways of life it will enable. A platform leaves the future open, rather than presuming to close it.[3] When it is designed correctly, it succeeds precisely by allowing people to build further developments on top of it. With a post-work platform, people may begin to participate more in political processes, or perhaps they will retreat into individualised worlds formed by media spectacles. But there are reasons for hope, given the shift in work ethic required for a post-work society. Such a project demands a subjective transformation in the process – it potentiates the conditions for a broader transformation from the selfish individuals formed by capitalism to communal and creative forms of social expression liberated by the end of work. Humanity has for too long been shaped by capitalist impulses, and a post-work world portends a future in which these constraints have been significantly loosened. This does not mean that a post-work society would simply be a realm of play. Rather, in such a society, the labour that remains will no longer be imposed upon us by an external force – by an employer or by the imperatives of survival. Work will become driven by our own desires, instead of by demands from outside.[4] Against the austerity of conservative forces, and the austere life promised by anti-modernists, the demand for a post-work world revels in the liberation of desire, abundance and freedom.

Such a future is undoubtedly risky, but so is any project to build a better world. There are no guarantees that things will work out as expected: a post-work world may generate immanent dynamics towards the rapid dissolution of capitalism, or the forces of reaction may co-opt the liberated desires under a new system of control. Concerns about the risks of political action have led parts of the contemporary left into a situation where they desire novelty, but a novelty without risk. Generic demands to experiment, create and prefigure are commonplace, but concrete proposals are all too often met with a wave of criticism outlining every possible point at which things might go wrong. In light of this dual tendency – for novelty, but against the risks inherent in social transformation – the allure of political ideas celebrating spontaneous 'events' becomes clearer. The event (as revolutionary rupture) becomes an expression of the desire for novelty without responsibility. The messianic event promises to shatter our stagnant world and bring us to a new stage of history, conveniently voided of the difficult work that *is* politics. The hard task ahead is to build new worlds while acknowledging that they will create novel problems. The best utopias are always riven by discord.

This imperative runs in opposition to the kind of precautionary principle that seeks to eliminate the contingency and risk involved in making decisions. On strong readings, the precautionary principle aims to convert epistemic uncertainty into a guardianship of the status quo, gently turning away those who would seek to build a better future with the imperative to 'do more research'. We might also consider here that the precautionary principle contains an almost inherent lacuna: it ignores the risks of its own application. In seeking to err always on the side of caution, and hence of eliminating risk, it contains a blindness to the dangers of inaction and omission.[5] While risks need to be reasonably hedged, a fuller appreciation of the travails of contingency implies that we are usually not better off taking the precautionary path. The precautionary principle is designed to close off the future and eliminate contingency, when in fact the contingency of high-risk adventures is precisely what leads to a more open future – in the words of conceptual artist Jenny

Holzer, 'You live the surprise results of old plans.' Building the future means accepting the risk of unintended consequences and imperfect solutions. We may always be trapped, but at least we can escape into better traps.[6]

AFTER CAPITALISM

The post-work project and, more broadly, the project of postcapitalism are progressive determinations of the commitment to universal emancipation. In practice, these projects involve 'a controlled dissolution of market forces . . . and a delinking of work from income'.[7] But the ultimate trajectory of universal emancipation is towards overcoming physical, biological, political and economic constraints. This ambition to undo constraints is one that, taken to its limits, leads inexorably towards grand and speculative frontiers. For the early Russian cosmists, even death and gravity were obstacles to be overcome through future ingenuity.[8] In these post-planetary speculations, we see the project of human emancipation transformed into an unceasing one that winds its way along two highly intertwined paths of development: technological and human.

Technological development follows a recombinant path, bringing together existing ideas, technologies and technological components into new combinations. Simple objects are united into increasingly complex technological systems, and each newly developed piece of technology forms the basis for a further technology. With this expansion, the combinatorial possibilities rapidly proliferate.[9] It would appear that capitalist competition has been a significant driver of this technological advancement. Under a popular narrative, intercapitalist competition is seen as driving technological changes in the production process, while consumer capitalism demands an increasingly differentiated set of products. But at the same time, capitalism has placed substantial obstacles in the way of technological development. While the carefully curated image of capitalism is one of dynamic risk-taking and technological innovation, this image in fact obscures the real sources of dynamism in the economy. Developments like railways, the internet, computing, supersonic flight, space travel, satellites, pharmaceuticals, voice-recognition software, nanotechnology, touch-screens and clean energy have all been nurtured and guided by states, not corporations. During the golden postwar era of research and development, two-thirds of research and development was publicly

funded.[10] Yet recent decades have seen corporate investment in high-risk technologies drastically decline.[11] And with neoliberalism's cutback in state
expenditure, it is therefore unsurprising that technological change has dimin-
ished since the 1970s.[12] In other words, it has been collective investment, not
private investment, that has been the primary driver of technological
development.[13] High-risk inventions and new technologies are too risky for
private capitalists to invest in; figures such as Steve Jobs and Elon Musk slyly
obscure their parasitical reliance on state-led developments.[14] Likewise, multi-
billion-dollar megascale projects are ultimately driven by non-economic goals
that exceed any cost–benefit analysis. Projects of this scale and ambition are in
fact hindered by market-based constraints, since a sober analysis of their
viability in capitalist terms reveals them to be profoundly underwhelming.[15] In
addition, some social benefits (those offered by an Ebola vaccine, for example)
are left unexplored because they have little profit potential, while in some
areas (such as solar power and electric cars) capitalists can be seen actively
impeding progress, lobbying governments to end green-energy subsidies and
implementing laws that obstruct further development. The entire
pharmaceuticals industry provides a particularly devastating illustration of the
effects of intellectual property monopolisation, while the technology industry
is increasingly plagued by patent trolling. Capitalism therefore misattributes
the sources of technological development, places creativity in a straitjacket of
capitalist accumulation, constrains the social imagination within the parameters of cost–benefit analyses and attacks profit-destroying innovations. To
unleash technological advancement, we must move beyond capitalism and
liberate creativity from its current strictures.[16] This would begin to liberate
technologies away from their current purview of control and exploitation, and
towards the quantitative and qualitative expansion of synthetic freedom. It
would enable the utopian ambitions of megaprojects to be unleashed, invoking
the classic dreams of invention and discovery. The dreams of space flight, the
decarbonisation of the economy, the automation of mundane labour, the
extension of human life, and so on, are all major technological projects that
find themselves hampered in various ways by capitalism. The boot-strapping
expansionary process of technology, once liberated from capitalist fetters, can
potentiate both positive and negative freedoms. It can form the basis for a fully
postcapitalist economy, enabling a shift away from scarcity, work and exploitation, and towards the full development of humanity.[17]

Intertwined with this picture of liberated technological transformation is therefore the future of human beings. The pathway towards a postcapitalist society requires a shift away from the proletarianisation of humanity and towards a transformed and newly mutable subject. This subject cannot be determined in advance; it can only be elaborated in the unfolding of practical and conceptual ramifications. There is no 'true' essence to humanity that could be discovered beyond our enmeshments in technological, natural and social webs.[18] The idea that a post-work society would simply inculcate further mindless consumption neglects humanity's capacity for novelty and creativity, and invokes a pessimism based upon current capitalist subjectivity.[19] Likewise, the development of new needs must be distinguished from their commodification. Whereas the latter locks new desires into a profit-seeking framework that constrains human flourishing, the former denotes a real form of progress. The 'extension and differentiation of needs as a whole' is to be lauded over any folk-political dream of returning to a 'primitive natural state of these needs'. The complexification of needs is disfigured under capitalist consumer society, to be sure, but, unbound from this mutation, 'their aim is necessarily the development of a "rich individuality" for the whole of mankind'.[20]

The postcapitalist subject would therefore not reveal an authentic self that had been obscured by capitalist social relations, but would instead unveil the space to create new modes of being. As Marx noted, 'all history is nothing but a continuous transformation of human nature', and the future of humanity cannot be determined abstractly in advance: it is first of all a practical matter, to be carried out in time. Nevertheless, some general notions might be entertained. For Marx, the primary principle of postcapitalism was the 'development of human powers which is an end in itself'.[21] Indeed, the fundamental aim of his project was universal emancipation. The various ideas that Marxists have advanced to get there – the socialisation of production, ending the value-form, eliminating wage labour – are simply means towards achieving this end. The immediate question is: What does this aim entail? The synthetic construction of freedom is the means by which human powers are to be developed. This freedom finds many different modes of expression, including economic and political ones,[22] experiments with sexuality and reproductive structures,[23] and the creation of new desires, expanded aesthetic capabilities,[24] new forms of thought and reasoning, and ultimately entirely new modes of being human.[25] The expansion of desires, of needs, of lifestyles, of communities, of ways of being, of capacities – all are invoked by the project of universal emancipation. This is a project of opening up the future, of undertaking a labour that elaborates what it might mean to be human, of producing a utopian project for new desires, and of aligning a political project with the trajectory of an endless universalising vector. Capitalism, for all its appearances of liberation and universality, has ultimately restrained these forces in an endless cycle of accumulation, ossifying the real potentials of humanity and constricting technological development to a series of banal marginal innovations. We move faster – capitalism demands it; yet we go nowhere. Instead, we must build a world in which we can accelerate out of our stasis.

BEFORE THE FUTURE

The argument of this book has been that the left can neither remain in the present nor return to the past. To construct a new and better future, we must begin taking the necessary steps to build a new kind of hegemony. This runs counter to much of our political common sense today. The tendencies towards folk politics – emphasising the local and the authentic, the temporary and the spontaneous, the autonomous and the particular – are explicable as reactions against a recent history of defeats, of partial, ambivalent victories, and of surging global complexity. But they remain radically insufficient for achieving broader victories against a planetary capitalism. Rather than seeking temporary and local relief in the various bunkers of folk politics, we must today move beyond these limits. Against ideas of resistance, withdrawal, exit or purity, the task of the left today is to engage the politics of scale and expansion, along with all the risks such a project entails. Doing so requires us to salvage the legacy of modernity and reappraise which parts of the post-Enlightenment matrix can be saved and which must be discarded; for it is only a new form of universal action that will be capable of supplanting neoliberal capitalism.

Without tabulae rasae or miraculous events, it is within the tendencies and affordances of our world today that we must locate the resources from which to build a new hegemony. While this book has focused on full automation and the end of work, there is a broad palette of political options for a contemporary left to choose from. This would mean, most immediately, rethinking classic leftist demands in light of the most advanced technologies. It would mean building upon the post-nation-state territory of 'the stack' – that global infrastructure that enables our digital world today.[26] A new type of production is already visible at the leading edges of contemporary technology. Additive manufacturing and the automation of work portend the possibility of production based on flexibility, decentralisation and post-scarcity for some goods. The rapid automation of logistics presents the utopian possibility of a globally interconnected system in which parts and goods can be shipped rapidly and efficiently without human labour. Cryptocurrencies and their block-chain technology could bring forth a new money of the commons, divorced from capitalist forms.[27]

The democratic guidance of the economy is also accelerated by emerging technologies. Famously, Oscar Wilde once said that the problem with socialism was that it took up too many evenings. Increasing economic democracy could require us to devote an overwhelming amount of time to discussions and decisions over the minutiae of everyday life.[28] The use of computing technology is essential in avoiding this problem, both by simplifying the decisions to be made and by automating decisions collectively deemed to be irrelevant. For example, rather than deliberating over every aspect of the economy, decisions could instead be made about certain key parameters (energy input, carbon output, level of inequality, level of research investment, and so on).[29] Social media – divorced from its drive to monetisation and tendency towards narcissism – could also foster economic democracy by bringing about a new public. New modes of deliberation and participation might emerge from a postcapitalist social media platform. And the perennial problem facing postcapitalist economies – that of how to distribute goods efficiently in the absence of market prices – can also be overcome through computers. Between the early Soviet attempts at economic planning and today, computing power has grown exponentially, to become 100 billion times more powerful.[30] The calculation of how to distribute our main productive resources is increasingly viable. Equally, data collection on resources and preferences through ubiquitous computing means that the raw data for running an economy are more readily available than ever before. And all of this could be mobilised towards the implementation of the Lucas Plan on national and global scales – redirecting our economies towards the self-conscious production of socially useful goods like renewable energy, cheap medicine and the expansion of our synthetic freedoms.

This is what a twenty-first-century left looks like. Any movement that wishes to remain relevant and politically potent must grapple with such potentials and developments in our technological world. We must expand our collective imagination beyond what capitalism allows. Rather than settling for marginal improvements in battery life and computer power, the left should mobilise dreams of decarbonising the economy, space travel, robot economies – all the traditional touchstones of science fiction – in order to prepare for a day beyond capitalism. Neoliberalism, as secure as it may seem today, contains no guarantee of future survival. Like every social system we have ever known, it will not last forever. Our task now is to invent what happens next.

Afterword: Reinventing the Future

Where are we now? In the nine months since the publication of *Inventing the Future*, there have been a number of significant developments. The election of Jeremy Corbyn to the leadership of the UK Labour Party and the unexpectedly successful run of Bernie Sanders in the US Democratic presidential primary have both transformed pre-existing expectations for the organised left. The (re)arrival of socialism in America is indicative of broader fragmentation at the level of political hegemony across the Western world. This is one of the defining features of the present moment: the technocratic parties of the neoliberal left and right are seeing their ability to manage polities increasingly threatened by the very economic forces they inculcated. Inequality, jobless growth, and general economic stagnation have all suspended the belief in the virtues of the political centre. Here there is cause both for enthusiasm and concern, with left *and* right populisms growing in this new environment. The common sense of politics is changing, and new possibilities are opening. While Corbyn and Sanders might have introduced entire new generations to socialist ideas, the potential for reactionary neo-nationalisms to take firmer command of the system has also increased. Without a clear strategy, a positive vision of the future, and a mobilised activist base, victory in the hegemonic struggle to come will be exceptionally difficult. Encouragingly, however, productive relationships are being built between the new socialisms, the remnants of the horizontalist movements (such as

Occupy), as well as more recently formed political movements such as Black Lives Matter, the Fight for 15, and various housing struggles. While they are not always entirely in sync, they do perhaps herald the arrival of a more dynamic and powerful political ecology – and importantly, one that is attuned to the interconnections beyond their local struggle.

Discussions around universal basic income have also greatly expanded since the release of the book. This has taken a number of forms, from becoming a topic of research for left-leaning think tanks, to increasing support among political parties, activists, and unions.[1] Though the Swiss referendum on introducing a UBI in June 2016 ultimately failed, the debate has shifted from one that introduces the idea to one about what form it might take. In this, we consider our political take on UBI to be absolutely necessary. To achieve a UBI that is genuinely universal and which provides an income above poverty levels will require the assemblage of a sizeable political movement to support it. Unavoidably, it will work to redistribute incomes and wealth in some form, and this remains an ineluctably political, rather than merely technocratic, issue. Simultaneously, a serious and redistributive UBI policy will inevitably open out onto a series of broader questions: What *is* the nature of work? What is the value of work? How does society create value? How should that value be shared?

The political project that we set out in *Inventing the Future* has itself played a small role in some of these events, having been read by a range of people from the ultra-left to trade unionists to journalists to politicians. The critique of folk politics and the need to think in more expansive, institutional, and hegemonic terms have been the focus of discussion for a number of groups on the left. The linkages of UBI, automation, and the need for a new anti-work politics has also been rejuvenated by activists, unions, and parties starting to take these ideas seriously. Yet, as with any project that seeks to supplant our present common sense, some elements of the project have been subjected to understandable criticism. With the benefit of hindsight, and the productive criticisms of numerous responses, it is worth reflecting on the contents of this book in order to clarify our arguments, to respond to the most significant questions, to acknowledge limitations and to correct some misunderstandings. We do so in a spirit of humility, given that we see this book as a contribution to a larger debate and, hopefully, an opportunity for reflection on what we think are important issues for the contemporary left.

POST-WORK FUTURES

In a number of pieces written about the book, some fundamental questions have been raised about what precisely a post-work world entails with respect to the environment, labour, social reproduction, and colonialism. Does a high-tech post-work world entail the exhaustion of resources and the decimation of the earth's climate? Does a post-work world mean the continued oppression and subjugation of low-income countries? What place does domestic and other unwaged labour have in this future? These are all essential questions to ask. To respond to these queries it is useful to sketch a series of alternative possible futures that indicate how a post-work project may play out. Roughly speaking, we can imagine four broad and potentially intersecting futures: a neocolonial and racist post-work world, an ecologically unsustainable post-work world, a misogynist post-work world, and a leftist post-work world.

A first possible future would be a neocolonial and racist post-work world. Here, post-work would be established in some of the advanced capitalist countries, but low-income countries would struggle to follow suit. The post-work countries would become large attractions for migrants, and the influx of people would exacerbate existing xenophobia and mobilise harsh state responses. Borders would be tightened up, and the European, American, and Australian borders would be littered with even more bodies than they are today. Cheap labour would continue to be exploited in the low-income countries, while domestic prison labour would continue, as much for its punitive potential as for its economic efficacy. The end result would be an exacerbation of existing global inequalities, an expansion of xenophobia and racism, and increasing political and military destabilisation as the Western world fortified itself against the rest of the world.

A second possible future would be an ecologically unsustainable vision of post-work. In this future, post-work would be established in some or many countries, but extensive automation would be achieved without a concern for long-term sustainability. Extraction processes around the world would intensify, and the pollution and environmental damage from them would continue to grow. The energy resources demanded by inefficient automation would be drawn from fossil fuel sources, and carbon emissions would rise above even current trends. Combined with this, consumption patterns would continue to expand at levels which transform any productivity gains into more and more output. The major result would be an accelerated climate catastrophe, leading towards mass climate-induced migration and xenophobia, significant political destabilisation, large losses of human life, the devastation of the biosphere, and the extinction of many species of life forms.

A third future would be a misogynist one. In this post-work future, most wage labour would have disappeared and there would be an immense increase in overall leisure time. Yet there would be no simultaneous shift in unpaid reproductive labour.[2] Women would continue to bear the burden of these tasks, and there would be no investment in the automation of household labour such as cooking and cleaning and laundry. Or alternatively, as has historically been the case, any household technologies would simply lead to higher standards of cleanliness, not less work. It would be a society where men were newly freed from wage labour, but where women continued to be constrained. A corresponding divide in politics would widen, with men freer than ever before to participate in public life, but with women still bound to the household.

In contrast to these depressing scenarios, we can imagine a fourth option: a leftist post-work future. This option would entail commitments to (at the very least) open borders, the abolition of spatial mechanisms of control (like prisons and ghettos), the reduction/socialisation of unwaged and waged work, the bolstering of the welfare state, and the provision of a global basic income. This would not yet be postcapitalist (for instance, commodities would still be bought within the market, private property would remain, and accumulative logics would still function), but it would be an immensely better world than the one we have now – both in terms of livelihoods and in terms of our political power.

Our book is an attempt to begin articulating a vision and a pathway to just such a post-work future. Though the responses to our book have covered many of the key themes and ideas, one crucial element is often missing from the discussion and that is the issue of surplus populations. It is not for nothing that the chapter on surplus populations forms the main turning point in the book, outlining the basic motive force of the post-work project.[3] That chapter tries to draw out the systemic connections between phenomena like the deadly functions of borders (see pp. 101–2), the violent management of jobless neighbourhoods (pp. 102–3), the hyper-exploitation of prison labour (pp. 90, 103), the continuation of outright slavery (p. 90), the rising density of informal slums (pp. 96–8), the proliferation of suicides and mental health issues (p. 94), the attacks on higher education (p. 99), and the devastating effects of a developing world becoming post-industrial (pp. 97–8). We raise the problem of automation and insist that developing countries and minority groups are the ones most at risk of being plunged even further into immiseration (pp. 97–8, 101–2, 104). As we argue, 'the maintenance of large portions of humanity within slums and informal, non-capitalist economies is likely to be consolidated by emerging technological trends'. The chapter is an attempt to explain the ongoing onslaught against the most marginalised, the ways in which increasing numbers of people are being tossed aside by capitalism, and the significant influence of gender, race, and colonialism in this expulsion.[4]

One of the fundamental arguments of this book is that some combination of the neocolonial, racist, unsustainable, and misogynist futures is the expected outcome of the current path of capitalist development. As we try to demonstrate in the surplus populations chapter, these futures are the endpoint of a business-as-usual approach – and we warn throughout the book that things will only get worse if we don't build up a significant movement to change course. We agree with the critics who claim that a post-work world may be built on colonialism, on a doubling down of unwaged reproductive labour, or the total destruction of the biosphere. Indeed it seems sadly quite likely, particularly given the rise of fascism, racism and xenophobia in recent years. However, it is precisely this analysis which motivates the book's claim that a leftist post-work world is both *necessary* and *possible* today. This is why the chapter on surplus populations appears immediately before the discussion of post-work – it establishes the conjunctural conditions within which the project becomes intelligible. The post-work future we envision is therefore not a free-floating project; it is not an abstract utopia. The image of the future is instead one which responds to and is conditioned by the deepening devastations around the world. This is important: *a post-work world must be seen as a response to existing and emerging neocolonial, racist, sexist, and exploitative conditions*. As such, any post-work project which continued or exacerbated those conditions would be anathema to our vision of a post-work future. Post-work has much to recommend itself on its own – and we spend sizeable chunks of the book elaborating on these reasons. But under today's conditions it is taking on a new urgency – 'these tendencies demand a response' (p. 23), and this is why 'a post-work world is an increasingly pressing option' (p. 86) and why 'the left [should] prepare for the coming crisis of work and surplus populations' (p. 86). This means that 'the political project for the twenty-first-century left must be to build an economy in which people are no longer dependent upon wage labour for survival' (p. 105). These, therefore, are the fundamental concerns which motivate our project of a post-work politics. Post-work cannot be premised on the rich countries continuing to plunder and exploit the poorest countries, nor on cis men dominating everyone else, nor on whites dominating people of colour. These are the basic coordinates of any leftist post-work vision, and they are nonnegotiable.

LIMITS OF ANALYSIS

Now we turn to two important limits of the book. The first of these are ecological concerns. We fully admit that issues of climate change and ecological sustainability are not dealt with in anywhere near enough depth in the text. A proper answer to these concerns about ecological sustainability would deserve a book-length response in itself. Nevertheless, we have tried to make it clear in the book that any vision of the future must be ecologically sustainable and not premised upon an accumulative and extractive economy that decimates our planet (hence the call throughout the book for a decarbonised economy). Whether extensive automation is compatible with ecological sustainability will depend on issues such as the replacement of fossil fuels, the expansion of renewable energy, the substitution of dwindling resources, the transformation of wasteful manufacturing processes, and the elimination of exploitative labour practices. In other words, any answer will have to draw upon an extensive array of both technical and political knowledge. However, we think a post-work politics has much to offer any attempt to overcome the division between a labour politics premised on growth and jobs, and a green politics premised on reining in pollution and greenhouse gas emissions. Post-work undercuts the primary reason to need growth and jobs – namely the attachment of income to work – thereby enabling new connections to be made between the movements. Less work is also an easy way to save an immense amount of energy consumption, with estimates of a 20 per cent reduction in energy consumption if the US moved to a European work week. Lastly, the basic premise of a post-work society is to use enhancements in productivity to lessen work rather than to expand production. The latter is of course a difficult task in a capitalist system, but that is why it must be the focus of political struggle.

The second limit to raise is the Western-centric nature of our prescriptive proposals. As we argued earlier, our analysis of the present conjuncture attempts to be resolutely global, and the picture of the coming crisis of work is equally global. Yet we are situated as white male Westerners, and our knowledge is primarily of conditions in the spaces within which we live and breathe. This is why we try to explicitly limit our strategic analysis to the Western world. Our intention here is to circumscribe the limits of our analysis and highlight our own situatedness. The alternative, it seems to us, would have been a hubristic claim that we know best how the rest of the world can and should build a post-work society – that two white men should lead the way. This would hardly be fitting with our claim that we must 'rely upon a global set of voices articulating and negotiating in practice what a common and plural future might be' (p. 83). That our strategic analysis is focused on the Western world is undoubtedly a limit of the book, but we believe it is a necessary limit. There is scope to breakdown this limit in the future, and we hope others will as well, by developing accounts of power and possibility in the context of other societies.

WHAT THE FOLK?

We now turn to what appears, perhaps unsurprisingly, to be the most contentious idea in our book: that of folk politics. Let us be clear about something up front: our critique of what we call folk politics is born neither out of a belief in the intrinsic desirability of alternative tactics and strategies, nor out of malice towards them. Rather, our critique arises from the experience of struggles in the past few decades. It has been over twenty years since the Zapatistas stormed onto the world stage, yet we have seen precious little evidence that any recent movements have posed a threat to the dominance of neoliberalism (let alone capitalism). Our own experiences in these movements, and particularly the brief moment of hope that emerged around Occupy, are why we started writing this book in the first place. We wanted them to succeed, and we were disappointed when they didn't. Our critique of folk politics stems from asking the question: What went wrong? We don't think our answers are particularly novel: they've been voiced in numerous forms by participants and external critics for some time now, and the book draws heavily upon this existing literature. Our novelty is perhaps in tracing these problems back to a preference for immediacy – namely, the kernel of contemporary 'folk politics'. (In fact, a better name for 'folk politics' might be 'the politics of immediacy'.) It is this valorisation of immediacy – and the way in which it has become a common sense – that we see played out in various ways across the left, both in the explicit statement of political theorists and in the implicit assumptions of various practices.

This leads us to an aspect of the concept which has yet to receive any attention: namely, its historically constructed character.[5] While this issue is not foregrounded in the book (it is only raised in one paragraph), our position is that folk politics changes over time. Certain ideas and values come to dominate and take on an intuitive place within the activist imagination. In the 1960s, in much of the Western world, folk politics would have meant building the revolutionary party. In the future, folk politics will again change. We may see, for instance, a folk political common sense come to rest upon social media clicktivism. We must therefore distinguish between two senses of folk politics. One is a historically constructed political common sense. The other is the contemporary manifestation of that common sense oriented around a politics of immediacy. Given its historical nature, it would be fair to say that *our own project is one of constructing a new folk politics*. It is only today that folk politics – 'a collective and *historically constructed* political common sense that has become out of joint with the actual mechanisms of power' (p. 10, emphasis added) – has come to overlap with another meaning of folk: as the locus of the small-scale and authentic grounded upon a valorisation of immediacy.

Ultimately, our desires are to transform the world, not to get the self-satisfaction of being proven right. If events were to show that our critique is wrong, we would be delighted to admit our error. For us, therefore, the essential components of the book are in its second half: the analysis of global surplus populations and the vision of the future. The four demands we set out to begin organising around for a post-work world should be taken as starting points for discussion, not dogmatic assertions.[6] A little humility is in order here, as we can make no claim to any certainty about our critiques and prescriptions for how these things should be achieved. The social world is complex and the assertive absoluteness with which many left thinkers put forth their ideas is belied by their repeated failures to change the world.

Returning to folk politics, though, we must insist upon three qualifications to place on our critique of the idea. Without these qualifications, the critique of folk politics steps outside its purview. The first is that folk politics is an implicit tendency, not an explicit position. This leads to a key point to insist upon: *folk politics is not equivalent to horizontalism, anarchism, prefigurative politics, or localism.* We constructed this concept because we find much of value in these movements, and we didn't want to simply denounce them in toto. Instead, the concept is designed to pick out a particular subset of characteristics from them. It is designed to describe a common element behind a variety of movements which have so far been incapable of transforming the world or stopping neoliberalism. But again: folk politics is not coterminous with horizontalism, anarchism, prefigurative politics, or localism. To the extent that particular practices embody our understanding of folk politics (as a politics of spatial, temporal, and conceptual immediacy), we argue that they are limited. But where they do not embody these features (for example, in the way that anarcho-syndicalism is focused on creating scalable political structures), we do not view them as being folk political in nature.

Let us give a simple example to reinforce our point. The Black Panthers operated a variety of community initiatives centred around health, education, and food. Some might take this to be an archetype of folk political thinking (community? local?). But it is anything but because the Black Panthers saw these efforts as part of a much grander strategic vision. In a wonderful phrase, they described these programmes as 'survival pending revolution'. Here is an effort to create new means of social reproduction – not as a space withdrawn from the rest of society, nor as a prefigurative paradise – but instead as a means within a larger struggle to overthrow racism, capitalism, and imperialism. This is not folk politics; it is premised upon a global analysis and seeks to scale its efforts in order to contend with vast structures of oppression. And this is why 'we hasten to add, [folk politics is] not intrinsically flawed' (p. 29). Tactics are only folk political relative to strategic orientation and historical conditions.

The next qualification that we place on the critique is also important for understanding how the term is being used. Our intention for the term has always been for it to be provocative, but never derogatory. This is clear in the second qualification: *we do not reject folk politics*. As we write in the book, 'Folk politics is a necessary component of any successful political project, but it can only be a starting point' (p. 12). Our critique is that it is insufficient, not that it is wrong. This is why we praise these movements throughout the book: 'The Occupy movements achieved real victories in creating solidarity, giving a voice to disenchanted and marginalised people, and raising public awareness' (p. 36). Later on, we note that 'operating under principles of direct democracy can be conducive to certain objectives, such as giving people a voice, creating a powerful sense of collective agency and enabling different perspectives to be articulated. It can foster the creation of a populist identity and empower people to start to see themselves as a collective' (p. 164). This is clearly very far from any wholesale dismissal of folk politics. And this is fundamentally different from setting up some old-fashioned binary between 'folk' and 'modernity'; instead the relationship we are trying to gesture towards is much more complex.

The third qualification is perhaps the most important one for understanding the limits of our critique: *folk politics is only a problem for projects which are attempting to overcome large-scale issues like capitalism and climate change*. Combine this with our earlier caveats and you get the claim that: *a politics of immediacy is necessary but insufficient to transform global capitalism*. And if that seems pretty modest, well, it's meant to be.

THE NECESSITY OF LEADERSHIP

Another scandalous moment of the book has been the assertion of the necessity of leadership, with more than a few commentators invoking fearful images of technocratic Leninists. Yet our approach to the question of political organisation is based on the rejection of such a perspective, and is grounded in the notion of an 'ecology of organisations' and a particular understanding of hegemonic politics. Here is a concise summary of how we envision a movement comprising an ecology of organisations:

> The overarching architecture of such an ecology is a relatively decentralised and networked form – but, unlike in the standard horizontalist vision, this ecology should also include hierarchical and closed groups as elements of the broader network. There is ultimately no privileged organisational form. Not all organisations need to aim for participation, openness and

horizontality as their regulative ideals. The divisions between spontaneous uprisings and organisational longevity, short-term desires and long-term strategy, have split what should be a broadly consistent project for building a post-work world. Organisational diversity should be combined with broad populist unity. (p. 163)

Note that there is no place for 'techno-fetishist vanguardism' here, though we do admit that 'hierarchical' and 'clandestine' organisations can have a role. But the need for secrecy and the inevitability of informal hierarchies have been roundly recognised by anarchists for a long time (indeed, we draw upon their insights in the book), so we don't think many would necessarily disagree with this aspect. Instead, it is the issue of vanguardism that seems to be the source of the problems – and it is a delicate one since it is prone to many misunderstandings.

We think the concern here lies in the *potential* for hierarchical and secretive groups to force the mantle of leadership upon themselves. We admit that we find this unlikely in our current era, where political promiscuity rules the day and an organisation that begins to centralise and distance itself from its members is doomed to collapse. But to spell out our own position: we argue for a horizontal architecture to any movement, which entails that *no one group or organisation should seek to dominate the movement.*

What we instead call for is mobile vanguard functions, with a reference pointing to the work of Rodrigo Nunes. In a quote distinguishing this notion from more traditional ideas, he writes,

The vanguard-function differs from the teleological understanding of the vanguard whose sway over the Marxist tradition helped engender vanguardism. It is objective to the extent that, once the change it introduces has propagated, it can be identified as the cause behind a growing number of effects. Yet it is not objective in the sense of a transitive determination, which would be made necessary by historical laws, between an objectively defined position (class, class fraction) and a subjective political breakthrough (consciousness, event). The vanguard-function is akin to what Deleuze and Guattari call the 'cutting edge of deterritorialisation' in an assemblage or situation; opening a new direction that, after it has communicated to others, can become something to follow, divert, resist etc.[7]

Given a more concrete formulation, this entails that:

> Leadership occurs as an event in those situations in which some initiatives manage to momentarily focus and structure collective action around a goal, a place or a kind of action. They may take several forms, at different scales and in different layers, from more to less 'spontaneous'. This could be a crowd at a protest suddenly following a handful of people in a change of direction, a small group's decision to camp attracting thousands of others, a newly created website attracting a lot of traffic and corporate media attention, and so forth. The most important characteristic of distributed leadership is precisely that these can, in principle, come from anywhere: not just anyone (a boost, no doubt, to activists' egalitarian sensibilities) but literally anywhere.[8]

We recommend reading his book, which is a superb analysis of how leadership functioned in Occupy and similar movements. Vanguardism, according to him, doesn't disappear – it just gets distributed and made mobile. What does this mean in practice? Let us take a simplified example of an ongoing and complex situation: the #BlackLivesMatter movement. Here we saw the initial emergence of a vanguard through social media, as the hashtag emerged in the wake of Trayvon Martin's murder. After Michael Brown was shot down by a cop, the residents of Ferguson became a vanguard in the streets, pushing back against the violence of the state and leading the movement to a new plateau of intensity. Social media continued to amplify this and a national (and eventually international) movement was born. In the wake of Freddie Gray's brutal murder, Baltimore's residents became the new vanguard: the struggle was expanding, led by the people in the streets. Today, however, the movement appears to be at risk of co-optation by a group of 'politically respectable' leaders. It is unclear, at the moment, where this leadership will take the movement should it become dominant, or whether other leaders will emerge in the streets and elsewhere.

This is vanguardism, but certainly not the type that many fear. We would even suggest it is a rather humble idea, attuned to the realities of on-the-ground activism as well as the larger issues of strategic planning.[9] It seems to us, this is how leadership always works in contemporary social movements. Our point is to make this explicit and to try and shift the debate around leadership to a more sophisticated level. Anarchists have much to add here since they have been discussing these issues for some time now. Our contribution is to suggest this needs to be thought at the level of an entire ecology of organisations, not just within organisations. This would encourage asking questions like: How do we get leadership in social movements for expansion and scaling, without installing permanent and unaccountable leaders?

But if not a central vanguard or leader imposing unity on a movement, then what gives it any consistency? The argument we make in the book is that it is 'the future'. Or rather, the common adherence to a desirable vision of a different world. This is not a vision which could be forced upon anyone. Rather, it 'involves a continual negotiation of differences and particularisms, seeking to establish a common language and programme in spite of any centrifugal forces' (p. 160). Building a counter-hegemony means undertaking the difficult labour of building and maintaining a common, collective project within and between differences. It is crucial here to understand what we mean by hegemony. Hegemony, as we set out the term in Chapter 7, is not to be identified as a system of domination. Reading it as such is a common error, and one which does a disservice to the subtlety of the concept and the history of its development since Gramsci. Instead, hegemony needs to be understood as a complex, emergent mode of power, dependent on the ability of groups within society to influence others in much more diffuse ways. This form of influence can take different forms, from rational debate to affective attraction, from educational practices to cultural codes, and from media framing to economic and infrastructural architectures. Hegemony, in this understanding, emerges out of the interactions and practices of a diverse array of groups, agents, and organisations within society. It does not flatten difference, but emerges from the interplay of differences.

Another key dimension of the hegemonic perspective on politics is the idea that no large-scale political project can proceed by dint of appealing only to those who are already consciously persuaded of its merits. Against such a perspective, we have seen some claim that changing others' desires is contrary to their freedom. But surely changing the desires, beliefs, and behaviours of racists, sexists, fascists, and capitalists is an absolutely essential part of politics. Indeed, one can only fully understand the successes of movements by the extent to which they are able to achieve broad-scaled transformations in the public 'common sense', and to change what people desire. The general public unacceptability of openly homophobic statements within the UK, for example, has only been made possible by a long-term hegemonic project to change the way people think. This has operated in part through explicit means, but it has also proceeded through a variety of other modes of action, from specific legal provisions to the framing of issues in the mass media, all of which was made possible by decades of campaigning. Taken together these methods create a different environment in which subjects are formed.

It might also be helpful to consider here what the alternative to this would look like. The alternative to a hegemonic framework is one which sees people as essentially inert, unchanging, and unchangeable, that would identify the creation of small enclaves of like-minded people as the only practicable goal, a kind of separatism. Such a position would lead to a reliance on spontaneous revolt, and would not only be likely to fail, but would also tend towards a rather unnuanced acceptance of essentialist social forms and categories. We have good reason to believe that any left politics worthy of the name would want to reject such a position. Indeed, the successes of anti-racism, feminism, and queer politics are related to their (at least implicit) embracing of hegemonic projects to change the conditions within which people form their beliefs, opinions, and desires. Such a process of transformation can rarely be understood as simply a matter of imposition. Instead, hegemonic politics works to reorient existing tendencies, desires, opinions, and beliefs, working with existing affordances and transforming them in turn. It is in this sense that hegemonic politics involves 'leadership' – not in the sense of individual leaders, but in the sense of changing the conditions which determine the trajectory of societies, by transforming the means by which subjectivities and desires are articulated and formed. This is politics, pure and simple.

A final word is called for on the suggestion of a Mont Pelerin of the left. This is, to be sure, intended to be somewhat scandalous (though we note that both Philip Mirowski and Owen Jones have recently echoed such a call). But the rise of neoliberalism is also arguably the greatest example of an ideological shift in the twenty-first century. This is why we find it of interest in terms of understanding how shifts in power operate on a global scale. A number of responses believe that we are arguing for a vanguardist Mont Pelerin of the left. From what has been said here, hopefully it is clear that this is resolutely not the case. That is why we specify that 'the call for a Mont Pelerin of the left should therefore not be taken as an argument to simply copy its mode of operation' (p. 67). Instead, we find three elements of it potentially useful for the left: its emphasis on a 'long-term vision', its intention and capacity to build 'methods of global expansion', and 'the pragmatic flexibility and the counter-hegemonic strategy that united an ecology of organisations with a diversity of interests' (p. 67). We find no value in the elitist and vanguardist aspects of the Mont Pelerin Society. As we argue in the book: 'in a world of complexity, no one has a privileged view of the totality' (p. 165). The challenge for a Mont Pelerin of the left is therefore to elaborate a way to instantiate these ideas – of vision, expansion, and flexible ideology – in novel forms that avoid the elitist vanguardism of the original Mont Pelerin Society and which respond to the different situation of the left (for instance, a lack of similar resources).

BUILDING FUTURES

There are a number of issues we have not touched upon, but this is already a lengthy response and we trust that our readers can make up their own minds on these matters. To conclude, we will turn to a discussion of the future – in particular, the relationship between the future in general and our particular vision of a post-work future. Throughout the chapter on left modernity, we consciously and consistently reference visions of the future in the plural: 'various modernities are possible, and new visions of the future are essential for the left' (p. 74). Elsewhere, we say that 'visions of the future are therefore indispensable for elaborating a movement against capitalism' (pp. 74–5). A little later, we write that a left modernity 'would be one that offered enticing and expansive visions of a better future' (p. 83). While we use the plural in this chapter, we later set out post-work as one option: 'we have outlined one possible project, in the form of a post-work politics' (p. 175). The second half of the book is a case for this particular vision – we 'argue for the desirability of a future without work' (p. 85) – and our confident tone comes from believing in it. But we recognise that this is not the only possible vision and thus we insist upon 'the necessity of [non-European and other] voices in building truly planetary and universal futures' (p. 78). We also situate ourselves in a broader debate and believe that 'any meaningful vision of the future will set out proposals and goals, and this [book] is a contribution to that potential discussion' (p. 107). We have, in some instances, given more rhetorical strength to the case for our post-work vision, but this should be tempered with our continual recognition that 'any particular image of modernity must be open to co-creation, and further transformation and alteration' (p. 78). In the end, the project set out in the book is an invitation. Post-work demands 'do not presume to know in advance who will be called into action by them' (p. 161). We hope that those who are persuaded by the call for a post-work politics will build upon the project, filling in the gaps we have missed, extending the project to new areas, and seeking to build connections across struggles. No one alone can invent the future.

Notes

INTRODUCTION

1. John Maynard Keynes, 'Economic Possibilities for Our Grandchildren', in *Essays in Persuasion* (New York: W. W. Norton & Co., 1963); George Young, *The Russian Cosmists: The Esoteric Futurism of Nikolai Fedorov and His Followers* (Oxford: Oxford University Press, 2012); Mark Dery, 'Black to the Future: Interviews with Samuel R. Delany, Greg Tate, and Tricia Rose', in Mark Dery, ed., *Flame Wars: The Discourse of Cyberculture* (Durham, NC: Duke University Press, 1994); Shulamith Firestone, *The Dialectic of Sex: The Case for Feminist Revolution* (New York: Morrow, 1970).

2. For exemplars of this stance, see Franco Berardi, *After the Future* (Edinburgh: AK Press, 2011); T. J. Clark, 'For a Left with No Future', *New Left Review* II/74 (March–April 2012); Fernando Coronil, 'The Future in Question: History and Utopia in Latin America (1989–2010)', in Craig Calhoun and Georgi Derluguian, eds, *Business as Usual: The Roots of the Global Financial Meltdown* (New York: New York University Press, 2011). Or, in the words of one popular recent essay: 'The future has no future': The Invisible Committee, *The Coming Insurrection* (Los Angeles: Semiotext(e), 2009), p. 23.

1. OUR POLITICAL COMMON SENSE: INTRODUCING FOLK POLITICS

1. Dave Mitchell, 'Stuff White People Smash,' *Rabble*, 26 June 2011, at rabble.ca.

2. It is telling that the main reason for the failure of the ongoing Doha Round negotiations at the WTO is because of divisions between states, rather than any social movement resistance.

3. Insight into some of the internal debates within Occupy around the issue of demands can be found in Astra Taylor and Keith Gessen, eds, *Occupy! Scenes from Occupied America* (London: Verso, 2011). For a detailed critique of the 'no demands' position, see Marco Desiriis and Jodi Dean, 'A Movement Without Demands?', *Possible Futures*, 3 January 2012, at possible-futures.org.

4. Zach Schwartz-Weinstein, 'Not Your Academy: Occupation and the Future of Student Struggles', in A. J. Bauer, Christina Beltran, Rana Jaleel and Andrew Ross, eds, *Is This What Democracy Looks Like?*, Social Text E-Book, 2012, at what-democracy-looks-like.com. For a piece that tracks the diminishing importance of concrete demands over time within a single student occupation at University College London in 2010, see Guy Aitchison, 'Reform, Rupture, or Re-Imagination: Understanding the Purpose of an Occupation', *Social Movement Studies* 10: 4 (2011), pp. 431–9.

5. Hakim Bey's work is perhaps the most infamous example of this self-sufficiency of the autonomous protest. See Hakim Bey, *TAZ: The Temporary Autonomous Zone, Ontological Anarchy, Poetic Terrorism*, 2nd rev. edn. (Brooklyn: Autonomedia, 2011). See also Jeremy Gilbert, *Anti-Capitalism and Culture: Radical Theory and Popular Politics* (Oxford/New York: Berg, 2008), pp. 203–9, for a comprehensive critique from within the social movement space of the dangers of 'the activist imaginary'.

6. Linda Polman, *The Crisis Caravan: What's Wrong with Humanitarian Aid?* (New York: Metropolitan Books, 2010).

7. Radix, 'Fracking Sussex: The Threat of Shale Oil & Gas', *Frack Off*, 2013, at frack-off.org.uk. In fact, the most successful force to stop fracking has been the market, with the recent drop in crude oil prices.

8. Eviction Free Zone, 'Direct Action, Occupy Wall Street, and the Future of Housing Justice: An Interview with Noam Chomsky', 2013, at libcom.org.

9. Adam Gabbatt, 'Occupy Wall Street Activists Buy $15m of Americans' Personal Debt', *Guardian*, 12 November 2013.

10. Paul Mason, *Live Working or Die Fighting: How the Working Class Went Global* (London: Vintage, 2008).

11. Stephen Stich, *From Folk Psychology to Cognitive Science: The Case Against Belief* (Cambridge, MA: MIT Press, 1983); Patricia Churchland, *Neurophilosophy: Towards a Unified Science of the Mind–Brain* (Cambridge, MA: MIT Press, 1986). While we want to draw a somewhat loose analogy with the neurophilosophical tradition here, we do not mean to argue that folk politics is in any sense *grounded* in folk psychology. Rather, our critique of it is similarly focused on the notion that the appearance of phenomena is both necessary and deceptive as to the reality of how a system operates.

12. For a history of these 'repertoires of contention', see Charles Tilly, *Social Movements, 1768–2004* (Boulder, CA: Paradigm, 2004).

13. James Doward, Tracy McVeigh, Mark Townsend and Matthew Taylor, 'March for the Alternative Sends a Noisy Message to the Government', *Guardian*, 26 March 2011.

14. Liza Featherstone, Doug Henwood and Christian Parenti, 'Left Anti-Intellectualism and Its Discontents', in Eddie Yuen, George Katsiaficas and Daniel Burton Rose,

eds, *Confronting Capitalism: Dispatches from a Global Movement* (New York: Soft Skull, 2004).

15. Bey, *TAZ*.

16. Paul Davidson, *The Keynes Solution: The Path to Global Economic Prosperity* (New York: Palgrave Macmillan, 2009).

17. The Invisible Committee, *The Coming Insurrection* (Los Angeles, CA/Cambridge, MA: Semiotext(e), distributed by the MIT Press, 2009).

18. Greg Sharzer, *No Local: Why Small-Scale Alternatives Won't Change the World* (Winchester: Zero, 2012).

19. Ernst Schumacher, *Small Is Beautiful: Economics as if People Mattered* (New York: Harper & Row, 1973).

20. Taylor and Gessen, *Occupy!*.

21. Richard J. F. Day, *Gramsci Is Dead: Anarchist Currents in the Newest Social Movements* (London: Pluto, 2005); Jon Beasley-Murray, *Posthegemony: Political Theory and Latin America* (Minneapolis: University of Minnesota Press, 2010).

22. Justin Healey, *Ethical Consumerism* (Thirroul, NSW: Spinney, 2013).

23. James Ladyman, James Lambert and Karoline Wiesner, 'What Is a Complex System?' *European Journal for Philosophy of Science* 3: 1 (2013), pp. 33–67.

24. Susan Buck-Morss, 'Envisioning Capital: Political Economy on Display', *Critical Inquiry* 21: 2 (1995), pp. 434–67.

25. Fredric Jameson, 'Cognitive Mapping', in C. Nelson and L. Grossberg, eds, *Marxism and the Interpretation of Culture* (Chicago: University of Illinois Press, 1990).

26. Ibid., p. 356.

27. Schumacher, *Small Is Beautiful*; Carl Honoré, *In Praise of Slow: Challenging the Cult of Speed* (New York: HarperSanFrancisco, 2005).

28. Rosa Luxemburg, *The Essential Rosa Luxemburg: Reform or Revolution and the Mass Strike*, ed. Helen Scott (Chicago: Haymarket, 2008), p. 68.

29. Friedrich Hayek, *The Road to Serfdom* (London: Routledge, 1962); and 'The Theory of Complex Phenomena', in Michael Martin and Lee McIntyre, eds, *Readings in the Philosophy of Social Science* (Cambridge, MA: MIT Press, 1964).

30. This is the question at the heart of the socialist calculation debate. See Oskar Lange and Fred M. Taylor, *On the Economic Theory of Socialism* (New York: McGraw-Hill, 1964); Fikret Adaman and Pat Devine, 'The Economics Calculation Debate: Lessons for Socialists', *Cambridge Journal of Economics* 20: 5 (September 1996); Allin Cottrell and Paul Cockshott, 'Calculation, Complexity and Planning: The Socialist Calculation Debate Once Again', *Review of Political Economy* 5: 1 (1993).

31. It is important to note here that 'the left' is an ultimately artificial if useful term, used to describe an incredibly diverse and potentially contradictory set of political and social forces. For a full discussion of the origins of the left/right distinction in post-revolutionary France, see Marcel Gauchet, 'Right and Left', in Lawrence Kritzman, ed., *Realms of Memory: Conflicts and Divisions* (New York: Columbia University Press, 1997). As a point of clarification, we consider 'the left' today in the broadest sense to consist of the following movements, positions and organisations: democratic socialism, communism, anarchism, left-libertarianism, anti-imperialism, anti-fascism, anti-racism, anti-capitalism, feminism, autonomism, trade unionism, queer

politics, and large sections of the green movement, among many groups allied or hybridised with the above. Any consistency these forces might have is a matter of political construction and articulation, rather than being in any sense natural or pre-given.

32. Gerassimos Moschonas, *In the Name of Social Democracy: The Great Transformation, 1945 to the Present*, translated by Gregory Elliott (London: Verso, 2002), pp. 15–17; John Gerard Ruggie, 'International Regimes, Transactions, and Change: Embedded Liberalism in the Postwar Economic Order', *International Organization* 36: 2 (1982).

33. After the demise of 1968, there was a brief reassertion of more classical Leninist and Maoist revolutionary thought. Yet these attempts to double down on traditional methods of organising remained numerically marginal and suffered eventual failure. For a history of this moment in America, see Max Elbaum, *Revolution in the Air: Sixties Radicals Turn to Lenin, Mao and Che* (London: Verso, 2006).

34. Moschonas, *In the Name of Social Democracy*, pp. 35–6.

35. For an early feminist critique of these modes of organising, see Jo Freeman, *The Tyranny of Structurelessness*, 1970, at struggle.ws.

36. Martin Klimke and Joachim Scharloth, eds, *1968 in Europe: A History of Protest and Activism, 1956–77* (New York: Palgrave Macmillan, 2008).

37. Ibid., p. 5.

38. Giovanni Arrighi, Terrence Hopkins and Immanuel Wallerstein, *Antisystemic Movements* (London/New York: Verso, 1989), pp. 45–7.

39. Ibid.

40. Peter Starr, *Logics of Failed Revolt: French Theory After May '68* (Stanford, CA: Stanford University Press, 1995).

41. Grant Kester, 'Lessons in Futility: Francis Alÿs and the Legacy of May '68', *Third Text* 23: 4 (2009).

42. Gilbert, *Anti-Capitalism and Culture*, pp. 23–4.

43. Daniel Yergin, *The Prize: The Epic Quest for Oil, Money, and Power* (New York: Simon & Schuster, 1991); Barry J. Eichengreen, *Global Imbalances and the Lessons of Bretton Woods* (Cambridge, MA: MIT Press, 2007).

44. Geoffrey Barlow, *The Labour Movement in Britain from Thatcher to Blair* (Frankfurt: Peter Lang, 2008).

45. As an indication of the success of the neoliberal project to crush union power definitively, the proportion of the total working-age population belonging to unions fell in seventeen out of twenty-one OECD nations in the period 1980–2000, and fell again in nineteen out of twenty-one in the period 2000–07. OECD, 'Trade Union Density', *OECD Stat Extracts*, at stats.oecd.org.

46. David Harvey, *A Brief History of Neoliberalism* (Oxford: Oxford University Press, 2007), pp. 11–14.

47. Ibid., p. 13.

48. Colin Crouch, *Post-Democracy* (Cambridge: Polity, 2004), Chapter 1.

49. Tim Jordan, *Activism! Direct Action, Hacktivism and the Future of Society* (London: Reaktion, 2001), p. 32.

50. Kimberlé Crenshaw, 'Demarginalizing the Intersection of Race and Sex: A Black Feminist Critique of Antidiscrimination Doctrine, Feminist Theory and Antiracist Politics', *University of Chicago Legal Forum* 140 (1988).

51. Shulamith Firestone, *The Dialectic of Sex: The Case for Feminist Revolution* (New York: Morrow, 1970); Mandy Merck and Stella Sandford, eds, *Further Adventures of the Dialectic of Sex: Critical Essays on Shulamith Firestone* (New York: Palgrave Macmillan, 2010).

52. See, for example, James A. Geschwender, *Class, Race, and Worker Insurgency* (New York: Cambridge University Press, 1977).

53. Amory Starr, *Naming the Enemy: Anti-Corporate Movements Confront Globalisation* (London: Zed, 2000).

54. Jordan, *Activism!*; Taylor and Gessen, *Occupy*.

55. This work builds upon and expands our earlier proposals set out in the 'Manifesto for an Accelerationist Politics'. We largely avoid using the term 'accelerationism' in this work, due to the miasma of competing understandings that has arisen around the concept, rather than from any abdication from its tenets as we understand them. See Alex Williams and Nick Srnicek, '#Accelerate: Manifesto for an Accelerationist Politics', in Robin Mackay and Armen Avanessian, eds, *#Accelerate: The Accelerationist Reader* (Falmouth: Urbanomic, 2014).

2. WHY AREN'T WE WINNING?
A CRITIQUE OF TODAY'S LEFT

1. These other positions can be seen in the various denunciations of Occupy for being too liberal. See Mark Bray, 'Five Liberal Tendencies that Plagued Occupy', *ROAR Magazine*, 14 March 2014, at roarmag.org. Similar arguments have also been made in the past. Marx, for example, argued that the peasantry provided an insufficient class basis for revolutionary politics, and that only the industrial working class would have interests in line with communism. Our argument is that, regardless of the class basis of horizontalism, localism and other folk politics, they all remain bound by notions of spatial, temporal and conceptual immediacy.

2. Anna Feigenbaum, Fabian Frenzel and Patrick McCurdy, *Protest Camps* (London: Zed, 2013), p. 159. We might observe that variants of horizontalism were present in left politics for some time before the early 1970s, with proto-horizontalist commitments clearly visible in nineteenth-century anarchism, as well as much earlier movements.

3. This chapter will leave aside the lengthy history of anarchist thought and practice, in order to focus solely on horizontalism as a contemporary embodiment of some of its principles and practices.

4. John Holloway, *Change the World Without Taking Power: The Meaning of Revolution Today* (London/Sterling, VA: Pluto, 2002).

5. Richard Day, *Gramsci Is Dead: Anarchist Currents in the Newest Social Movements* (London: Pluto, 2005), p. 8. See also Jon Beasley-Murray, *Posthegemony: Political Theory and Latin America* (Minneapolis: University of Minnesota Press, 2010).

6. A commitment to consensus decision-making is not always an explicit mainstay of horizontalism as such, but is rather a popular contemporary way of procedurally embodying horizontality in practice. Some forms of anarchism, such as South American 'platformism', explicitly avoid consensus decision-making.

7. Uri Gordon, *Anarchy Alive! Anti-Authoritarian Politics from Practice to Theory* (London: Pluto, 2007), p. 20.

8. While we remain unconvinced of the large-scale prospects for direct democracy in its face-to-face and/or consensus-driven forms, this certainly does not preclude thinking about how participative democracy might be conceived along more complex, technologically mediated lines.

9. Murray Bookchin, *Post-Scarcity Anarchism* (Edinburgh: AK Press, 2004), p. xxviii.

10. Ibid., p. 58.

11. Manuel Castells, *Networks of Outrage and Hope: Social Movements in the Internet Age* (Cambridge, UK/Malden, MA: Polity, 2012), p. 11.

12. The origin of the form of consensus decision-making used in contemporary left activism is generally thought to have been with the Quaker religious movement around 300 years ago. The procedure was introduced to political activism via Quaker participants in anti-nuclear campaigns. L. A. Kauffmann, 'The Theology of Consensus', in Astra Taylor and Keith Gessen, eds, *Occupy! Scenes from Occupied America* (London: Verso, 2011).

13. Marina Sitrin, 'Occupy: Making Democracy a Question', in Federico Campagna and Emanuele Campiglio, eds, *What We Are Fighting For: A Radical Collective Manifesto* (London: Pluto, 2012), pp. 86–7.

14. Colin Crouch, *Post-Democracy* (Cambridge: Polity, 2004).

15. Kauffmann, 'Theology of Consensus'.

16. Federico Campagna and Emanuele Campiglio. 'What Are We Struggling For?', in Campagna and Campiglio, *What Are We Fighting For?*, p. 5.

17. Bookchin, *Post-Scarcity Anarchism*, p. 11.

18. South London Solidarity Federation, 'Direct Action and Unmediated Struggle', in Campagna and Campiglio, *What Are We Fighting For?*, p. 192.

19. Perhaps the best-known form of direct action, the mass strike, was the most powerful weapon of labour movements in the nineteenth and twentieth centuries, and remains a significant tool when used appropriately today. But this often requires scaling up (to a national or industry-wide level) as well as persistence, solidarity, consistent membership and organised systems of funding. The structure of horizontalist movements often militates against the success of this kind of tactic.

20. Feigenbaum et al., *Protest Camps*, p. 161.

21. The relative successes of Egypt, Tunisia and Iceland in using the tactic of occupation stem from a variety of conditions that render them significantly different from the conditions in Europe and North America – for instance, the relatively homogeneous religious and ethno-cultural composition of Tunisia and Iceland; the strong links forged between the occupations and other institutional forms of resistance in all three countries; the different (more visible) form of state repression in Egypt and Tunisia; the small size of Iceland (and the conscious attempt to express the movement in parliamentary terms); and the distinctive affective hurdles (namely,

fear) to be overcome in Egypt and Tunisia. For these and other reasons, these countries managed more success with the tactic.

22. Research and Destroy, 'The Wreck of the Plaza', *Research and Destroy*, 14 June 2014, at researchanddestroy.wordpress.com.

23. Josh MacPhee, 'A Qualitative Quilt Born of Pizzatopia', in Kate Khatib, Margaret Killjoy and Mike McGuire, eds, *We Are Many: Reflections on Movement Strategy from Occupation to Liberation* (Edinburgh: AK Press, 2012), p. 27.

24. Taylor and Gessen, *Occupy!*.

25. George Ciccariello-Maher, 'From Oscar Grant to Occupy: The Long Arc of Rebellion in Oakland,' in Khatib et al., *We Are Many*, p. 42.

26. Castells, *Networks of Outrage and Hope*, p. 59.

27. Feigenbaum et al., *Protest Camps*, p. 35.

28. Ibid., pp. 52–3.

29. Ibid., p. 42.

30. See, for example, the Australian Tent Embassy built around aboriginal land rights (ibid., p. 45); Castells, *Networks of Outrage and Hope*, pp. 59–60.

31. Lester Spence and Mike McGuire, 'Occupy and the 99%', in Khatib et al., *We Are Many*, p. 58.

32. Raúl Zibechi, 'Latin America Today, Seen from Below', *Upside Down World*, 26 June 2014, at upsidedownworld.org, pp. 42–4. We would argue that, while spontaneous political and social movements lasting a relatively short time have a role to play, a politics that consists *entirely* of such entities will find it extremely difficult to take apart and replace the relatively long-lasting embedded phenomena that characterise advanced capitalism.

33. Anton Pannekoek, *Workers' Councils* (Edinburgh: AK Press, 2003); Gregory Fossedal, *Direct Democracy in Switzerland* (New Brunswick, NJ: Transaction, 2007); Keir Milburn, 'Beyond Assemblyism: The Processual Calling of the 21st-Century Left', in Shannon Brincat, ed., *Communism in the 21st Century, Volume 3: The Future of Communism* (Santa Barbara: Praeger, 2013).

34. Isabel Ortiz, Sara Burke, Mohamed Berrada and Hernán Cortés, *World Protests 2006–2013* (New York: Initiative for Policy Dialogue and Friedrich-Ebert-Stiftung, 2013), pdf available at fes-globalization.org.

35. Michael Albert, *Parecon: Life After Capitalism* (London: Verso, 2004).

36. Samuel Farber, 'Reflections on "Prefigurative Politics"', *International Socialist Review* 92 (March 2011), at isreview.org.

37. Jane McAlevey, *Raising Expectations (and Raising Hell): My Decade Fighting for the Labor Movement* (London: Verso, 2014), p. 11.

38. Not An Alternative, 'Counter Power as Common Power', *Journal of Aesthetics and Protest* 9 (2014), at joaap.org.

39. Martin Gilens and Benjamin Page, 'Testing Theories of American Politics: Elites, Interest Groups, and Average Citizens', *Perspectives on Politics* 12: 3 (2014).

40. Rodrigo Nunes, *Organisation of the Organisationless: Collective Action After Networks* (London: Mute, 2014), p. 36.

41. David Graeber, *Fragments of an Anarchist Anthropology* (Chicago, IL: Prickly Paradigm, 2004), p. 89.

42. Helen Hester, 'Synthetic Genders and the Limits of Micropolitics', . . . *ment* 6 (2015).

43. Marco Desiriis and Jodi Dean, 'A Movement Without Demands?' *Possible Futures*, 3 January 2012, at possible-futures.org.

44. Noam Chomsky, *Occupy* (London: Penguin, 2012), p. 58.

45. Not An Alternative, 'Counter Power as Common Power'.

46. Ibid.

47. Jeroen Gunning and Ilan Zvi Baron, *Why Occupy a Square? People, Protests and Movements in the Egyptian Revolution* (London: Hurst, 2013), pp. 180–1.

48. Ibid., p. 181.

49. Hakim Bey, *TAZ: The Temporary Autonomous Zone, Ontological Anarchy, Poetic Terrorism*, 2nd rev. edn (Brooklyn: Autonomedia, 2011), p. xi.

50. 'Communiqué from an Absent Future', *We Want Everything*, 24 September 2009, at wewanteverything.wordpress.com, p. 19.

51. Desiriis and Dean, 'A Movement Without Demands?'.

52. See, for example, Theodore Schatzki's discussions of Shaker villages: Theodore Schatzki, *The Site of the Social: A Philosophical Account of the Constitution of Social Life and Change* (University Park, PA: Pennsylvania State University, 2002).

53. Farber, 'Reflections on "Prefigurative Politics"'.

54. Bruno Bosteels, 'The Mexican Commune', at academia.edu, p. 12.

55. This is an old question, often invoked in debates between anarchism and Marxism. See, for example, historical reflections on anarchism and communism in Mexico in ibid., p. 6.

56. The Invisible Committee, *The Coming Insurrection* (Los Angeles: Semiotext(e), 2009), p. 12; John Holloway, *Crack Capitalism* (London: Pluto, 2010); Nathan Brown, 'Rational Kernel, Real Movement: Badiou and Theorie Communiste in the Age of Riots', *Lana Turner: A Journal of Poetry and Opinion* 5 (2012); David Graeber, 'Afterword', in Khatib et al., *We Are Many*, p. 425.

57. Spence and McGuire, 'Occupy and the 99%', p. 61.

58. Paul Mason, *Why It's Kicking Off Everywhere: The New Global Revolutions* (London: Verso, 2012), p. 63.

59. In light of the emergence of Occupy, McKenzie Wark memorably asked: How do you occupy an abstraction? See McKenzie Wark, 'How to Occupy an Abstraction', at versobooks.com.

60. R. I. M. Dunbar, 'Neocortex Size as a Constraint on Group Size in Primates', *Journal of Human Evolution* 22: 6 (1992).

61. For the most extensive study of this, see Marina Sitrin, *Everyday Revolutions: Horizontalism and Autonomy in Argentina* (London: Zed, 2012).

62. Silvia Federici, 'Feminism, Finance and the Future of #Occupy – An Interview', *ZNet*, 26 November 2011, at zcomm.org.

63. A similar problem arose with the general assemblies at Occupy Wall Street. Milburn, 'Beyond Assemblyism, p. 191; Sitrin, *Everyday Revolutions*, p. 67–8.

64. Sitrin, *Everyday Revolutions*, p. 130; Juan Alcorta, 'Solidarity Economies in Argentina and Japan', *Studies of Modern Society* 40: 12 (2007), p. 270.

65. Farber, 'Reflections on "Prefigurative Politics"'.

66. Estimates are that the barter economy went from between 1 and 2.5 million people to just 100,000 people once the economy recovered. Alcorta, 'Solidarity Economies', pp. 272–3; Sitrin, *Everyday Revolutions*, p. 77.

67. Feigenbaum et al., *Protest Camps*, p. 159.

68. Holloway, *Change the World Without Taking Power*.

69. Ernst Schumacher, *Small Is Beautiful: Economics as if People Mattered* (New York: Harper & Row, 1973).

70. Phillip Blond, *Red Tory: How Left and Right Have Broken Britain and How We Can Fix It* (London: Faber & Faber, 2010).

71. Justin Healey, *Ethical Consumerism* (Thirroul, NSW: Spinney, 2013).

72. Uri Gordon, *Anarchy Alive! Anti-Authoritarian Politics from Practice to Theory* (London: Pluto, 2007).

73. Alan Ducasse, 'The Slow Revolutionary', *Time*, 3 October 2004.

74. Carl Honoré, *In Praise of Slow: Challenging the Cult of Speed* (New York: HarperSanFrancisco, 2005).

75. Ibid., p. 84.

76. Sarah Bowen, Sinikka Elliott and Joslyn Brenton, 'The Joy of Cooking?' *Contexts* 13: 3 (2014).

77. Miriam Glucksmann and Jane Nolan, 'New Technologies and the Transformations of Women's Labour at Home and Work', *Equal Opportunities International* 26: 2 (20 February 2007).

78. Will Boisvert, 'An Environmentalist on the Lie of Locavorism', *New York Observer*, 16 April 2013.

79. Alison Smith, Paul Watkiss, Geoff Tweddle, Alan McKinnon, Mike Browne, Alistair Hunt, Colin Treleven, Chris Nash and Sam Cross, *The Validity of Food Miles as an Indicator of Sustainable Development: Final Report* (London: Department for Environment, Food and Rural Affairs, 2005).

80. Caroline Saunders, Andrew Barber and Greg Taylor, *Food Miles: Comparative Energy/Emissions Performance of New Zealand's Agriculture Industry*, Agribusiness and Economics Research Unit, Lincoln University, Canterbury, NZ, July 2006, pdf available at lincoln.ac.nz.

81. In the UK in 2005, air freight made up just 1 per cent of food tonne miles travelled, but 11 per cent of food-related emissions. Smith et al., *Validity of Food Miles*, p. 3.

82. Doug Henwood, 'Moving Money (Revisited)', *LBO News*, 2010, at lbo-news.com.

83. Stephen Gandel, 'By Every Measure, the Big Banks Are Bigger', *Fortune*, 13 September 2013, at fortune.com.

84. Victoria McGrane and Tan Gillian, 'Lenders Are Warned on Risk', *Wall Street Journal*, 25 June 2014.

85. *OTC Derivatives Statistics at End-June 2014*, Basel: Bank for International Settlements, 2014, p. 2, at bis.org.

86. David Boyle, *A Local Banking System: The Urgent Need to Reinvigorate UK High Street Banking* (London: New Economics Foundation, 2011), p. 8.

87. Ibid., pp. 8–9.

88. Giles Tremlett, 'Spain's Savings Banks' Culture of Greed, Cronyism, and Political Meddling', *Guardian*, 8 June 2012.

89. Boyle, *Local Banking System*, p. 10.
90. Andrew Bibby, 'Co-op Bank Crisis: What Next for the Co-operative Sector?', *Guardian*, 21 January 2014.
91. Greg Sharzer, *No Local: Why Small-Scale Alternatives Won't Change the World* (Winchester: Zero Books, 2012), p. 3.
92. Philip Mirowski, *Never Let a Serious Crisis Go to Waste: How Neoliberalism Survived the Financial Meltdown* (London: Verso, 2013), p. 326.
93. Zibechi, 'Latin America Today'.
94. Christian Marazzi, 'Exodus Without Promised Land', in Campagna and Campiglio, eds, *What We Are Fighting For*, p. viii.
95. Such an approach has also been labelled 'alternativism' by communisation theorists. Endnotes, 'What Are We to Do?' in Benjamin Noys, ed., *Communization and Its Discontents: Contestation, Critique, and Contemporary Struggles* (Brooklyn: Minor Compositions, 2012), p. 30.
96. Day, *Gramsci Is Dead*, pp. 20–1.
97. Bey, *TAZ*, p. 99.
98. Invisible Committee, *Coming Insurrection*, p. 96.
99. Ibid., p. 113.
100. Ibid., p. 102.
101. Ibid., pp. 107, 114.
102. Vivek Chibber, *Postcolonial Theory and the Specter of Capital* (London: Verso, 2013), pp. 228–9.
103. Dan Hancox, *The Village Against the World* (London: Verso, 2013), Chapter 8; Ulrike Fokken, 'Die Rote Insel', *Die Tageszeitung*, 16 February 2013, at taz.de; Jason E. Smith, 'The Day After the Insurrection', *Radical Philosophy* 189 (2015), p. 43.
104. See also Alberto Toscano, 'The Prejudice Against Prometheus', *STIR*, 2011, at stirtoaction.com.
105. Chris Dixon, 'Organizing to Win the World', *Briarpatch Magazine*, 18 March 2015, at briarpatchmagazine.com; Keir Milburn, 'On Social Strikes and Directional Demands', *Plan C*, 7 May 2015, at weareplanc.org.

3. WHY ARE THEY WINNING?
THE MAKING OF NEOLIBERAL HEGEMONY

1. Jamie Peck, *Constructions of Neoliberal Reason* (Oxford: Oxford University Press, 2010), p. 40.
2. This standard history is now in the process of being rewritten, and this chapter relies heavily on the pioneers of this research, including the unpublished work of Alex Andrews. See, for example, Philip Mirowski and Dieter Plehwe, eds, *The Road from Mont Pelerin: The Making of the Neoliberal Thought Collective* (Cambridge, MA: Harvard University Press, 2009); Philip Mirowski, *Never Let a Serious Crisis Go to Waste: How Neoliberalism Survived the Financial Meltdown* (London: Verso, 2013); Peck, *Constructions of Neoliberal Reason*; Daniel Stedman Jones, *Masters of the Universe: Hayek, Friedman, and the Birth of Neoliberal Politics* (Princeton, NJ:

Princeton University Press, 2012); Richard Cockett, *Thinking the Unthinkable: Think-Tanks and the Economic Counter-Revolution, 1931–1983* (London: Fontana, 1995); Michel Foucault, *The Birth of Biopolitics: Lectures at the College de France 1978–1979* (New York: Palgrave Macmillan, 2010).

3. Witness, for instance, the unlikely but immensely productive alliance in the United States between economic neoliberals and radical social conservatives. Peck, *Constructions of Neoliberal Reason*, p. 6; David Harvey, *A Brief History of Neoliberalism* (Oxford: Oxford University Press, 2005), pp. 49–50.

4. Pierre Dardot and Christian Laval, *The New Way of the World: On Neoliberal Society*, transl. Gregory Elliot (London: Verso, 2014).

5. Rob Van Horn, 'Reinventing Monopoly and the Role of Corporations: The Roots of Chicago Law and Economics', in Mirowski and Plehwe, *Road from Mont Pelerin*, pp. 204–37.

6. Harvey, *Brief History of Neoliberalism*.

7. Philip Cerny, *Rethinking World Politics: A Theory of Transnational Neopluralism* (New York: Oxford University Press, 2010), p. 128.

8. Karl Polanyi is a notable exception, having long ago recognised the role of the state in building markets in labour and land. Karl Polanyi, *The Great Transformation: The Political and Economic Origins of Our Time* (Boston: Beacon Press, 2001); Peck, *Constructions of Neoliberalism Reason*, p. 4.

9. This gendering of rights is appropriate for the historical context.

10. It is worth mentioning that this political construction of economies negates the possibility of any simple economism. Thomas Lemke, 'The Birth of Biopolitics: Michel Foucault's Lecture at the Collège de France on Neoliberal Governmentality', *Economy and Society* 30: 2 (2001), p. 194.

11. Harvey, *Brief History of Neoliberalism*, p. 2.

12. The construction of markets has been exceptionally well studied within the sociology of finance and economic sociology. See Donald MacKenzie, *Material Markets: How Economic Agents Are Constructed* (Oxford: Oxford University Press, 2009), Chapter 7; Donald MacKenzie, Fabian Muniesa and Lucia Siu, eds, *Do Economists Make Markets? On the Performativity of Economics* (Princeton, NJ: Princeton University Press, 2007); Michel Callon, 'An Essay on Framing and Overflowing: Economic Externalities Revisited by Sociology', in Michel Callon, ed., *The Laws of Markets* (Oxford: Blackwell, 1998), pp. 244–69; Michel Callon, 'The Embeddedness of Economic Markets in Economics', in Callon, *Laws of Markets*; Andrew Barry, *Political Machines: Governing a Technological Society* (London: Athlone, 2001).

13. Nick Srnicek, 'Representing Complexity: The Material Construction of World Politics', PhD thesis, London School of Economics and Political Science, 2013, Chapter 5; Donald MacKenzie, *An Engine, Not a Camera: How Financial Models Shape Markets* (Cambridge: MIT Press, 2008).

14. Callon, 'Essay on Framing and Overflowing'.

15. This create-and-sustain movement in many ways parallels Jamie Peck's notion of the roll-back and roll-out phases of neoliberalisation. See Peck, *Constructions of Neoliberal Reason*, pp. 22–3.

16. Mirowski and Plehwe, *Road from Mont Pelerin*.

17. Peck, *Constructions of Neoliberal Reason*, p. 48.

18. Plehwe, 'Introduction', in Mirowski and Plehwe, *Road from Mont Pelerin*, p. 16.

19. Cockett, *Thinking the Unthinkable*, p. 109.

20. Peck, *Constructions of Neoliberal Reason*, p. 50; Cockett, *Thinking the Unthinkable*, p. 4.

21. Peck, *Constructions of Neoliberal Reason*, p. 50.

22. Cited in Cockett, *Thinking the Unthinkable*, p. 104.

23. Peck, *Constructions of Neoliberal Reason*, p. 49.

24. Cited in Cockett, *Thinking the Unthinkable*, p. 111.

25. Plehwe, 'Introduction', p. 7.

26. Dardot and Laval, *New Way of the World*, p. 55.

27. Plehwe, 'Introduction', p. 4.

28. Peck, *Constructions of Neoliberal Reason*, p. 276.

29. Colin Crouch, *The Strange Non-Death of Neoliberalism* (Cambridge: Polity, 2011), p. 23.

30. Cockett, *Thinking the Unthinkable*, p. 117.

31. Peck, *Constructions of Neoliberal Reason*, p. 51.

32. Ibid., p. 84.

33. Peck, *Constructions of Neoliberal Reason*, p. 57.

34. Quantitative social network analysis highlights the significance of Fisher as well, placing him alongside Hayek at the centre of the MPS network. See Plehwe, 'Introduction', p. 20.

35. Cockett, *Thinking the Unthinkable*, p. 131.

36. Ibid., p. 132.

37. Ibid., p. 141.

38. Ibid., p. 142.

39. Ibid., pp. 156–7.

40. Ibid., Chapter 5.

41. Harvey, *Brief History of Neoliberalism*, p. 44.

42. Ibid.

43. Cockett, *Thinking the Unthinkable*, p. 184.

44. Leo Panitch and Sam Gindin, *The Making of Global Capitalism: The Political Economy of American Empire* (London: Verso, 2012), p. 114.

45. Harvey, *Brief History of Neoliberalism*, p. 54.

46. Plehwe, 'Introduction', p. 6.

47. Harvey, *Brief History of Neoliberalism*, p. 13.

48. Ann Pettifor, 'The Power to "Create Money out of Thin Air"', openDemocracy, 18 January 2013, at opendemocracy.net.

49. This desire for an answer can also be seen in the choice of macroeconomic models. Peter Kenway, *From Keynesianism to Monetarism: The Evolution of UK Macroeconometric Models* (London: Routledge, 1994), p. 39.

50. Cockett, *Thinking the Unthinkable*, p. 196.

51. Milton Friedman, *Capitalism and Freedom: Fortieth Anniversary Edition* (Chicago: University of Chicago Press, 2002), p. xiv.

52. Some argue that neoliberalism was necessary because of the crisis of accumulation facing capitalism in the 1970s. But this argument neglects alternative ways in which that crisis could have been resolved and attributes immense clarity of self-interest to capitalists.

53. Philip Cerny, *Rethinking World Politics: A Theory of Transnational Neopluralism* (New York: Oxford University Press, 2010), p. 139.

54. David Stuckler, Lawrence King and Martin McKee, 'Mass Privatisation and the Post-Communist Mortality Crisis: A Cross-National Analysis', *Lancet* 373: 9,661 (2009).

55. Harvey, *Brief History of Neoliberalism*, p. 41.

56. This is one source of the common claim that postmodernism is the cultural expression of neoliberalism.

57. Harvey, *Brief History of Neoliberalism*, p. 53.

58. Dardot and Laval, *New Way of the World*, p. 3.

59. Ibid., p. 265.

60. Mark Fisher, *Capitalist Realism: Is There No Alternative?* (Winchester: Zero, 2009), Chapter 4.

61. Wanda Vrasti, 'Struggling with Precarity: From More and Better Jobs to Less and Lesser Work', *Disorder of Things*, 12 October 2013, at thedisorderofthings.com.

62. Harvey, *Brief History of Neoliberalism*, p. 61.

63. For evidence of the austerity narrative and its adoption in popular consciousness, see Liam Stanley, '"We're Reaping What We Sowed": Everyday Crisis Narratives and Acquiescence to the Age of Austerity', *New Political Economy* 19: 6 (2014).

64. Ernesto Laclau, 'Identity and Hegemony: The Role of Universality in the Constitution of Political Logics', in Judith Butler, Ernesto Laclau and Slavoj Žižek, eds, *Contingency, Hegemony and Universality: Contemporary Dialogues on the Left* (London: Verso, 2011), p. 50.

65. The classical mark of ideology today is that it feeds on cynicism, or, as Slavoj Žižek puts it, ideology works even (and especially) if you *do not believe in it*. See Slavoj Žižek, *The Sublime Object of Ideology* (London/New York: Verso, 1989).

66. Mirowski, *Never Let a Serious Crisis Go to Waste*, p. 356.

67. Ibid., p. 332.

4. LEFT MODERNITY

1. This expansionary process has been conceived of in a variety of (not incompatible) ways – for instance, through uneven and combined development, spatial fixes, and expanding cycles of hegemony. In each case, though, the expansionary nature of capitalist universalism is readily apparent. See, respectively, Neil Smith, *Uneven Development: Nature, Capital and the Production of Space* (London: Verso, 2010); David Harvey, *The Limits to Capital* (London: Verso, 2006); Giovanni Arrighi, *The Long Twentieth Century: Money, Power and the Origins of Our Time* (London: Verso, 2009).

2. For a lengthy defence of this claim, see Vivek Chibber, *Postcolonial Theory and the Specter of Capital* (London: Verso, 2013), ¶ 9.4.

3. 'For it is finally the universal . . . which furnishes the only true denial of established universalisms.' François Jullien, *On the Universal: The Uniform, the Common and Dialogue Between Cultures* (Cambridge: Polity, 2014), p. 90.

4. Mark Fisher and Jeremy Gilbert, *Reclaim Modernity: Beyond Markets, Beyond Machines* (London: Compass, 2014), pp. 12–14.

5. Sandro Mezzadra, 'How Many Histories of Labor? Towards a Theory of Postcolonial Capitalism', *European Institute for Progressive Cultural Policies*, 2012, at eipcp.net.

6. Mark Fisher, *Capitalist Realism: Is There No Alternative?* (Winchester: Zero, 2009).

7. Similar arguments have also been made about postmodernity. See Harvey, *The Condition of Postmodernity: An Enquiry into the Origins of Cultural Change* (Oxford: Wiley-Blackwell, 1991).

8. Peter Wagner, *Modernity: Understanding the Present* (Cambridge: Polity, 2012), p. 23.

9. For a similar argument with respect to 'development', see Kalyan Sanyal, *Rethinking Capitalist Development: Primitive Accumulation, Governmentality and Post-Colonial Capitalism* (New Delhi: Routledge India, 2013), p. 92.

10. To give a sense of this variety, Jameson outlines fourteen different proposals for the beginning of modernity as historical period. Fredric Jameson, *A Singular Modernity: Essay on the Ontology of the Present* (London: Verso, 2002), p. 32.

11. Alberto Toscano, *Fanaticism: On the Uses of an Idea* (London: Verso, 2010); Frederick Cooper, *Decolonization and African Society: The Labor Question in French and British Africa* (Cambridge: Cambridge University Press, 1996).

12. Chibber, *Postcolonial Theory*, p. 233.

13. We seek to follow Susan Buck-Morss when she writes: 'The rejection of Western-centrism does not place a taboo on using the tools of Western thought. On the contrary, it frees the critical tools of the Enlightenment . . . for original and creative application.' Susan Buck-Morss, *Thinking Past Terror: Islamism and Critical Theory on the Left* (London: Verso, 2003), p. 99.

14. Wang Hui, *The End of the Revolution: China and the Limits of Modernity* (London: Verso, 2011), pp. 69–70.

15. Göran Therborn, *European Modernity and Beyond: The Trajectory of European Societies, 1945–2000* (London: Sage, 1995), p. 4.

16. Jameson, *Singular Modernity*, p. 18.

17. Corey Robin, *The Reactionary Mind: Conservatism from Edmund Burke to Sarah Palin* (New York: Oxford University Press, 2011).

18. Simon Critchley, 'Ideas for Modern Living: The Future', *Guardian*, 21 November 2010.

19. Kamran Matin, 'Redeeming the Universal: Postcolonialism and the Inner Life of Eurocentrism', *European Journal of International Relations* 19: 2 (2013), p. 354.

20. Walt Whitman Rostow, *The Stages of Economic Growth: A Non-Communist Manifesto* (Cambridge: Cambridge University Press, 1990).

21. Walter Mignolo, *The Darker Side of Western Modernity: Global Futures, Decolonial Options* (Durham, NC: Duke University Press, 2011), pp. xxiv–xxv.

22. S. N. Eisenstadt, 'Multiple Modernities', *Daedalus* 129: 1 (2000), p. 1.

23. Theodor Adorno and Max Horkheimer, *Dialectic of Enlightenment* (London: Verso, 1997); Zygmunt Bauman, *Modernity and the Holocaust* (Cambridge: Polity, 1991).

24. David Priestland, *The Red Flag: A History of Communism* (New York: Grove, 2009).

25. Stephen Eric Bronner, *Reclaiming the Enlightenment: Toward a Politics of Radical Engagement* (New York: Columbia University Press, 2004), p. 28.

26. Lyotard, *The Postmodern Condition: A Report on Knowledge*, transl. Geoffrey Bennington and Brian Massumi (Manchester: Manchester University Press, 1984).

27. Walter Mignolo and He Weihua, 'The Prospect of Harmony and the Decolonial View of the World', *Marxism and Reality* 4 (2012).

28. Wagner, *Modernity*, p. 81.

29. S. N. Eisenstadt, 'Multiple Modernities', *Daedalus* 129: 1 (2000).

30. For contemporary reflections on this concept, see the debates collected in Alex Anievas, ed., *Marxism and World Politics: Contesting Global Capitalism* (London: Routledge, 2012).

31. For a philosophical–political–religious genealogy of the universal, see Jullien, *On the Universal*, Chapters 4–7.

32. It should be clear that the discussion of the universal here is within a political rather than a philosophical register.

33. Étienne Balibar, 'Sub Specie Universitatis', *Topoi* 25: 1–2 (2006), p. 11.

34. Broadly, we can divide these criticisms between Latin American decolonialism, South Asian subaltern studies and African postcolonialism, which each inflect modernity and colonialism through their regional history.

35. Mignolo, *Darker Side of Western Modernity*.

36. Ibid., Chapter 2; Ramón Grosfoguel, 'Decolonizing Western Uni-Versalisms: Decolonial Pluri-Versalism from Aimé Césaire to the Zapatistas', transl. George Ciccariello-Maher, *Transmodernity: Journal of Peripheral Cultural Production of the Luso-Hispanic World* 1: 3 (2012).

37. Jullien, *On the Universal*, p. 92.

38. Jullien argues that Islamic thought does have a degree of ethico-political universal normativity, but this is in any case significantly less apparent than that emerging from European modernity and is qualified by the priority given to community (ibid., p. 74). John Hobson, *The Eastern Origins of Western Civilisation* (Cambridge: Cambridge University Press, 2004); Amartya Sen, 'East and West: The Reach of Reason', *New York Review of Books* 47: 12 (2000).

39. 'The project of provincializing Europe cannot . . . originate from the stance that the reason/science/universals that help define Europe as the modern are simply "culture-specific" and therefore only belong to the European cultures. [This] simple rejection of modernity would be, in many situations, politically suicidal.' Dipesh Chakrabarty, *Provincializing Europe: Postcolonial Thought and Historical Difference* (Princeton, NJ: Princeton University Press, 2007), pp. 43–5; Matin, 'Redeeming the Universal, Duy Lap Nguyen, 'The Universal Province of Modernity', *Interventions* 16: 3 (2014), p. 447; Mignolo, *Darker Side of Western Modernity*, p. 275.

40. There have been a number of alternative approaches posed in light of the critiques of classic substantialist universalism. We will not elaborate on them here, but a few quick comments are in order. 'Negative universalism' grounds universalism on a common opposition, but this remains a folk-political, defensive and negative approach. It does not elaborate an alternative future. 'Minimal universalism' argues

for a few basic principles common to all, but is simply a reduced version of classical universalism and remains subject to all its problems. Finally, 'pluri-versalism' is the most intriguing perspective, and the one we would most closely align with. It argues for self-determination of cultures in mutual horizontal engagement. But it requires three quick comments. First, it neglects the medium of engagement between cultures, which we argue requires a sophisticated theory of reasoning in order to avoid domination. (See Anthony Laden's work for a non-dominating and collective conception of reasoning.) Secondly, it rightly opposes a homogeneous vision of universalism, but overlooks the ways in which universalism can already incorporate the sorts of differences it highlights. Pluri-versalism too easily suggests neglecting the common aspect required in a globalised world. Humanity exists not simply as mutually exclusive ways of being, but instead as a deeply intertwined set of differences. Thirdly, pluri-versalism recognises that capitalist universalism needs to be eliminated first in order for it to stand a chance. Until then, it is bound to resistance and defensive gestures against expansionary capitalism. Pluri-versalism thus relies upon the elimination of capitalism and is dependent upon a counter-hegemonic postcapitalist project as its presupposed condition of existence. The problem of universalism – especially actually-existing universalism – cannot be dispensed with by theoretical fiat. Grosfoguel, 'Decolonizing Western Uni-Versalisms', p. 101; Bhikhu Parekh, 'Non-Ethnocentric Universalism', in Tim Dunne and Nicholas J. Wheeler, eds, *Human Rights in Global Politics* (Cambridge: Cambridge University Press, 1999), pp. 128–59; Mignolo, *Darker Side of Western Modernity*, p. 275; Anthony Simon Laden, *Reasoning: A Social Picture* (Oxford: Oxford University Press, 2014).

41. Ernesto Laclau, 'Identity and Hegemony: The Role of Universality in the Constitution of Political Logics', in Judith Butler, Ernesto Laclau and Slavoj Žižek, eds, *Contingency, Hegemony and Universality: Contemporary Dialogues on the Left* (London: Verso, 2011).

42. Nora Sternfeld, 'Whose Universalism Is It?', transl. Mary O'Neill, 2007, at eipcp.net; Jullien, *On the Universal*, p. 92.

43. Butler, 'Restaging the Universal: Hegemony and the Limits of Formalism', in Butler et al., *Contingency, Hegemony and Universality*, pp. 33.

44. Stefan Jonsson, 'The Ideology of Universalism', *New Left Review* II/63 (May–June 2010), p. 117.

45. Matin, 'Redeeming the Universal'.

46. For the classic reference point on negative freedom, see Isaiah Berlin, 'Two Concepts of Liberty', in Henry Hardy, ed., *Liberty* (Oxford: Oxford University Press, 2002).

47. Milton Friedman, *Capitalism and Freedom: Fortieth Anniversary Edition* (Chicago: University of Chicago Press, 2002), Chapter 1.

48. Friedrich Hayek, *The Constitution of Liberty* (London: Routledge, 2006).

49. This has overlaps with Philippe van Parijs's (as well as many other theorists') distinction between formal and real freedom, but the notion of 'synthetic' freedom highlights that it is not a natural aspect of humanity, but something constructed. See Philippe Van Parijs, *Real Freedom for All: What (If Anything) Can Justify Capitalism?* (Oxford: Oxford University Press, 1997), pp. 21–4.

50. Daniel Raventós, *Basic Income: The Material Conditions of Freedom*, transl. Julie Wark (London: Pluto, 2007), p. 68; Mignolo, *Darker Side of Western Modernity*, pp. 300–1.

51. Karl Marx and Friedrich Engels, *The German Ideology* (London: Prometheus, 1976), p. 44.

52. Steven Lukes, *Power: A Radical View*, 2nd edn (Houndmills: Palgrave Macmillan, 2005), p. 65.

53. As Erik Olin Wright puts it, 'The idea of "flourishing" includes not just the development of human intellectual, psychological and social capacities during childhood, but also the lifelong opportunity to exercise those capacities, and to develop new capacities as life circumstances change.' Erik Olin Wright, *Envisioning Real Utopias* (London: Verso, 2010), pp. 47–8.

54. There is no strict order of preference for these three elements, even though the remainder of this book will focus predominantly on the first.

55. Alex Gourevitch, 'Labor Republicanism and the Transformation of Work', *Political Theory* 41: 4 (2013), p. 597.

56. Slavoj Žižek, 'Utopia and Its Discontents', interview with Slawomir Sierakowski, 23 February 2015, at lareviewofbooks.org.

57. Karl Marx, *Wage-Labour and Capital & Value, Price and Profit* (New York: International Publishers, 1976), p. 54; *Grundrisse: Introduction to the Critique of Political Economy*, transl. Martin Nicolaus (Middlesex: Penguin, 1973), p. 706; and *Capital: A Critique of Political Economy, Volume III* (London: Lawrence & Wishart, 1977), p. 820.

58. There is an alternative republican argument for this position, which rightly argues that wage labour involves domination (as distinct from interference), and that only the provision of the basic means of existence enables us to overcome this domination. This tradition has a long line of thinkers associated with it, from Aristotle to Robespierre to nineteenth-century labour activists. While we will not rely on it here to support the argument for a post-work society, it nevertheless has important contributions to make over and above liberal conceptions of freedom. See Raventós, *Basic Income*, Chapter 3; Gourevitch, 'Labor Republicanism and the Transformation of Work', pp. 593–8.

59. Antonella Corsani, 'Beyond the Myth of Woman: The Becoming-Transfeminist of (Post-)Marxism', transl. Timothy S. Murphy, *SubStance* 36: 1 (2007), p. 127.

60. For this argument, see Parijs, *Real Freedom for All*, pp. 17–20.

61. This shares similarities with the ideas of power-with and power-to. See Uri Gordon, *Anarchy Alive! Anti-Authoritarian Politics from Practice to Theory* (London: Pluto Press, 2007), pp. 54–5; John Holloway, *Change the World Without Taking Power: The Meaning of Revolution Today* (London/Sterling, VA: Pluto, 2002), p. 28.

62. Laden, *Reasoning*, pp. 14–23; Gordon, *Anarchy Alive!*, p. 54.

63. For the notion of language as cognitive scaffolding, see Andy Clark, *Supersizing the Mind: Embodiment, Action, and Cognitive Extension* (New York: Oxford University Press, 2008), Chapter 3.

64. Cited in Gregory Elliott, *Althusser: The Detour of Theory* (Leiden: Brill, 2006), p. 16.

65. Krafft Ehricke, 'The Extraterrestrial Imperative', *Air University Review*, February 1978.

66. Marx and Engels, *German Ideology*, p. 44.

67. For a defence of this Promethean spirit, see Ray Brassier, 'Prometheanism and Its Critics', in Robin Mackay and Armen Avanessian, eds, *#Accelerate: The Accelerationist Reader* (Falmouth: Urbanomic, 2014).

68. For an earlier, historicized interpretation of our cyborg nature, see Donna Haraway, 'A Cyborg Manifesto: Science, Technology, and Socialist-Feminism in the Late Twentieth Century', in *Simians, Cyborgs and Women: The Reinvention of Nature* (London: Free Association Books, 1991). For a contemporary updating, see the Laboria Cuboniks manifesto in Helen Hester and Armen Avanessian, eds, *Dea Ex Machina* (Berlin: Merve Verlag, 2015).

69. Benedict Singleton, 'Maximum Jailbreak', in Mackay and Avanessian, *#Accelerate*.

70. Alfred Schmidt, *The Concept of Nature in Marx* (London: Verso, 2014), pp. 144–5.

71. Sadie Plant, 'Binary Sexes, Binary Codes', 3 June 1996, at future-nonstop.org.

72. Reza Negarestani, 'The Labor of the Inhuman', in Mackay and Avanessian, *#Accelerate*, 452.

73. Ibid., p. 438.

74. For examples of these parochial defences, see Jürgen Habermas, *The Future of Human Nature* (Cambridge: Polity, 2003); Francis Fukuyama, *Our Posthuman Future: Consequences of the Biotechnology Revolution* (London: Profile, 2003).

75. For two fascinating accounts of bodily experimentation, see Shannon Bell, *Fast Feminism* (New York: Autonomedia, 2010); and Beatriz Preciado, *Testo Junkie: Sex, Drugs and Biopolitics in the Pharmacopornographic Era* (New York: Feminist Press CUNY, 2013).

76. The remainder of this book will be concerned mostly with the first two aspects of synthetic freedom: the basic conditions of existence, and the collective capacities to act. We will, however, return to the technological augmentation of humanity in the Conclusion.

77. Susan Buck-Morss, *Hegel, Haiti, and Universal History* (Pittsburgh, PA: University of Pittsburgh Press, 2009), p. 106.

5. THE FUTURE ISN'T WORKING

1. Two recent manifestos from India and Germany have also attacked the glorification of work: Kamunist Kranti, 'A Ballad Against Work', 1997, at libcom.org; and Krisis-Group, 'Manifesto Against Labour', 1999, at krisis.org.

2. Karl Marx, *Capital: A Critique of Political Economy, Volume III* (London: Lawrence & Wishart, 1977), p. 820.

3. Research suggests that changes in opportunities (provided by moments such as an economic crisis) are far more important than the level of grievances in generating a social movement. In other words, the idea that making things worse will lead to revolution has little empirical support. Sidney Tarrow, *Power in Movement: Social Movements and Contentious Politics*, 2nd edn (Cambridge: Cambridge University Press, 1998), Chapter 5.

4. Karl Marx, *Capital: A Critique of Political Economy, Volume I*, transl. Ben Fowkes (London: Penguin, 1990), Part 8.

5. Michael Perelman, *The Invention of Capitalism: Classical Political Economy and the Secret History of Primitive Accumulation* (Durham, NC: Duke University Press, 2000), p. 14.

6. As Marx writes, '"Proletarian" must be understood to mean, economically speaking, nothing other than "wage-labourer", the man who produces and valorises "capital", and *is thrown onto the street as soon as he becomes superfluous to the need for valorisation.'* Marx, *Capital, Volume I*, p. 764 n. 1 (emphasis added).

7. In the case of groups like unpaid domestic labourers, the proletariat can also rely upon the wages of another for its survival, along with all the problematic dependencies this fosters. In this case, the proletariat is *indirectly* reliant upon waged labour for its survival.

8. Richard Freeman, 'The Great Doubling: The Challenge of the New Global Labor Market', in John Edwards, Marion Crain and Arne Kalleberg, eds, *Ending Poverty in America: How to Restore the American Dream* (New York: New Press, 2007).

9. Steve Fraser, *The Age of Acquiescence: The Life and Death of American Resistance to Organized Wealth and Power* (New York: Little, Brown US, 2015), p. 60.

10. The problem of how to define the surplus population is one which is often assumed away in the literature. But there are important issues here that cannot simply be passed by. If the surplus is defined in terms of waged versus non-waged, then are working prison populations not part of the surplus? What about the vast amounts of informal labour that works for a wage and produces for a market? Other problems arise if one defines the surplus in terms of productive and unproductive labour. In particular, one is led to the conclusion Negri and Hardt draw – that since socially productive labour exists everywhere under conditions of post-Fordism, the term no longer has meaning. (Michael Hardt and Antonio Negri, *Multitude: War and Democracy in the Age of Empire* [New York: Penguin, 2005], p. 131.) We reject that conclusion and attempt to demonstrate here that the concept still has important analytical and explanatory utility. We believe that the surplus can be defined as those who are outside of waged labour under capitalist conditions of production. The latter qualification means that most informal labour (not under capitalist conditions of production) is included in the category. We are particularly influenced here by the work of Kalyan Sanyal.

11. Joan Robinson, *Economic Philosophy* (Harmondsworth: Penguin, 1964), p. 46.

12. In economics this is associated with the non-accelerating inflation rate of unemployment (NAIRU). Hiring workers when unemployment is at this level is thought to raise wages and eventually cause inflation, thereby setting a floor to how low the unemployment rate should go.

13. For classic statements about the political uses of unemployment, see Michał Kalecki, 'Political Aspects of Full Employment', *Political Quarterly* 14: 4 (1943); Samuel Bowles, 'The Production Process in a Competitive Economy: Walrasian, Neo-Hobbesian, and Marxian Models', *American Economic Review* 75: 1 (1985).

14. This emphasis on secular trends, we would argue, is one of the unique characteristics of a Marxist understanding of unemployment.

15. The fear of automation taking jobs has a long history, of which the Luddites were one of the earliest examples. More recently this fear was a major issue in the 1960s

with discussions about the idea of cybernation and in the 1980s and 1990s with headline-grabbing journalistic commentary, and has re-emerged again over the past few years. The large number of relevant texts include: Ad Hoc Committee, 'The Triple Revolution', *International Socialist Review* 24: 3 (1964); Donald Michael, *Cybernation: The Silent Conquest* (Santa Barbara, CA: Center for the Study of Democratic Institutions, 1962); Paul Mattick, 'The Economics of Cybernation', *New Politics* 1: 4 (1962); David Noble, *Progress Without People: In Defense of Luddism* (Toronto: Between the Lines, 1995); Jeremy Rifkin, *The End of Work: The Decline of the Global Labor Force and the Dawn of the Post-Market Era* (New York: Putnam, 1997); Martin Ford, *The Lights in the Tunnel: Automation, Accelerating Technology and the Economy of the Future* (US: CreateSpace Independent Publishing Platform, 2009); Erik Brynjolfsson and Andrew McAfee, *The Second Machine Age: Work, Progress, and Prosperity in a Time of Brilliant Technologies* (New York: W. W. Norton, 2014).

16. These estimates are for the US and European labour markets, though similar numbers undoubtedly hold globally and, as we argue later, may even be worse in developing economies. Carl Benedikt Frey and Michael Osborne, *The Future of Employment: How Susceptible Are Jobs to Computerisation?* 2013, pdf available at oxfordmartin.ox.ac.uk; Jeremy Bowles, 'The Computerisation of European Jobs', *Bruegel* (2014), at bruegel.org; Stuart Elliott, 'Anticipating a Luddite Revival', *Issues in Science and Technology* 30: 3 (2014).

17. Karl Marx, *Capital: A Critique of Political Economy, Volume I*, transl. Ben Fowkes (London: Penguin, 1990), p. 566–7.

18. Paul Einzig, *The Economic Consequences of Automation* (New York: W. W. Norton, 1957), p. 78.

19. Thor Berger and Carl Benedikt Frey, *Technology Shocks and Urban Evolutions: Did the Computer Revolution Shift the Fortunes of US Cities?* (Oxford Martin School Working Paper, 2014), p. 6.

20. James Bessen, 'Toil and Technology', *Finance & Development* 52: 1 (2015), p. 17.

21. Evidence already suggests that the global density of bank branches is retreating. Carl Benedikt Frey and Michael Osborne, *Technology at Work: The Future of Innovation and Employment* (Citi – Global Perspectives and Solutions, 2015), pp. 25–6, pdf available at ir.citi.com.

22. Wassily Leontief, 'National Perspectives: The Definition of Problems and Opportunities', in *The Long-Term Impact of Technology on Employment and Unemployment*, a National Academy of Engineering symposium (1983).

23. There is some evidence for this currently happening, with businesses reporting difficulties in finding skilled workers and rising wage disparities within occupations between the most and least skilled. Bessen, 'Toil and Technology', p. 19.

24. Boyan Jovanovic and Peter L. Rousseau, *General Purpose Technologies*, Working Paper, National Bureau of Economic Research, January 2005, at nber.org; George Terbough, *The Automation Hysteria: An Appraisal of the Alarmist View of the Technological Revolution* (New York: W. W. Norton, 1966), pp. 54–5; Aaron Benanav and Endnotes, 'Misery and Debt', in *Endnotes 2: Misery and the Value Form* (London: Endnotes, 2010), p. 31.

25. Barry Eichengreen, *Secular Stagnation: The Long View* (Working Paper, National Bureau of Economic Research, January 2015), p. 5, pdf available at nber.org.

26. Kalyan Sanyal, *Rethinking Capitalist Development: Primitive Accumulation, Governmentality and Post-Colonial Capitalism* (New Delhi: Routledge India, 2013), p. 55. Notably, this means that this economic sector is eminently contemporary, rather than being a residue of some pre-capitalist mode of production.

27. Gabriel Wildau, 'China Migration: At the Turning Point', *Financial Times*, 4 May 2015, at ft.com; 'Global Labor Glut Sinking Wages Means U.S. Needs to Get Schooled', *Bloomberg*, 4 May 2015, at bloomberg.com. While Africa has yet to be fully integrated into the global capitalist system, it is worth emphasising that the integration of China and the post-Soviet states was a one-off surge in the global labour force. The trend from here on out will be a general decline in the importance of this mechanism for producing surplus populations.

28. We note here that while the first two mechanisms are integral to capitalist accumulation (changes in the productive forces and the expansion of capitalist social relations), the third is a logic distinct from just accumulation. The empirical characteristics of this group also change over time (as with, for instance, the integration of women into the workforce over the past four decades). Lynda Yanz and David Smith, 'Women as a Reserve Army of Labour: A Critique', *Review of Radical Political Economics* 15:1 (1983), p. 104.

29. In other words, these dominations can often be functional for capitalism, even if their function does not explain their genesis.

30. A full 36 million people are considered to be in slavery today: *Global Slavery Index 2014* (Dalkeith, Western Australia: Walk Free Foundation, 2014).

31. Edward E. Baptist, *Half Has Never Been Told: Slavery and the Making of American Capitalism* (New York: Basic Books, 2014); Silvia Federici, 'Wages Against Housework', in *Revolution at Point Zero: Housework, Reproduction, and Feminist Struggle* (Oakland, CA: PM Press, 2012).

32. In terms of global unemployment, women have faced the brunt of the crisis in recent years. ILO, *World Employment and Social Outlook: The Changing Nature of Jobs* (Geneva: International Labour Organization, 2015), p. 18.

33. For example, black males in the United States were particularly affected by the automation and outsourcing of manufacturing. William Julius Wilson, *When Work Disappears: The World of the New Urban Poor* (New York: Vintage Books, 1997), pp. 29–31.

34. Michael McIntyre, 'Race, Surplus Population, and the Marxist Theory of Imperialism', *Antipode* 43:5 (2011), p. 1500–2.

35. These draw broadly upon the divisions Marx drew between the floating/reserve army, latent and stagnant, but are here offered as an updating of his historical example.

36. Gary Fields, *Working Hard, Working Poor: A Global Journey* (New York: Oxford University Press, 2012), p. 46.

37. This is what Kalyan Sanyal describes as 'need economies'. See Sanyal, *Rethinking Capitalist Development*.

38. The area of 'vulnerable employment' now accounts for 48 per cent of global employment – five times higher than pre-crisis levels. This number is also thought to

underestimate the amount of vulnerably employed, given its informal, off-the-books nature. ILO, *Global Employment Trends 2014: Risk of a Jobless Recovery?* (Geneva: International Labour Organization, 2014), p. 12; David Neilson and Thomas Stubbs, 'Relative Surplus Population and Uneven Development in the Neoliberal Era: Theory and Empirical Application', *Capital & Class* 35 (2011), p. 443.

39. In Marx's schema, this can be understood as C-M-C, where commodities are produced and sold on the market in order to receive money to buy goods for subsistence. This differs from pre-capitalist subsistence economies in that goods are not produced for personal consumption, but instead must be mediated through the market. Sanyal, *Rethinking Capitalist Development*, pp. 69–70.

40. Michael Denning, 'Wageless Life', *New Left Review* II/66 (November–December 2010), p. 86; ILO, *G20 Labour Markets: Outlook, Key Challenges and Policy Responses* (Geneva: International Labour Organization/OECD/World Bank, 2014), at ilo.org, p. 8.

41. Marilyn Power, 'From Home Production to Wage Labor: Women as a Reserve Army of Labor', *Review of Radical Political Economics* 15:1 (1983).

42. David Harvey, *A Companion to Marx's Capital, Volume 1* (London: Verso, 2010), p. 280.

43. ILO, *Key Indicators of the Labour Market, 8th edn* (Geneva: International Labour Organization, 2013), at ilo.org.

44. *State of the Global Workplace: Employee Engagement Insights for Business Leaders Worldwide*, Gallup, 2013, at ihrim.org, p. 27; John Bellamy Foster, Robert W. McChesney and R. Jamil Jonna, 'The Global Reserve Army of Labor and the New Imperialism', *Monthly Review*, November 2011; Neilson and Stubbs, 'Relative Surplus Population'. The International Labour Organization currently estimates that 5.9 per cent of the working population (201 million people) are unemployed – but this relies on a very stringent definition of unemployment. ILO, *World Employment and Social Outlook – Trends 2015* (Geneva: International Labour Organization, 2015), at ilo.org, p. 16. If one works for an hour mowing a lawn, makes a few dollars selling homemade wares on a street, or has a doctorate and works in a call centre, the ILO counts this as employment. In other words, part-time workers, informal workers and underemployed workers all count as employed. The ILO definition of unemployment also *improves* when people drop out of the labour force: a smaller workforce means lower unemployment. A more meaningful measure is therefore the level of employment among the working-age population, according to which the ILO estimates that over 40 per cent of the world's population is not employed. ILO, *Global Employment Trends 2014*, p. 18. In a similar measure, they estimate that only half the global labour force is in waged or salaried work. ILO, *World Employment and Social Outlook: The Changing Nature of Jobs* (Geneva: International Labour Organization, 2015), p. 28. But these measures still overestimate the number of people employed, and so other measures have attempted to overcome these deficiencies. Gallup, for instance, defines 'employment' as formal work for thirty hours or more per week – and concludes that 74 per cent of the global labour force fails to meet this definition. *State of the Global Workplace: Employee Engagement Insights for Business Leaders Worldwide*, Gallup, 2013, pdf available at

ihrim.org, p. 27. Another study, based on ILO data on the unemployed, vulnerably employed and economically inactive, estimates the surplus population at 61 per cent of the total working-age population (calculated from data by Neilson and Stubbs, 'Relative Surplus Population, p. 444). The conclusion to draw from these alternative measures is simple: the global surplus population is massive, and in fact outnumbers the formal working class.

45. Frantz Fanon, *The Wretched of the Earth*, transl. Constance Farrington (London: Penguin Classics, 2001), Chapter 2; Patricia Connelly, *Last Hired First Fired: Women and the Canadian Work Force* (Toronto: The Women's Press, 1978).

46. Cleaver here uses the term 'Lumpen' to refer to what we have called the 'proletariat' condition. Eldridge Cleaver, 'On Lumpen Ideology', *The Black Scholar*, 4:3 (1972), pp. 9–10.

47. Mattick, 'Economics of Cybernation', p. 19.

48. Benanav and Endnotes, 'Misery and Debt'; Fredric Jameson, *Representing Capital: A Reading of Volume One* (London: Verso, 2011), p. 2. Broadly speaking, we can discern two ways in which the concept of surplus populations has functioned in recent debates. One set of arguments is concerned with the overlapping of particular social groups (for example, black minorities) with the concept of the surplus population. Another, much smaller, set of arguments has been interested in the claim that the surplus population has a secular trend to grow in size.

49. Marx, *Capital, Volume I*, p. 798.

50. Richard Duboff, 'Full Employment: The History of a Receding Target', *Politics & Society* 7: 1 (1977), pp. 7–8.

51. While NAIRU is debatable as a measure of full employment, the postwar period saw unemployment typically below NAIRU, and the neoliberal period has seen unemployment consistently above NAIRU. Jared Bernstein and Dean Baker, 'Full Employment: The Recovery's Missing Ingredient', *Washington Post*, 3 November 2014, p. 10; José Nun, 'The End of Work and the "Marginal Mass" Thesis', *Latin American Perspectives* 27: 1 (2000), p. 8; Guy Standing, *The Precariat: The New Dangerous Class* (London: Bloomsbury Academic, 2011), pp. 46–7; Jeffrey Straussman, 'The "Reserve Army" of Unemployed Revisited', *Society* 14: 3 (1977), p. 42.

52. *Economic Projections of Federal Reserve Board Members and Federal Reserve Bank Presidents, December 2014*, Federal Reserve Board, 2014, pdf available at federalreserve.gov, p. 1.

53. Claire Cain Miller, 'As Robots Grow Smarter, American Workers Struggle to Keep Up', *New York Times*, 15 December 2014.

54. Bureau of Labor Statistics, 'Civilian Employment–Population Ratio', Federal Reserve Bank of St Louis, 2014, at research.stlouisfed.org; Deepankar Basu, *The Reserve Army of Labour in the Postwar US Economy: Some Stock and Flow Estimates*, Working Paper (Amherst: University of Massachusetts, 2012), p. 7.

55. ILO, *Global Employment Trends 2014*, p. 17.

56. The job growth rate dropped from 1.7 per cent between 1991 and 2007 to 1.2 per cent between 2007 and 2014. ILO, *World Employment and Social Outlook*, p. 16; ILO, *World Employment and Social Outlook*, p. 29.

57. Ibid., p. 20.

58. Workers in developing economies, of course, have long lived under conditions of precarity. The new concern for precarity is therefore a symptom of the collapse of a model of work peculiar to developed economies in the postwar period.

59. A more thorough exploration of these characteristics can be found in Standing, *Precariat*, pp. 10–11.

60. Marx, *Capital, Volume I*, p. 789.

61. Francis Green, Tarek Mostafa, Agnès Parent-Thirion, Greet Vermeylen, Gijs van Houten, Isabella Biletta and Maija Lyly-Yrjanainen, 'Is Job Quality Becoming More Unequal?', *Industrial & Labor Relations Review* 66: 4 (2013), pp. 770–1; Andrew Glyn, *Capitalism Unleashed: Finance, Globalization, and Welfare* (Oxford: Oxford University Press, 2007), p. 114.

62. Carrie Gleason and Susan Lambert, *Uncertainty by the Hour*, pp. 1–3, pdf available at opensocietyfoundations.org.

63. While this aspect of precarity has often been emphasised, irregular work still remains a small portion of the labour market in most advanced capitalist countries. Kim Moody, 'Precarious Work, "Compression" and Class Struggle "Leaps"', *RS21*, 10 February 2015, at rs21.org.uk. It is estimated that about a quarter of workers in developed economies are on temporary contracts or without a contract. ILO, *World Employment and Social Outlook*, p. 30.

64. *Self-Employed Workers in the UK – 2014* (London: Office for National Statistics, 2014), pdf available at ons.gov.uk.

65. Bureau of Labor Statistics, 'Employment Level – Part-Time for Economic Reasons, All Industries'.

66. Official business surveys find that 1.4 million people are working under zero-hours contracts in the UK. See *Analysis of Employee Contracts that Do Not Guarantee a Minimum Number of Hours* (London: Office for National Statistics, 30 April 2014), pdf available at ons.gov.uk.

67. Dean Baker and Jared Bernstein, *Getting Back to Full Employment: A Better Bargain for Working People* (Washington, DC: Center for Economic and Policy Research, 2013), p. 12.

68. Bernstein and Baker, 'Full Employment'.

69. In a poll of mainstream economic experts, a weighted 43 per cent of respondents agreed that technology played a central role in wage stagnation, versus 28 per cent who disagreed. 'Poll Results: Robots', *IGM Forum*, 25 February 2014, at igmchicago.org.

70. ILO, *G20 Labour Markets*, p. 5; *The Slow Recovery of the Labor Market*, US Congressional Budget Office, February 2014, at cbo.gov, p. 6; Ciaren Taylor, Andrew Jowett and Michael Hardie, 'An Examination of Falling Real Wages, 2010–2013' (London: Office for National Statistics, 2014), at ons.gov.uk.

71. The level of personal savings in America has dropped drastically since the 1970s. US Bureau of Economic Analysis, 'Personal Saving Rate'.

72. 'Share of U.S. Workers Living Paycheck to Paycheck Continues Decline from Recession-Era Peak, Finds Annual CareerBuilder Survey', CareerBuilder, 25 September 2013, at careerbuilder.com; *8 Million People One Paycheque Away from Losing Their Home*, Shelter, 11 April 2013, at england.shelter.org.uk.

73. Saskia Sassen, *Expulsions: Brutality and Complexity in the Global Economy* (Cambridge: Harvard University Press, 2014), p. 54.

74. Carlos Nordt, Ingeborg Warnke, Erich Seifritz and Wolfram Kawohl, 'Modelling Suicide and Unemployment: A Longitudinal Analysis Covering 63 Countries, 2000–11', *Lancet*, 2015, p. 5; Justin Wolfers, *Is Business Cycle Volatility Costly? Evidence from Surveys of Subjective Wellbeing*, Working Paper, National Bureau of Economic Research, 2003, at nber.org; Nikolaos Antonakakis and Alan Collins, 'The Impact of Fiscal Austerity on Suicide: On the Empirics of a Modern Greek Tragedy', *Social Science & Medicine* 112 (July 2014); Karen McVeigh, 'DWP Urged to Publish Inquiries on Benefit Claimant Suicides', *Guardian*, 14 December 2014.

75. Ben Bernanke, 'The Jobless Recovery', paper presented at the Global Economic and Investment Outlook Conference, Carnegie Mellon University, Pittsburgh, Pennsylvania, 6 November 2003, at federalreserve.gov.

76. Olivier Coibon, Yuriy Gorodnichenko and Dmitri Koustas, *Amerisclerosis? The Puzzle of Rising US Unemployment Persistence*, Brookings Papers on Economic Activity, Brookings Institution, Fall 2013, pdf available at brookings.edu.

77. Natalia Kolesnikova and Yang Liu, 'Jobless Recoveries: Causes and Consequences', *Regional Economist*, April 2011, at stlouisfed.org.

78. *Slow Recovery of the Labor Market*, p. 2; Bureau of Labor Statistics, 'Employed, Usually Work Full Time'.

79. ILO, *G20 Labour Markets*, p. 4.

80. It has been suggested that one reason for this connection is that, in the wake of a recession, firms are risk-averse in relation to hiring for occupations that are automatable. Nir Jaimovich and Henry E. Siu, *The Trend Is the Cycle: Job Polarization and Jobless Recoveries*, Working Paper, National Bureau of Economic Research, 2012, at nber.org, p. 29.

81. The distinction between routine and non-routine better explains the data than either a division between low and high levels of education, or between manufacturing and service jobs. Ibid., pp. 3, 16–19.

82. Over the past three decades, a full 92 per cent of the job losses in automatable mid-skill positions have occurred in the twelve months from the onset of a recession. Ibid., p. 2.

83. In previous recessions, the routine jobs have never returned. Ibid., p. 14.

84. ILO, *Global Employment Trends 2014*, pp. 11–12; Bureau of Labor Statistics, 'Of Total Unemployed, Percent Unemployed 27 Weeks and Over', Federal Reserve Economic Data, Federal Reserve Bank of St Louis, 1 January 1948; Eurostat, 'Long-Term Unemployment Rate', *Eurostat*, 2015, at ec.europa.eu.

85. Alan Krueger, Judd Cramer and David Cho, 'Are the Long-Term Unemployed on the Margins of the Labor Market?', Brookings Papers on Economic Activity, Spring 2014.

86. Loïc Wacquant, 'The Rise of Advanced Marginality: Notes on Its Nature and Implications', *Acta Sociologica* 39: 2 (1996), p. 125; Richard Florida, Zara Matheson, Patrick Adler and Taylor Brydges, *The Divided City and the Shape of the New Metropolis*, Martin Prosperity Institute, 2014, at martinprosperity.org.

87. William Julius Wilson, *When Work Disappears: The World of the New Urban Poor* (New York: Vintage Books, 1997), p. 15.

88. Loïc Wacquant, 'Class, Race and Hyperincarceration in Revanchist America', *Socialism and Democracy* 28: 3 (2014), p. 46.

89. Frances Fox Piven and Richard Cloward, *Poor People's Movements: Why They Succeed, How They Fail* (New York: Random House, 1988), p. 191.

90. Michelle Alexander, *The New Jim Crow* (New York: New Press, 2012), p. 218.

91. The number of black males working in manufacturing was nearly cut in half between 1973 and 1987. Wilson, *When Work Disappears*, pp. 29–31.

92. Ibid., p. 42.

93. Ibid., p. 19.

94. Wacquant, 'Rise of Advanced Marginality,' p. 127.

95. While the size of the informal economy is notoriously difficult to measure, by all accounts it forms a significant part of the global economy. For an overview of methods to measure the global shadow economy, see Friedrich Schneider and Andreas Buehn, *Estimating the Size of the Shadow Economy: Methods, Problems, and Open Questions* (CESifo Working Paper Series No. 4448, 2013), pdf available at papers. ssrn.com. For a more detailed, ethnographic account of one urban informal economy, see: Sudhir Alladi Venkatesh, *Off the Books: The Underground Economy of the Urban Poor* (Cambridge: Harvard University Press, 2006).

96. The United Nations suggests that two-fifths of workers in developing economies are in the informal sector, while other research notes a significant growth in this proportion between 1985 and 2007. Mike Davis, *Planet of Slums* (London: Verso, 2006), p. 176; Friedrich Schneider, *Outside the State: The Shadow Economy and the Shadow Economy Labour Force*, Working Paper, 2014, pdf available at econ. jku.at, p. 20.

97. UN-Habitat, *The Challenge of Slums: Global Report on Human Settlements 2003* (Nairobi: UN-Habitat, 2003), at mirror.unhabitat.org, p. 46.

98. Karl Polanyi, *The Great Transformation: The Political and Economic Origins of Our Time* (Boston, MA: Beacon, 2001), p. 41.

99. Jan Breman, 'Introduction: The Great Transformation in the Setting of Asia', in *Outcast Labour in Asia: Circulation and Informalization of the Workforce at the Bottom of the Economy* (New Delhi: Oxford University Press, 2012), pp. 8–9; Nicholas Kaldor, *Strategic Factors in Economic Development* (Ithaca, NY: New York State School of Industrial and Labor Relations, 1967).

100. Jan Breman, 'A Bogus Concept?', *New Left Review* II/84 (November–December 2013), p. 137.

101. Sukti Dasgupta and Ajit Singh, *Manufacturing, Services and Premature Deindustrialization in Developing Countries: A Kaldorian Analysis*, Working Paper Series, World Institute for Development Economics Research, 2006, at ideas.repec. org, p. 6; Breman, 'Introduction', p. 2; Fields, *Working Hard, Working Poor*, p. 58; Davis, *Planet of Slums*, p. 15.

102. Davis, *Planet of Slums*, p. 175; Breman, 'Introduction', pp. 3–8; George Ciccariello-Maher, *We Created Chávez: A People's History of the Venezuelan Revolution* (Durham, NC: Duke University Press, 2013), Chapter 9.

103. Sassen, *Expulsions*, Chapter 2.

104. Sanyal, *Rethinking Capitalist Development*, p. 69.

105. Davis, *Planet of Slums*, pp. 181–2.

106. Rather than a 30–40 per cent manufacturing share of total employment, the numbers are closer to 15–20 per cent, and manufacturing now begins to decline as a share of GDP at per capita levels of around $3,000, rather than $10,000. Dani Rodrik, 'The Perils of Premature Deindustrialization', *Project Syndicate*, 11 October 2013, at project-syndicate.org, p. 5.

107. Over 30 million manufacturing jobs have been lost since 1996. Erik Brynjolfsson, Andrew McAfee and Michael Spence, 'New World Order', *Foreign Affairs*, August 2014.

108. Manfred Elfstrom and Sarosh Kuruvilla, 'The Changing Nature of Labor Unrest in China', *ILR Review* 67: 2 (2014)

109. Real wages rose by 300 per cent between 2000 and 2010. ILO, *Global Wage Report 2012/13: Wages and Equitable Growth* (Geneva: International Labour Organization, 2013), pdf available at ilo.org, p. 20.

110. ILO, *Global Employment Trends 2014*, p. 29.

111. International Federation of Robotics, *World Robotics: Industrial Robots 2014* (Frankfurt: International Federation of Robotics, 2014), pdf available at worldrobotics.org, p. 19; Lee Chyen Yee and Clare Jim, 'Foxconn to Rely More on Robots; Could Use 1 Million in 3 Years', *Reuters*, 1 August 2011; 'Guangzhou Spurs Robot Use amid Rising Labor Costs', *China Daily*, 16 April 2014, at chinadaily.com.cn; Angelo Young, 'Nike Unloads Contract Factory Workers, Showing How Automation Is Costing Jobs of Vulnerable Emerging Market Laborers', *International Business Times*, 20 May 2014.

112. *Majority of Large Manufacturers Are Now Planning or Considering 'Reshoring' from China to the US*, Boston Consulting Group, 24 September 2013, at bcg.com; Stephanie Clifford, 'US Textile Plants Return, with Floors Largely Empty of People', *New York Times*, 19 September 2013.

113. Dani Rodrik, *Premature Deindustrialization*, BREAD Working Paper No. 439, Bureau for Research and Economic Analysis of Development, 2015, at ipl.econ. duke.edu, p. 2.

114. Fiona Tregenna, *Manufacturing Productivity, Deindustrialization, and Reindustrialization*, World Institute for Development Economics Research, 2011, at econstor.eu, p. 11.

115. Out of a labour force of 481 million, approximately 1 million work in this sector. Fields, *Working Hard, Working Poor*, p. 51.

116. Frey and Osborne, *Technology at Work*, p. 62; Brynjolfsson and McAfee, *Second Machine Age*, pp. 184–5.

117. Rosa Luxemburg, *The Accumulation of Capital* (London: Routledge, 2003), pp. 344–5.

118. This is why, despite the massive size of China's proletarian population, this surplus labour supply is becoming a problem as real wages surge upwards.

119. Göran Therborn, *Why Some People Are More Unemployed than Others: The Strange Paradox of Growth and Unemployment* (London: Verso, 1991), pp. 23–4.

120. Harvey, *A Companion to Marx's Capital, Volume 1*, p. 280.

121. The political intervention to bring this about is often missed by commentators who are sanguine about the historical experience of automation. See, for example, George Terbough, *The Automation Hysteria: An Appraisal of the Alarmist View of the Technological Revolution* (New York: W. W. Norton, 1966), Chapter 5.

122. Lewis Corey, *The Decline of American Capitalism* (New York: Covici Friede, 1934), p. 272.

123. Harry Braverman, 'Automation: Promise and Menace', *American Socialist*, October 1955, at marxists.org; Benanav and Endnotes, 'Misery and Debt', p. 36; Duboff, 'Full Employment', p. 1.

124. Benjamin Kline Hunnicutt, *Work Without End: Abandoning Shorter Hours for the Right to Work* (Philadelphia: Temple University Press, 1988), pp. 259–60.

125. Pierre Dardot and Christian Laval, *The New Way of the World: On Neoliberal Society*, transl. Gregory Elliot (London: Verso, 2014), p. 67.

126. ILO, 'Trends', *World Employment and Social Outlook*, p. 23.

127. Peter Cappelli, 'The Path Not Studied: Schools of Dreams More Education Is Not an Economic Elixir', *Issues in Science and Technology*, 27 November 2013, at issues. org; Stanley Aronowitz, Dawn Esposito, William DiFazio and Margaret Yard, 'The Post-Work Manifesto', in Stanley Aronowitz and Jonathan Cutler, eds, *Post-Work: The Wages of Cybernation* (New York: Routledge, 1998), p. 48; Stefan Collini, *What Are Universities For?* (London: Penguin, 2012); Andrew McGettigan, *The Great University Gamble: Money, Markets and the Future of Higher Education* (London: Pluto Press, 2013).

128. Standing, *Precariat*, p. 45.

129. Notably, even Paul Krugman and Lawrence Summers are doubtful that skills training will be able to solve the upcoming problems. Paul Krugman, 'Sympathy for the Luddites', *New York Times*, 13 June 2013; Lawrence Summers, 'Roundtable: The Future of Jobs', presented at The Future of Work in the Age of the Machine, Hamilton Project, Washington, DC, 19 February 2015, at hamiltonproject.org.

130. Glyn, *Capitalism Unleashed*, pp. 27–31.

131. Harvey, *Companion to Marx's Capital, Volume 1*, pp. 284–5.

132. PMI surveys suggest the annual growth rate has been 2 per cent, which is far below what has been standard for global GDP growth. (Chris Williamson, 'January's PMI Surveys Signal First Global Growth Upturn for Six Months', *Markit*, 4 February 2015, at markit.com.) Other studies find that growth is higher than this, but potential output has been declining in developed economies since before the crisis, and estimates of global potential output have continually been revised down after the crisis. *World Economic Outlook 2015: Uneven Growth: Short- and Long-Term Factors* (Washington, DC: International Monetary Fund, 2015), pp. 69–71, pdf available at imf.org.

133. We do not pretend to adjudicate between the competing explanations here, but merely point to the growing consensus about a new era of lower growth: Andrew Kliman, 'What Lies Ahead: Accelerating Growth or Secular Stagnation?' *E-International Relations*, 24 January 2014, at e-ir.info; Robert Gordon, *Is US Economic Growth Over? Faltering Innovation Confronts the Six Headwinds*, Working Paper, National Bureau of Economic Research, August 2012, at nber.org;

Lawrence Summers, 'US Economic Prospects: Secular Stagnation, Hysteresis, and the Zero Lower Bound', *Business Economics* 49: 2 (2014); Tyler Cowen, *The Great Stagnation: How America Ate All the Low-Hanging Fruit of Modern History, Got Sick, and Will (Eventually) Feel Better* (New York: Dutton, 2011); Coen Teulings and Richard Baldwin, eds, *Secular Stagnation: Facts, Causes and Cures* (London: CEPR, 2014).

134. Cowen, *Great Stagnation*, pp. 47–8.

135. Thor Berger and Carl Benedikt Frey, *Industrial Renewal in the 21st Century: Evidence from US Cities?* (Oxford Martin School Working Paper, 2014).

136. Calculated based on data from: Bureau of Labor Statistics, 'Table 1. Private Sector Gross Jobs Gains and Losses by Establishment Age'; Bureau of Labor Statistics, 'Table 5. Number of Private Sector Establishments by Age'.

137. This is the position of a variety of centre-left economists. See Baker and Bernstein, *Getting Back to Full Employment*; Pavlina Tcherneva, *Beyond Full Employment: The Employer of Last Resort as an Institution for Change*, Annandale-on-Hudson: Levy Economics Institute of Bard College, September 2012, pdf available at levyinstitute.org.

138. Denning, 'Wageless Life', pp. 84–6.

139. Aaron Bastani, 'Weaponising Workfare', *openDemocracy*, 22 March 2013, at opendemocracy.net; Joe Davidson, 'Workfare and the Management of the Consolidated Surplus Population', *Spectre* 1 (2013), at spectrecambridge.wordpress. com; Marta Russell, 'The New Reserve Army of Labor?' *Review of Radical Political Economics* 33: 2 (2001).

140. Aufheben, 'Editorial: The "New" Workfare Schemes in Historical and Class Context', *Aufheben* 21 (2012), pdf available at libcom.org, p. 4.

141. 'In 1820 Britain had a population of 12 million, while between 1820 and 1915 emigration was 16 million. Put differently, more than half the increase in British population emigrated each year during this period. The total emigration from Europe as a whole to the "new world" (of "temperate regions of white settlement") over this period was 50 million.' Foster, McChesney and Jonna, 'The Global Reserve Army of Labor and the New Imperialism'; Davis, *Planet of Slums*, p. 183.

142. For example, in the 1970s and 1980s Switzerland maintained low unemployment despite slow growth by repatriating Italian immigrants. Therborn, *Why Some People Are More Unemployed than Others*, p. 28.

143. Tara Brian and Frank Laczko, eds, *Fatal Journeys: Tracking Lives Lost During Migration* (Geneva: International Organization for Migration, 2014), pdf available at publications.iom.int, p. 12.

144. Dennis Arnold and John Pickles, 'Global Work, Surplus Labor, and the Precarious Economies of the Border', *Antipode* 43: 5 (2011).

145. Between 1998 and 2013, prison populations have increased from 25 to 30 per cent, while the overall world population has increased by 20 per cent. Roy Walmsley, *World Prison Population List* (London: International Centre for Prison Studies, 2013), 10th edn, pdf available at prisonstudies.org, p. 1.

146. Molly Moore, 'In France, Prisons Filled with Muslims', *Washington Post*, 29 April 2008; Scott Gilmore, 'Canada's Racism Problem? It's Even Worse than America's',

Macleans, 22 January 2015, at macleans.ca; Jaime Amparo-Alves, 'Living in the Necropolis: Homo Sacer and the Black Inhuman Condition in Sao Paulo/Brazil', presented at Critical Ethnic Studies and the Future of Genocide, University of California at Riverside, March 2011, at repositories.lib.utexas.edu.

147. Alexander, *New Jim Crow*, p. 13.

148. George S. Rigakos and Aysegul Ergul, 'Policing the Industrial Reserve Army: An International Study', *Crime, Law and Social Change* 56: 4 (2011), p. 355.

149. Angela Y. Davis, 'Deepening the Debate over Mass Incarceration', *Socialism and Democracy* 28: 3 (2014), p. 16.

150. It suffices to point to two facts here: that the spike in prison construction came during a period of declining crime rates, and that if the crime rate is held constant over the past thirty years, the United States is six times more punitive now. Alexander, *New Jim Crow*, p. 218; Wacquant, 'Class, Race and Hyperincarceration', p. 45.

151. Wacquant, 'Class, Race and Hyperincarceration', p. 42.

152. In California, 80 per cent of defendants required representation by state-appointed lawyers. Ruth Wilson Gilmore, 'Globalisation and US Prison Growth: From Military Keynesianism to Post-Keynesian Militarism', *Race & Class* 40: 2–3 (1998–99), p. 172.

153. Wacquant, 'Class, Race and Hyperincarceration', p. 44.

154. Derek Neal and Armin Rick, *The Prison Boom and the Lack of Black Progress After Smith and Welch*, Working Paper, National Bureau of Economic Research, 2014, at nber.org, p. 2.

155. Wacquant, 'Class, Race and Hyperincarceration', p. 43.

156. Wacquant, 'From Slavery to Mass Incarceration: Rethinking the "Race" Question in America', *New Left Review* II/13 (January–February 2002), p. 42.

157. Ibid., p. 53; Alexander, *New Jim Crow*, p. 219.

158. Wacquant, 'From Slavery to Mass Incarceration', pp. 57–8; Rocamadur, 'The Feral Underclass Hits the Streets: On the English Riots and Other Ordeals', *Sic* 2 (2014), at communisation.net, p. 104 n. 10.

159. Jeremy Travis, Bruce Western and Steve Redburn, *The Growth of Incarceration in the United States: Exploring Causes and Consequences* (Washington, DC: National Academies Press, 2014), p. 258; Neal and Rick, *Prison Boom and the Lack of Black Progress*, p. 34.

160. The mechanics of getting unions and social movements to adapt to new goals must necessarily be worked out in practice and in the context of local conditions. Union habits and structures differ from country to country and from sector to sector, making tailored responses necessary.

161. For example, recent fast food strikes brought forth numerous predictions that raising the minimum wage would lead to automation. Given how deplorable these jobs are, we consider their automation an unambiguous positive. Steven Greenhouse, '$15 Wage in Fast Food Stirs Debate on Effects', *New York Times*, 4 December 2013.

162. Paul Lafargue, 'The Right to Be Lazy', in Bernard Marszalek, ed., *The Right to Be Lazy: Essays by Paul Lafargue* (Oakland: AK Press, 2011), p. 45.

163. For thoughts on how this might practically be achieved, see Angela Y. Davis, *Are Prisons Obsolete?* (New York: Seven Stories, 2003), Chapter 6.

6. POST-WORK IMAGINARIES

1. Both explicitly and implicitly, this chapter owes much to Kathi Weeks's work. See Kathi Weeks, *The Problem with Work: Feminism, Marxism, Antiwork Politics, and Postwork Imaginaries* (Durham, NC: Duke University Press, 2011).

2. 'Communiqué from an Absent Future', *We Want Everything*, 24 September 2009, at wewanteverything.wordpress.com.

3. Ben Trott, 'Walking in the Right Direction?' *Turbulence* 1 (2007), at turbulence.org. uk; Marco Desiriis and Jodi Dean, 'A Movement Without Demands?' *Possible Futures*, 3 January 2012, at possible-futures.org; Bertie Russell, 'Demanding the Future? What a Demand Can Do', *Journal of Aesthetics and Protest*, 2014, at joaap.org.

4. Weeks, *Problem with Work*, pp. 218–24, 175.

5. This is one aspect that distinguishes them from the concept of 'transitional demands' articulated by Trotsky. See Trott, 'Walking in the Right Direction?'; Leon Trotsky, *The Transitional Program: Death Agony of Capitalism and the Tasks of the Fourth International* (London: Bolshevik Publications, 1999).

6. On the criteria of desirability, viability and achievability, see Erik Olin Wright, *Envisioning Real Utopias* (London: Verso, 2010), pp. 20–5.

7. For an example of the former, see the Stakhanovite movement, or Lenin's comments on Taylorist management methods: 'The Russian is a bad worker compared with people in advanced countries . . . We must organise in Russia the study and teaching of the Taylor system and systematically try it out and adapt it to our own ends.' Vladimir Lenin, 'The Immediate Tasks of the Soviet Government', 1918, Marxists Internet Archive, at marxists.org; Lewis H. Siegelbaum, *Stakhanovism and the Politics of Productivity in the USSR, 1935–1941* (Cambridge: Cambridge University Press, 1990). For a critique of the idea of freedom without abundance, see: '[T]his development of productive forces . . . is an absolutely necessary practical premise, because without it privation, *want*, is merely made general'. Karl Marx and Friedrich Engels, *The German Ideology* (London: Prometheus, 1976), p. 54.

8. While we do not have the space to discuss them here, there are important ethical questions surrounding machines and work – particularly in the area of artificial intelligence. Such issues are bound to become more significant in the coming decades. For more, see Thomas Metzinger, *The Ego Tunnel: The Science of the Mind and the Myth of the Self* (New York: Basic Books, 2009); Illah Reza Nourbakhsh, *Robot Futures* (Cambridge, MA: MIT Press, 2013).

9. While ending work is a common theme of the left, the demand for full automation surprisingly finds few explicit expressions. See, for example, Eldridge Cleaver, 'On Lumpen Ideology', *The Black Scholar* 4: 3 (1972); Valerie Solanas, *S.C.U.M. Manifesto (Society for Cutting Up Men)* (London: Verso, 2004), p. 3; J. Jesse Ramírez, 'Marcuse Among the Technocrats: America, Automation, and Postcapitalist Utopias, 1900–1941', *American Studies* 57: 1 (2012). More recently, Aaron Bastani of NovaraMedia has made calls for a 'fully automated luxury communism' and members of the Plan C collective have similarly called for 'luxury communism' – discussions which this book attempts to contribute to.

10. 'Development of the productive forces of social labour is the historical task and justification of capital. This is just the way in which it unconsciously creates the material requirements of a higher mode of production.' Karl Marx, *Capital: A Critique of Political Economy, Volume III* (London: Lawrence & Wishart, 1977), p. 259.

11. Marilyn Fischer, 'Tensions from Technology in Marx's Communist Society', *Journal of Value Inquiry* 16: 2 (1982), pp. 125–6; Carl Benedikt Frey and Michael Osborne, *The Future of Employment: How Susceptible Are Jobs to Computerisation?* 17 September 2013, pdf available at oxfordmartin.ox.ac.uk, p. 8; Karl Marx, *Capital: A Critique of Political Economy, Volume I*, transl. Ben Fowkes (London: Penguin, 1990), Chapters 13–15.

12. Karl Marx, *Grundrisse: Introduction to the Critique of Political Economy*, transl. Martin Nicolaus (Middlesex: Penguin, 1973), p. 693.

13. Marx, *Capital, Volume I*, p. 517.

14. Maarten Goos, *How the World of Work Is Changing: A Review of the Evidence* (Geneva: International Labour Organization, 2013), pdf available at ilo.org, pp. 10–12; Frey and Osborne, *Future of Employment*, p. 10.

15. Bruno Latour, 'How to Write "The Prince" for Machines as Well as Machinations', in Brian Elliot, ed., *Technology and Social Change* (Edinburgh: Edinburgh University Press, 1988), p. 27.

16. Fiona Tregenna, *Manufacturing Productivity, Deindustrialization, and Reindustrialization*, World Institute for Development Economics Research, 2011, at econstor.eu, p. 7.

17. Colin Gill, *Work, Unemployment and the New Technology* (Cambridge: Polity, 1985), p. 95.

18. Tessa Morris-Suzuki, 'Robots and Capitalism', in Jim Davis, Thomas Hirschl and Michael Stack, eds, *Cutting Edge: Technology, Information, Capitalism and Social Revolution* (London: Verso, 1997), p. 15; *World Robotics: Industrial Robots 2014*, Frankfurt: International Federation of Robotics, 2014, pdf available at worldrobotics.org, p. 15.

19. Globally, 45 per cent of workers are involved in services, 32 per cent in agriculture and 23 per cent in manufacturing, with over half of recent job growth coming from the service sector. ILO, *Global Employment Trends 2014: Risk of a Jobless Recovery?* (Geneva: International Labour Organization, 2014), p. 23.

20. Frey and Osborne, *Future of Employment*, p. 11.

21. This does not include the numerous robots sold for entertainment, domestic and personal services. *World Robotics: Service Robots 2014*, Frankfurt: International Federation of Robotics, 2014, pdf available at worldrobotics.org, p. 20.

22. Routine jobs have declined from 60 per cent to 40 per cent of total jobs in the United States in this period. David Autor, Frank Levy and Richard Murnane, 'The Skill Content of Recent Technological Change: An Empirical Exploration', *Quarterly Journal of Economics* 118: 4 (2003), p. 1,296; Stefania Albanesi, Victoria Gregory, Christina Patterson and Ayşegül Şahin, 'Is Job Polarization Holding Back the Job Market?' *Liberty Street Economics*, 27 March 2013, at libertystreeteconomics. newyorkfed.org.

23. Guido Matias Cortes, Nir Jaimovich, Christopher J. Nekarda and Henry E. Siu, *The*

Micro and Macro of Disappearing Routine Jobs: A Flows Approach, Working Paper, National Bureau of Economic Research, July 2014, at nber.org.

24. David Autor, *Polanyi's Paradox and the Shape of Employment Growth*, Working Paper, National Bureau of Economic Research, September 2014, at nber.org; Maarten Goos, Alan Manning and Anna Salomons, 'Job Polarization in Europe', *American Economic Review* 99: 2 (2009).

25. Morris-Suzuki, 'Robots and Capitalism', p. 17.

26. The significance of 3D printing (or additive manufacturing) lies first in its generic capacity to create complexity with a simple technology – anything from houses to jet engines to living organs can be created in this way. Second, its ability to drastically reduce the costs of construction (in terms of both material and labour) portend a new era in the building of basic infrastructure and housing. Finally, its flexibility is a significant advance, overcoming the traditional costs associated with revamping fixed investment for new production lines.

27. Businesses will easily be the quickest adopters of this technology, since it can achieve significant cost savings. Governments and public services (such as the automated overground railways already in London) are likely to be the second wave of adopters. Eventually, with legal and insurance changes, consumers will be forced into adopting this technology.

28. Isaac Arnsdorf, 'Rolls-Royce Drone Ships Challenge $375 Billion Industry: Freight', *Bloomberg*, 25 February 2014, at bloomberg.com; BBC News, 'Amazon Testing Drones for Deliveries', BBC News, 2 December 2013; Danielle Kucera, 'Amazon Acquires Kiva Systems in Second-Biggest Takeover', *Bloomberg*, 19 March 2012, at bloomberg.com; Vicky Validakis, 'Rio's Driverless Trucks Move 100 Million Tonnes', *Mining Australia*, 24 April 2013, at miningaustralia.com.au; Elise Hu, 'The Fast-Food Restaurants that Require Few Human Workers', NPR.org, 29 August 2013, at npr.org; Christopher Steiner, *Automate This: How Algorithms Came to Rule Our World* (New York: Portfolio/Penguin, 2012); Mark Levinson, *The Box: How the Shipping Container Made the World Smaller and the World Economy Bigger* (Princeton, NJ: Princeton University Press, 2008); Daniel Beunza, Donald MacKenzie, Yuval Millo and Juan Pablo Pardo-Guerra, *Impersonal Efficiency and the Dangers of a Fully Automated Securities Exchange* (London: Foresight, 2011).

29. For a slightly outdated but still useful summary of various automation processes, see Ramin Ramtin, *Capitalism and Automation: Revolution in Technology and Capitalist Breakdown* (London: Pluto, 1991), Chapter 4.

30. Erik Brynjolfsson and Andrew McAfee, *The Second Machine Age: Work, Progress, and Prosperity in a Time of Brilliant Technologies* (New York: W. W. Norton, 2014), Chapters 2–4.

31. Ibid., Chapter 1; Frey and Osborne, *Future of Employment*, p. 44.

32. Paul Lippe and Daniel Martin Katz, '10 Predictions About How IBM's Watson Will Impact the Legal Profession', *ABA Journal*, 2 October 2014, at abajournal.com.

33. Brynjolfsson and McAfee, *Second Machine Age*, Chapter 2.

34. Dave Cliff, Dan Brown and Philip Treleaven, *Technology Trends in the Financial Markets: A 2020 Vision* (London: Foresight, 2011), p. 36. The exact timeline of automation of financial markets depends on the product under consideration. For

an outline of the uneven adoption of trading automation, see Carl Benedikt Frey and Michael Osborne, *Technology at Work: The Future of Innovation and Employment*, (Citi – Global Perspectives and Solutions, 2015), pp. 26–7, pdf available at ir.citi.com

35. Vauhini Vara, 'The Lowe's Robot and the Future of Service Work', *New Yorker*, 29 October 2014.

36. Frey and Osborne, *Future of Employment*, p. 19.

37. Ibid., p. 42.

38. In an unexpected revival of an old Marxist theory, two recent models have suggested that automation will lead to the immiseration of workers: Jeffrey Sachs, Seth Benzell and Guillermo LaGarda, *Robots: Curse or Blessing? A Basic Framework*, Working Paper, National Bureau of Economic Research, April 2015, at nber.org; Seth Benzell, Laurence Kotlikoff, Guillermo LaGarda and Jeffrey Sachs, *Robots Are Us: Some Economics of Human Replacement*, Working Paper, National Bureau of Economic Research, February 2015, at nber.org.

39. Lawrence Summers, 'Roundtable: The Future of Jobs', presented at The Future of Work in the Age of the Machine, Hamilton Project, Washington, DC, 19 February 2015, at hamiltonproject.org. The ILO also argues that today's sluggish global job growth is related largely to sluggish economic growth, but they also note that productivity growth has recovered quicker than employment growth. ILO, *World Employment and Social Outlook: The Changing Nature of Jobs* (Geneva: International Labour Organization, 2015), pp. 19, 23.

40. Bank of International Settlements, *Annual Report, 2013/2014* (Basel: Bank for International Settlements, 2014), at bis.org, pp. 58–60; Robert Gordon, 'US Productivity Growth: The Slowdown Has Returned After a Temporary Revival', *International Productivity Monitor* 25 (2013); David Autor, 'Roundtable: The Future of Jobs', presented at the The Future of Work in the Age of the Machine, Hamilton Project, Washington, DC, 19 February 2015, at hamiltonproject.org.

41. Susantu Basu and John Fernald, *Information and Communications Technology as a General-Purpose Technology: Evidence from U.S. Industry Data* (San Francisco: Federal Reserve Bank of San Francisco Working Paper, 2006), p. 17, pdf available at frbsf.org.

42. However, emerging research suggests industrial robots have already contributed around 16 per cent of recent labour productivity growth. Georg Graetz and Guy Michaels, *Robots at Work* (London: Centre for Economic Performance, 2015), p. 21, pdf available at events.crei.cat.

43. Frey and Osborne, *Technology at Work*, p. 40.

44. Frey and Osborne, *Future of Employment*, p. 38; Stuart Elliott, 'Anticipating a Luddite Revival', *Issues in Science and Technology* 30: 3 (2014), at issues.org.

45. The standard Marxist response to full automation is to point to its 'objective' limits by arguing that capitalism will never eliminate its source of surplus value (i.e. labour). But this argument confuses a systemic outcome with an individual incentive, an internal barrier with an absolute limit, and a political struggle with a theoretical tension. In the first place, the individual imperatives are to increase the productivity of technology in order to gain extra surplus value relative to other

capitalists. The systemic outcome of this is detrimental for all capitalists (less surplus value being produced), but still remains beneficial for individual capitalists, and will therefore continue. In the second place, the limits of the capitalist mode of production are mistakenly taken to be the limits of any possible change. If capitalism cannot survive with full automation, it is deemed that full automation must not be possible. Such a position makes capitalism the end-point of history, rejecting in advance any postcapitalist possibility. Finally, the theoretically derived tension between increased productivity, rising organic composition and a reduced rate of profit is taken to present a situation that capital will never allow to occur because of its systemic effects. Missing from this account is a political movement that would struggle to push capitalism beyond itself. In other words, the argument that full automation will never occur simply posits that political struggle is ineffective. In the end, such a line of reasoning gives up on every critical account of capitalism, and accepts it as the final stage of history. As Ramin Ramtin bluntly puts it, 'The fact that [full automation] would result in explosive socioeconomic and political contradictions does not make it impossible' (Ramtin, *Capitalism and Automation*, p. 103). The simple wager of the demand for full automation is that wealth can be produced in non-capitalist ways. For representative critiques of full automation, see Ernest Mandel, *Late Capitalism* (London: Verso, 1998), p. 205; George Caffentzis, 'The End of Work or the Renaissance of Slavery? A Critique of Rifkin and Negri', in *In Letters of Blood and Fire* (Oakland, CA: PM Press, 2012), p. 78.

46. It should be mentioned that, increasingly, tacit knowledge tasks are being automated through environmental control and machine learning, with more recent innovations eliminating even the need for a controlled environment. Frey and Osborne, *Future of Employment*, p. 27; Autor, *Polanyi's Paradox*; Sarah Yang, 'New "Deep Learning" Technique Enables Robot Mastery of Skills via Trial and Error', *Phys.org*, 21 May 2015, at phys.org.

47. As Marx notes, because of this 'the field of application for machinery would therefore be entirely different in a communist society from what it is in bourgeois society.' Marx, *Capital, Volume I*, p. 515 n. 33.

48. Silvia Federici, 'Permanent Reproductive Crisis: An Interview', *Mute*, 7 March 2013, at metamute.org.

49. For an excellent overview of historical experiences of alternative domestic arrangements, see Dolores Hayden, *Grand Domestic Revolution: A History of Feminist Designs for American Homes, Neighbourhoods and Cities* (Cambridge: MIT Press, 1996).

50. However, it is important to recognise that, historically, domestic labour-saving devices have tended to place greater demands on household maintenance, rather than allowing more free time. Ruth Schwartz Cowan, *More Work for Mother: The Ironies of Household Technology from the Open Hearth to the Microwave* (New York: Basic Books, 1985); Leopoldina Fortunati, *The Arcane of Reproduction: Housework, Prostitution, Labor and Capital* (Brooklyn: Autonomedia, 1995), p. 145; Silvia Federici, 'The Reproduction of Labor Power in the Global Economy and the Unfinished Feminist Revolution', in *Revolution at Point Zero: Housework, Reproduction, and Feminist Struggle* (Oakland, CA: PM Press, 2012), pp. 106–7.

51. We mean 'productivity' here in the strictly Marxist sense, and not as a suggestion that domestic work is idle.

52. 'Robot Capable of Sorting Through and Folding Piles of Rumpled Clothes' *Phys.org*, 16 March 2015, at phys.org.

53. Thanks to Helen Hester for emphasizing this point to us.

54. Shulamith Firestone, *The Dialectic of Sex: The Case for Feminist Revolution* (New York: Farrar, Straus & Giroux, 2003), pp. 180–1.

55. E. P. Thompson, 'Time, Work-Discipline, and Industrial Capitalism', *Past & Present* 38: 1 (1967), p. 85; Stanley Aronowitz, Dawn Esposito, William DiFazio and Margaret Yard, 'The Post-Work Manifesto', in Stanley Aronowitz and Jonathan Cutler, eds, *Post-Work: The Wages of Cybernation* (New York: Routledge, 1998), pp. 59–60; David Graeber, 'Revolution at the Level of Common Sense', in Federico Campagna and Emanuele Campiglio, eds, *What We Are Fighting For: A Radical Collective Manifesto* (London: Pluto, 2012), p. 171.

56. Benjamin Kline Hunnicutt, *Work Without End: Abandoning Shorter Hours for the Right to Work* (Philadelphia: Temple University Press, 1988), p. 9.

57. Roland Paulsen, 'Non-Work at Work: Resistance or What?', *Organization*, 2013, at sagepub.com.

58. Witold Rybczynski, *Waiting for the Weekend* (New York: Penguin, 1991), pp. 115–17; Thompson, 'Time, Work-Discipline, and Industrial Capitalism', p. 76.

59. Rybczynski, *Waiting for the Weekend*, p. 133.

60. Hunnicutt, *Work Without End*, p. 1.

61. Ibid., p. 155.

62. Ibid., pp. 147–9.

63. Paul Lafargue, 'The Right to Be Lazy', in Bernard Marszalek, ed., *The Right to Be Lazy: Essays by Paul Lafargue* (Oakland: AK Press, 2011), p. 34.

64. John Maynard Keynes, 'Economic Possibilities for Our Grandchildren', in *Essays in Persuasion* (New York: W. W. Norton, 1963); Hunnicutt, *Work Without End*, p. 155.

65. Marx, *Capital, Volume III*, p. 820.

66. Hunnicutt, *Work Without End*, Chapter 7.

67. A handful of EU countries – most notably France – have reduced the working week to as little as thirty-five hours, but the overall trend has been to maintain a forty-hour working week. The 1970s also saw some sectors strike explicitly in support of a shorter working week. Ibid., p. 198; Anders Hayden, 'Patterns and Purpose of Work-Time Reduction: A Cross-National Comparison', in Anna Coote and Jane Franklin, eds, *Time on Our Side: Why We All Need a Shorter Working Week* (London: New Economics Foundation, 2013), p. 128; Aronowitz et al., 'Post-Work Manifesto', p. 63; Chris Harman, *Is a Machine After Your Job? New Technology and the Struggle for Socialism* (London, 1979), at marxists.org, Part 8.

68. Hunnicutt, *Work Without End*, p. 2.

69. Notably, this appears to have reached a turning point in the US. Despite the addition of 40 million new workers, overall labour hours remained the same between 1998 and 2013. Shawn Sprague, 'What Can Labor Productivity Tell Us About the U.S. Economy?', *Beyond the Numbers: Productivity* 3: 12 (2014), p. 1.

70. Jonathan Crary, 24/7: Terminal Capitalism and the Ends of Sleep (London: Verso, 2013).

71. Lydia Saad, 'The "40-Hour" Workweek Is Actually Longer – by Seven Hours', Gallup, 29 August 2014, at gallup.com.

72. Valerie Bryson, 'Time, Care and Gender Inequalities', in Coote and Franklin, Time on Our Side, p. 56.

73. Craig Lambert, 'The Second Job You Don't Know You Have', Politico, 20 May 2015, at politico.eu.

74. Guy Standing, The Precariat: The New Dangerous Class (London: Bloomsbury Academic, 2011), pp. 120–7.

75. The manifold arguments for shorter working weeks have been repeated throughout history: the physical and mental health benefits, the response to technological unemployment, the improved productivity it could bring about, and the better bargaining position it would generate for labour. These arguments were as dominant in the early twentieth century as they are now.

76. David Rosnick and Mark Weisbrot, Are Shorter Work Hours Good for the Environment? A Comparison of US and European Energy Consumption, Center for Economic and Policy Research, December 2006, pdf available at cepr.net, p. 7; Anders Hayden and John M. Shandra, 'Hours of Work and the Ecological Footprint of Nations: An Exploratory Analysis', Local Environment 14: 6 (2009).

77. Juliet Schor, 'The Triple Dividend', in Coote and Franklin, Time on Our Side, pp. 9–10.

78. Denis Campbell, 'UK Needs Four-Day Week to Combat Stress, Says Top Doctor', Guardian, 1 July 2014.

79. Ibid., pp. 20–1.

80. Mondli Hlatshwayo, 'NUMSA and Solidarity's Responses to Technological Changes at the ArcelorMittal Vanderbijlpark Plant: Unions Caught on the Back Foot', Global Labour Journal 5: 3 (2014); Ramtin, Capitalism and Automation, p. 132.

81. This was a position floated by the TUC in the UK during the 1970s, and which achieved some success with metalworkers in West Germany. Gill, Work, Unemployment and the New Technology, pp. 171–2.

82. This was what occurred in the 1996 French truck drivers' strike. Alan Riding, 'French Trucker Strike Ends with Indirect Defeat for Government', New York Times, 30 November 1996.

83. André Gorz, Paths to Paradise: On the Liberation from Work, transl. Malcolm Imrie (Boston: South End Press, 1985), p. 46.

84. Anna Coote, Jane Franklin and Andrew Simms, 21 Hours (London: New Economics Foundation, 2010), at neweconomics.org; Tom Hodgkinson, 'Campaigners Call for 30-Hour Working Week to Allow for Healthier, Fairer Society – and More Time for Fun', Independent, 24 April 2014.

85. Jo Littler, Nina Power and Precarious Workers Brigade, 'Life After Work', New Left Project, 20 May 2014, at newleftproject.org.

86. Will Dahlgreen, 'Introduce a Four Day Week, Say Public', YouGov, 16 April 2014, at yougov.co.uk.

87. Schor, 'Triple Dividend', p. 8.

88. Anna Coote, 'Introduction: A New Economics of Work and Time', in Coote and Franklin, *Time on Our Side*, p. xxi; Hayden, 'Patterns and Purpose of Work-Time Reduction'.

89. The above subheading is from Sleaford Mods' song of the same name.

90. Paul Mattick, 'The Economics of Cybernation', *New Politics* 1: 4 (1962), p. 30.

91. The idea has also been called a guaranteed income, a social dividend, a citizen's income and a negative income tax. Each of these invokes a slightly different variation. We prefer the term 'universal basic income' because it does not immediately limit who can receive the income (as does the idea of a 'citizen's income'), and it does not rely on an income ceiling (as does a 'negative income tax').

92. UBI has been advocated by numerous thinkers. See, among many other sources, Thomas Paine, 'Agrarian Justice', in *Rights of Man, Common Sense, and Other Political Writings*, ed. Mark Philp (Oxford: Oxford University Press, 2008); Bertrand Russell, *Roads to Freedom: Socialism, Anarchism and Syndicalism* (Nottingham: Spokesman, 2006); Robert Theobald, ed., *The Guaranteed Income: Next Step in Economic Evolution?* (Garden City, NY: Doubleday, 1966); Martin Luther King, *Where Do We Go from Here? Chaos or Community?* (Boston, MA: Beacon, 2010); Milton Friedman, *Capitalism and Freedom: Fortieth Anniversary Edition* (Chicago: University of Chicago Press, 2002); Murray Bookchin, *Post-Scarcity Anarchism* (Edinburgh: AK Press, 2004); Michael Hardt and Antonio Negri, *Empire* (Cambridge, MA: Harvard University Press, 2001); Weeks, *Problem with Work*.

93. Walter Van Trier, 'Who Framed "Social Dividend"?', presented at the First USBIG Conference, CUNY, New York, 8 March 2002, at econpapers.repec.org, p. 29.

94. Lynn Chancer, 'Benefitting from Pragmatic Vision, Part I: The Case for Guaranteed Income in Principle', in Aronowitz and Cutler, *Post-Work*, p. 86.

95. Evelyn Forget, *The Town with No Poverty: Using Health Administration Data to Revisit Outcomes of a Canadian Guaranteed Annual Income Field Experiment* (Winnipeg: University of Manitoba, 2011); Derek Hum and Wayne Simpson, 'A Guaranteed Annual Income? From Mincome to the Millennium', *Policy Options/ Options Politique*, February 2001.

96. Chancer, 'Benefitting from Pragmatic Vision, Part I', p. 86.

97. Specifically, in the United States these included Nixon's Family Assistance Plan and Carter's Better Jobs and Income Program, neither of which was passed. In Australia, a guaranteed income was also recommended by the Poverty Commission in 1973, but support for it evaporated after elections brought in a new government. Ibid., pp. 87–9; Barry Jones, *Sleepers Wake! Technology and The Future of Work* (London: Oxford University Press, 1982), pp. 204–5.

98. An indispensable resource for the story behind this rise and fall in a basic income policy, along with an essential guide to how cultural framing affects the viability of the policy, is Brian Steensland, *The Failed Welfare Revolution: America's Struggle over Guaranteed Income Policy* (Princeton, NJ: Princeton University Press, 2007).

99. Daniel Raventós, *Basic Income: The Material Conditions of Freedom*, transl. Julie Wark (London: Pluto Press, 2007), p. 12.

100. Paul Krugman, 'Sympathy for the Luddites', *New York Times*, 13 June 2013; Martin Wolf, 'Enslave the Robots and Free the Poor', *Financial Times*, 11 February 2014.

101. More specifically, the Green Party of England and Wales has included it in its manifesto; the Liberal Party of Canada has put the idea on their agenda, and its leader pushed for it in 2001; in Canada, the Standing Senate Committee on Social Affairs recommended it as a way to deal with poverty; and the Swiss will be voting in a referendum on the idea. Denis Balibouse, 'Swiss to Vote on 2,500 Franc Basic Income for Every Adult', *Reuters*, 4 October 2013; Hum and Simpson, 'A Guaranteed Annual Income?'; Rigmar Osterkamp, 'The Basic Income Grant Pilot Project in Namibia: A Critical Assessment', *Basic Income Studies* 8: 1 (2013); Davala et al., *Basic Income*; Forget, *The Town with No Poverty*, p. 2.

102. Davala et al., *Basic Income*; Barbara Jacobson, 'Basic Income Is a Human Right! A Report on the Demonstration in Berlin', *Basic Income UK*, 29 September 2013, at basicincome.org.uk; Alfredo Mazzamauro, '"Only One Big Project": Italy's Burgeoning Social Movements', *ROAR Magazine*, 20 January 2014. The Basic Income Earth Network (BIEN), which has been campaigning for a UBI since 1986.

103. This is a design choice, however – as the conservative proposal for a UBI (or the functionally similar negative income tax) often invokes means-testing. See, for example, Lewis Meriam, *Relief and Social Security* (Washington, DC: Brookings Institution, 1946); Friedman, *Capitalism and Freedom*.

104. A UBI programme would ideally involve a transformation of the welfare state. Programmes that provide services must be kept and expanded – for example, healthcare, childcare, housing, public transport and internet access. All of these should be immediate goals of the left, not only for their inherent good but also because expanding public services is necessary for reducing overall energy consumption. Alyssa Battistoni, 'Alive in the Sunshine', *Jacobin* 13 (2014), at jacobinmag.com; Wright, *Envisioning Real Utopias*, p. 4.

105. Forget, *The Town with No Poverty*; Hum and Simpson, 'A Guaranteed Annual Income?'; Chancer, 'Benefitting from Pragmatic Vision, Part I', pp. 99–109.

106. The rise of UBI in the 1960s and 1970s was largely a result of this capacity to generate support across political divisions. Steensland, *Failed Welfare Revolution*, pp. 18–19.

107. Wright, *Envisioning Real Utopias*, p. 218.

108. Cutler and Aronowitz, 'Quitting Time', p. 8.

109. Michał Kalecki, 'Political Aspects of Full Employment', *Political Quarterly* 14: 4 (1943).

110. The influential Holmes and Rahe Stress Scale found the loss of a job to be one of the most stressful life events an adult can face. Richard H. Rahe and Ransom J. Arthur, 'Life Change and Illness Studies: Past History and Future Directions', *Journal of Human Stress* 4: 1 (1978).

111. A basic income has been a centrepiece proposal of the Japanese Blue Grass Collective, a group of disability activists who have been mobilizing for the idea since the 1970s. Toru Yamamori, 'Una Sola Moltitudine: Struggles for Basic Income and the Common Logic that Emerged from Italy, the UK, and Japan', presented at Immaterial Labour, Multitudes and New Social Subjects, King's College, University of Cambridge, 29 April 2006, pp. 9–12, pdf available at academia.edu.

112. Paolo Virno, *A Grammar of the Multitude* (Cambridge: Semiotext(e), 2004), pp. 98–9.

113. Marx and Engels, *German Ideology*, p. 53.

114. Robert J. Van Der Veen and Philippe Van Parijs, 'A Capitalist Road to Communism', *Theory and Society* 15: 5 (1986), pp. 645–6.

115. Weeks, *Problem with Work*, p. 230.

116. Ailsa Mckay and Jo Vanevery, 'Gender, Family, and Income Maintenance: A Feminist Case for Citizens Basic Income', *Social Politics: International Studies in Gender, State and Society* 7: 2 (2000), p. 281; Gorz, *Paths to Paradise*, p. 42.

117. Notably, this also fundamentally distinguishes the position here from a number of other proposals (such as Parecon or New Socialism) which explicitly identify effort and sacrifice as the bases for reward. Michael Albert, *Parecon: Life After Capitalism* (London: Verso, 2004), p. 157; W. Paul Cockshott and Allin Cottrell, *Towards a New Socialism* (Nottingham: Spokesman, 1993), p. 27; Karl Marx, *Critique of the Gotha Program* (New York: International, 1966), pp. 8–10.

118. Weeks, *Problem with Work*, p. 149.

119. Mckay and Vanevery, 'Gender, Family, and Income Maintenance', p. 280.

120. Hum and Simpson, 'A Guaranteed Annual Income?', p. 81.

121. This is one reason why the UBI is a better demand than that of wages for housework. Weeks, *Problem with Work*, p. 144.

122. Raventós, *Basic Income*, Chapter 8; Chancer, 'Benefitting from Pragmatic Vision, Part I', pp. 120–2; Guy Standing, 'The Precariat Needs a Basic Income' *Financial Times*, 21 November 2013; Gorz, *Paths to Paradise*, p. 45.

123. For an eloquent polemic against the work ethic, see Federico Campagna, *The Last Night: Anti-Work, Atheism, Adventure* (Winchester: Zero, 2013).

124. Steensland, *Failed Welfare Revolution*, pp. 13–18.

125. Ibid., p. 17.

126. Pierre Dardot and Christian Laval, *The New Way of the World: On Neoliberal Society*, transl. Gregory Elliot (London: Verso, 2014), p. 260.

127. Campagna, *Last Night*, p. 16.

128. Weeks, *Problem with Work*, p. 44.

129. Ibid., p. 46.

130. Ibid., pp. 70–1.

131. Youngjoo Cha and Kim A. Weeden, 'Overwork and the Slow Convergence in the Gender Gap in Wages', *American Sociological Review* 79: 3 (2014).

132. Keir Milburn, 'On Social Strikes and Directional Demands', *Plan C*, 7 May 2015, at weareplanc.org.

133. *State of the Global Workplace: Employee Engagement Insights for Business Leaders Worldwide*, Gallup, 2013, pdf available at ihrim.org, p. 12.

134. As usual, the satirical newspaper *The Onion* is ahead of the curve, with a recent headline declaring: 'Chinese Factory Workers Fear They May Never Be Replaced with Machines'.

135. Gáspár Miklós Tamás, 'Telling the Truth About Class', *Grundrisse* 22 (2007), at grundrisse.net.

136. While it adhered to unscalable folk-political practices, the 'back to the land' movement of the 1970s was in many ways an expression of the desire to escape the dominant work ethic. Bernard Marszalek, 'Lafargue for Today', in *The Right to Be Lazy*, p. 13.

137. Gorz, *Paths to Paradise*, p. 10.
138. Steensland, *Failed Welfare Revolution* p. 220.

7. A NEW COMMON SENSE

1. Lesley Wood, *Crisis and Control: The Militarization of Protest Policing* (London: Pluto, 2014).

2. For an overview of some of the debates around capitalism's origins, see Ellen Meiksins Wood, *The Origin of Capitalism: A Longer View* (London: Verso, 2002), Chapters 1–3.

3. For a foundational step towards understanding the conditions of postcolonial capitalism and the hegemony of 'development', see Kalyan Sanyal, *Rethinking Capitalist Development: Primitive Accumulation, Governmentality and Post-Colonial Capitalism* (New Delhi: Routledge India, 2013).

4. The unique conditions of Venezuela appear to have produced the only space in which this strategy is being meaningfully adopted, albeit in an intriguingly modified form. See George Ciccariello-Maher, 'Dual Power in the Venezuelan Revolution', *Monthly Review* 59: 4 (2007); Vladimir Lenin, 'The Dual Power', *Pravda*, 9 April 1917, at marxists.org.

5. For a critique of communisation's tendency to make this supposition, see Alberto Toscano, 'Now and Never', in Benjamin Noys, ed., *Communization and Its Discontents: Contestation, Critique, and Contemporary Struggles* (Brooklyn: Minor Compositions, 2012).

6. While agreeing with their counter-hegemonic approach and insistence on a postcapitalist vision, we diverge from J. K. Gibson-Graham's goal of folk-political community economies and their discursive understanding of hegemony. The major difference in analysis is in their denial of capitalist universalism, which enables them to see small-scale particularities as sufficient for changing economies. For the critique of capitalist universalism and the articulation of a postcapitalist hegemony, see, respectively, J. K. Gibson-Graham, *The End of Capitalism (as We Knew It): A Feminist Critique of Political Economy* (Minneapolis: University of Minnesota Press, 2006); and J. K. Gibson-Graham, *A Postcapitalist Politics* (Minneapolis: University of Minnesota Press, 2006).

7. The full story of the evolution of the term within Marxist thought begins with its inclusion in the writings of G. V. Plekhanov in 1884 as *gegemoniya*, which by the time of Lenin had evolved into an idea of political leadership within a class alliance. This idea was developed considerably by Gramsci into a more ramified and complex understanding of rule by consent, to analyse both Marxist strategy and the existing state of capitalist power. G. F. Plekhanov, 'Socialism and the Political Struggle', in *Selected Philosophical Works*, vol. 1 (Moscow: Progress, 1974); V. I. Lenin, *What Is to Be Done?* (Moscow: Progress, 1971); Antonio Gramsci, *Selections from the Prison Notebooks*, ed. Quintin Hoare and Geoffrey Nowell-Smith (London: Lawrence & Wishart, 1971).

8. There have been a number of critiques of hegemony, including Richard Day, *Gramsci Is Dead: Anarchist Currents in the Newest Social Movements* (London: Pluto, 2005); Scott Lash, 'Power After Hegemony: Cultural Studies in Mutation?'

Theory, Culture & Society 24: 3 (2007); Athina Karatzogianni and Andrew Robinson, *Power, Resistance, and Conflict in the Contemporary World: Social Movements, Networks, and Hierarchies* (London/New York: Routledge, 2010); Jon Beasley-Murray, *Posthegemony: Political Theory and Latin America* (Minneapolis: University of Minnesota Press, 2010). It suffices to say that the majority of these critiques rest upon a misconstruction of hegemony, either as being equivalent to domination (which in all its post-Gramscian formulations it is explicitly not) or as relying upon active assent (which it does not). While other theoretical understandings of power – such as those offered by thinkers like Foucault, Deleuze and Guattari, and Bourdieu – might be usefully applied as supplements to the perspective offered by the idea of hegemony, we do not agree with those who have recently argued that they can effectively replace it.

9. It is useful to note here that, while hegemonic governance is generally within the order of (at least passive) consent, it does not mean the total absence of dominance or coercive force. It indicates simply a situation in which coercive force must be cloaked in the respectable garb of consensuality. See Gramsci, *Selections from the Prison Notebooks*, p. 80. This clarification is necessary to avoid charges of the kind levelled against Gramscian hegemony theory by critics who want to attest to the historical–cultural specificity of the idea, especially given its apparent incompatibility with very different political situations such as those of India under British colonialism, or the United States during slavery. See Ranajit Guha, *Dominance Without Hegemony: History and Power in Colonial India* (Cambridge, MA: Harvard University Press, 1998); Frank Wilderson, 'Gramsci's Black Marx: Whither the Slave in Civil Society?' *Social Identities* 9: 2 (2003). We will presume that hegemony in the generalised sense we outline in this chapter will pertain in any complex society where domination is *not* the primary mode of governance.

10. This is a point also made by Podemos leader Pablo Iglesias. Pablo Iglesias, 'The Left Can Win', *Jacobin*, 9 December 2014, at jacobinmag.com.

11. John Holloway, *Change the World Without Taking Power: The Meaning of Revolution Today* (London: Pluto Press, 2010).

12. While Gramscianism has often been associated with the Eurocommunist political tendency, we would distinguish the basic political analysis and strategic insights of hegemony theory from this particular historical manifestation. Indeed, an overt focus on electoralism in preference to achieving broader hegemonic transformations would seem to us to be an abandonment of the fundamental insights of hegemony itself – not the least of which is an understanding of power as resting in multiple interlocking loci, of which the state is only one.

13. While we endorse the expansion of the concept of hegemony contained in the work of Ernesto Laclau and Chantal Mouffe, in particular its expansion of the range of political subjectivities included within it, it is not without problems. The use of discourse theory as a social ontology results in an effectively anti-realist account, which does unnecessary harm to the broader project of understanding the complexity of the political world. See Ernesto Laclau and Chantal Mouffe, *Hegemony and Socialist Strategy* (London/New York: Verso, 1985); Ernesto Laclau, *New Reflections on the Revolution of Our Time* (London/New York: Verso, 1990). For a lengthy

critique of Laclau and Mouffe's discourse-based hegemony theory, see Geoff Boucher, *The Charmed Circle of Ideology: A Critique of Laclau and Mouffe, Butler and Žižek* (Melbourne: re.press, 2009).

14. David Harvey, *A Brief History of Neoliberalism* (Oxford: Oxford University Press, 2005), p. 40.

15. This concept was originally devised by Joseph Overton, in relation to the proper operational purpose of a think tank. See Nathan J. Russell, 'An Introduction to the Overton Window of Political Possibilities', Mackinac Center for Public Policy, 4 January 2006, at mackinac.org.

16. This can be conceived in cultural terms as the creation of 'capitalist realism'. See Mark Fisher, *Capitalist Realism: Is There No Alternative?* (Winchester: Zero, 2009).

17. 'In such a situation, hegemony has nothing to do with the capacity to make people believe in you; it has everything to do with the strategic capacity to render their belief or disbelief irrelevant.' Jeremy Gilbert, 'Hegemony Now', 2013, at academia. edu, p. 16.

18. David Harvey, *Spaces of Hope* (Berkeley, CA: University of California Press, 2000), p. 159.

19. Judy Wajcman, *TechnoFeminism* (Cambridge: Polity, 2004), p. 35.

20. Jonathan Joseph, *Hegemony: A Realist Analysis* (New York: Routledge, 2002).

21. Thomas Hughes, 'Technological Momentum', in Merritt Roe Smith and Leo Marx, eds, *Does Technology Drive History? The Dilemma of Technological Determinism* (Cambridge, MA: MIT Press, 1994); and *Networks of Power: Electrification in Western Society, 1880–1930* (Baltimore, MD: Johns Hopkins University Press, 1993).

22. This is what Peter Thomas argues: 'Gramsci . . . was aware that all social practices are interrelated, precisely because of his Marxist emphasis on social practices as social relations within a social totality, not merely as the expressions of some regional logics. That led him to conceive of what I would describe as the "political constitution of the social".' Peter Thomas, '"The Gramscian Moment": An Interview with Peter Thomas', in Adam Thomas, ed., *Antonio Gramsci: Working-Class Revolutionary: Essays and Interviews* (London: Workers' Liberty, 2012).

23. De Witt Douglas Kilgore, *Astrofuturism: Science, Race, and Visions of Utopia in Space* (Philadelphia: University of Pennsylvania Press, 2003), p. 21.

24. Asif A. Siddiqi, *The Red Rockets' Glare: Spaceflight and the Russian Imagination, 1857–1957* (Cambridge: Cambridge University Press, 2014), p. 78.

25. Nikolai Federovich Federov, 'The Philosophy of the Common Task', in *What Was Man Created For?*, transl. Elisabeth Kouitaissof and Marilyn Minto (London: Honeyglen, 1990), p. 98.

26. For one example, see Alexander Bogdanov, *Red Star: The First Bolshevik Utopia*, ed. Loren Graham and Richard Stites, transl. Charles Rougle (Bloomington, IN: Indiana University Press, 1984).

27. Siddiqi, *Red Rockets' Glare*, pp. 86–7.

28. Richard Stites, *Revolutionary Dreams: Utopian Vision and Experimental Life in the Russian Revolution* (Oxford: Oxford University Press, 1989), p. 36.

29. Francis Spufford, *Red Plenty: Inside the Fifties' Soviet Dream* (London: Faber & Faber, 2010); Siddiqi, *Red Rockets' Glare*, Chapter 8.

30. While the Soviet Union is now often deemed an economic failure, between 1928 and 1970 its economy did exceptionally well, outpacing every country except Japan. Robert Allen, *Farm to Factory: A Reinterpretation of the Soviet Industrial Economy* (Princeton, NJ: Princeton University Press, 2003), pp. 6–7.

31. Steve Fraser, *The Age of Acquiescence: The Life and Death of American Resistance to Organized Wealth and Power* (New York: Little, Brown US, 2015), Chapter 6.

32. Fisher, *Capitalist Realism*.

33. The shift from the secular, postcapitalist techno-optimism of *Star Trek* to the fundamentalist techno-pessimism of *Battlestar Galactica* is one example of this. Barry Buzan, 'America in Space: The International Relations of *Star Trek* and *Battlestar Galactica*', *Millennium: Journal of International Studies* 39: 1 (2010).

34. See, for example, Kathi Weeks, *The Problem with Work: Feminism, Marxism, Antiwork Politics, and Postwork Imaginaries* (Durham, NC: Duke University Press, 2011), pp. 182–3; Nancy Fraser, *The Fortunes of Feminism: From Women's Liberation to Identity Politics to Anti-Capitalism* (London: Verso, 2013); Helen Hester, 'Promethean Labours and Domestic Realism', in Joshua Johnson, ed., *The Scales of Our Eyes: The Scope of Leftist Thought* (London: Mimesis International, 2015); José Esteban Muñoz, *Cruising Utopia: The Then and There of Queer Futurity* (New York: New York University Press, 2009), pp. 19–21; Shulamith Firestone, *The Dialectic of Sex: The Case for Feminist Revolution* (New York: Morrow, 1970).

35. Fredric Jameson, *Valences of the Dialectic* (London: Verso, 2010), p. 413.

36. 'Marx alone sought to combine the politics of revolt with the "poetry of the future" and applied himself to demonstrate that socialism was more modern than capitalism and more productive. To recover that futurism and that excitement is surely the fundamental task of any left "discursive struggle" today.' Fredric Jameson, *Representing Capital: A Reading of Volume One* (London: Verso, 2011), p. 90.

37. Fredric Jameson, *A Singular Modernity: Essay on the Ontology of the Present* (London: Verso, 2002), p. 8.

38. We can draw a distinction here between abstract and concrete utopias. Whereas the former project an image of the future unbound from current political conditions, the latter are guided by a rigorous analysis of the given conjuncture and aimed at intervention in the here and now. Alfred Schmidt, *The Concept of Nature in Marx* (London: Verso, 2014), p. 128; Ernst Bloch, *The Principle of Hope* (Cambridge, MA: MIT Press, 1995).

39. George Young, *The Russian Cosmists: The Esoteric Futurism of Nikolai Fedorov and His Followers* (Oxford: Oxford University Press, 2012).

40. Richard Stites, 'Fantasy and Revolution: Alexander Bogdanov and the Origins of Bolshevik Science Fiction', in Bogdanov, *Red Star*, p. 15; Siddiqi, *Red Rockets' Glare*, Chapter 4.

41. Erik Olin Wright, *Envisioning Real Utopias* (London: Verso, 2010), p. 23.

42. Jameson, *Singular Modernity*, p. 26; Vincent Geoghegan, *Utopianism and Marxism* (Oxford: Peter Lang, 2008), p. 16.

43. Zygmunt Bauman, *Socialism: The Active Utopia* (London: Routledge, 2011), p. 13.

44. Kilgore, *Astrofuturism*, pp. 237–8; Stites, *Revolutionary Dreams*, p. 33.

45. Slavoj Žižek, 'Towards a Materialist Theory of Subjectivity', Birkbeck, London, 22 May 2014, podcast available at backdoorbroadcasting.net.

46. Weeks, *Problem with Work*, p. 204.

47. Ruth Levitas, *The Concept of Utopia* (Oxford: Peter Lang, 2011).

48. E. P. Thompson, 'Romanticism, Utopianism and Moralism: The Case of William Morris', *New Left Review* I/99 (September–October 1976), p. 97.

49. The most condensed and interventionist form of this utopian dimension is the manifesto. See Weeks, *Problem with Work*, pp. 213–18.

50. Manuel Castells, *Networks of Outrage and Hope: Social Movements in the Internet Age* (Cambridge: Polity, 2012), p. 15.

51. Patricia Reed, 'Seven Prescriptions for Accelerationism', in Robin Mackay and Armen Avanessian, eds, *#Accelerate: The Accelerationist Reader* (Falmouth: Urbanomic, 2014), pp. 528–31.

52. Wendy Brown, 'Resisting Left Melancholy', *Boundary 2* 26: 3 (1999).

53. Paul Mason, *Why It's Kicking Off Everywhere: The New Global Revolutions* (London: Verso, 2012), pp. 66–73.

54. Mark Fisher, 'Going Overground', *K-Punk*, 5 January 2014, at k-punk.org.

55. Bloch, *Principle of Hope*.

56. Paul Gilroy, *The Black Atlantic: Modernity and Double Consciousness* (London: Verso, 1993), p. 37; Weeks, *Problem with Work*, pp. 190–3; Geoghegan, *Utopianism and Marxism*, p. 20.

57. Curiously, this lack of a profit motive has led some on the left to see space exploration perversely as a 'capitalist utopia'. George Caffentzis and Silvia Federici, 'Mormons in Space', in George Caffentzis, *In Letters of Blood and Fire* (Oakland: PM Press, 2012), p. 65.

58. Louis Althusser, 'Ideology and Ideological State Apparatus (Notes Towards an Investigation)', in *Lenin and Philosophy and Other Essays* (New York: Monthly Review, 2001), pp. 88–9.

59. Gramsci, *Selections from the Prison Notebooks*, p. 10.

60. Mary Morgan and Malcolm Rutherford, 'American Economics: The Character of the Transformation', *History of Political Economy* 30 (1998).

61. G. C. Harcourt, *Some Cambridge Controversies in the Theory of Capital* (Cambridge: Cambridge University Press, 1972).

62. Paul A. Samuelson, 'Understanding the Marxian Notion of Exploitation: A Summary of the So-Called Transformation Problem Between Marxian Values and Competitive Prices', *Journal of Economic Literature* 9: 2 (1971).

63. Edward Fullbrook, 'Introduction', in Edward Fullbrook, ed., *Pluralist Economics* (London: Zed, 2008), pp. 1–2.

64. More information can be found on their website: rethinkeconomics.org.

65. David Colander and Harry Landreth, 'Pluralism, Formalism and American Economics', in Fullbrook, *Pluralist Economics*, pp. 31–5.

66. The most dominant textbook is by Greg Mankiw, a former Bush lackey and courageous defender of the 1 per cent: N. Gregory Mankiw, *Macroeconomics*, 8th edn (New York: Worth, 2012).

67. William Mitchell and L. Randall Wray, 'Modern Monetary Theory and Practice', 2014, pdf available at mmtonline.net.

68. For two brief but excellent exceptions, see Tiziana Terranova, 'Red Stack Attack!', in Mackay and Avanessian, *#Accelerate*.

69. For some of the existing research on this topic, see Oskar Lange and Fred M. Taylor, *On the Economic Theory of Socialism* (New York: McGraw-Hill, 1964); W. Paul Cockshott and Allin Cottrell, *Towards a New Socialism* (Nottingham: Spokesman, 1993); W. Paul Cockshott, Allin Cottrell, Gregory Michaelson, Ian Wright and Victor Yakovenko, *Classical Econophysics* (London: Routledge, 2009); Andy Pollack, 'Information Technology and Socialist Self-Management', *Monthly Review* 49: 4 (1997); Dan Greenwood, 'From Market to Non-Market: An Autonomous Agent Approach to Central Planning', *Knowledge Engineering Review* 22: 4 (2007).

70. There are already a number of economists working on these issues. The problem is hindered by the existence of multiple measures (many of which nonetheless reach similar conclusions about the cyclical and secular trends), and by studies remaining at the level of appearances and not digging deeper into the causal mechanisms behind them. There seems to be a correlation between increasing use of fixed capital in the production process and a long-term secular decline in profitability, but any causal connection so far remains at the level of assertion. For more, see Minqi Li, Feng Xiao and Andong Zhu, 'Long Waves, Institutional Changes, and Historical Trends: A Study of the Long-Term Movement of the Profit Rate in the Capitalist World-Economy', *Journal of World-Systems Research* 13: 1 (2007); Guglielmo Carchedi, *Behind the Crisis: Marx's Dialectic of Value and Knowledge* (Chicago: Haymarket, 2012); Deepankar Basu and Ramaa Vasudevan, 'Technology, Distribution and the Rate of Profit in the US Economy: Understanding the Current Crisis', *Cambridge Journal of Economics* 37: 1 (2013); Gerard Dumenil and Dominique Levy, 'The Profit Rate: Where and How Much Did It Fall? Did It Recover? (USA 1948–2000)', *Review of Radical Political Economics* 34: 4 (2002).

71. Mary Morgan, *The World in the Model: How Economists Work and Think* (Cambridge: Cambridge University Press, 2012).

72. For more information, see wea.org.uk.

73. Andy Clark, *Supersizing the Mind: Embodiment, Action, and Cognitive Extension* (New York: Oxford University Press, 2008).

74. John Zerzan, *Future Primitive and Other Essays* (Brooklyn: Semiotext(e), 1996); Derrick Jensen, *Endgame: The Problem of Civilization, Volume 1* (New York: Seven Stories, 2006).

75. Gavin Mueller, 'The Rise of the Machines', *Jacobin* 10 (2013), at jacobinmag.com.

76. This has been one of the main focuses of science and technology studies and feminist approaches to technology. For representative examples of this research, see Wajcman, *TechnoFeminism*; Wiebe Bijker, Thomas Hughes and Trevor Pinch, eds, *The Social Construction of Technological Systems* (Cambridge, MA: MIT Press, 1987); Wiebe Bijker, *Of Bicycles, Bakelites, and Bulbs: Toward a Theory of Sociotechnical Change* (Cambridge, MA: MIT Press, 1997); Donald MacKenzie, Fabian Muniesa and Lucia Siu, eds, *Do Economists Make Markets? On the*

Performativity of Economics (Princeton, NJ: Princeton University Press, 2007); Thomas Hughes, *Networks of Power: Electrification in Western Society, 1880–1930* (Baltimore, MD: Johns Hopkins University Press, 1993).

77. This is the subject of recent debates over the 'reconfiguration thesis'. Alberto Toscano, 'Logistics and Opposition', *Mute*, 2011, at metamute.org; Jasper Bernes, 'Logistics, Counterlogistics and the Communist Project', in *End Notes 3: Gender, Race, Class and Other Misfortunes* (September 2013); Alberto Toscano, 'Lineaments of the Logistical State', *Viewpoint*, 2015, at viewpointmag.com.

78. 'Machinery does not lose its use value as soon as it ceases to be capital. While machinery is the most appropriate form of the use value of fixed capital, it does not at all follow that therefore subsumption under the social relation of capital is the most appropriate and ultimate social relation of production for the application of machinery.' Karl Marx, *Grundrisse: Introduction to the Critique of Political Economy*, transl. Martin Nicolaus (Harmondsworth: Penguin, 1973), pp. 699–700.

79. As the examples here will show, repurposing and creation are ultimately highly intertwined, given that every repurposing involves a creative use of old material, and every creation involves a repurposing of existing material to hand. The distinction between the two is ultimately a matter of emphasis rather than opposition.

80. Andrew Feenberg, *Transforming Technology: A Critical Theory Revisited* (New York: Oxford University Press, 2002).

81. For a series of useful guidelines for how workers can adopt technology into the workplace, see Chris Harman, *Is a Machine After Your Job? New Technology and the Struggle for Socialism* (London, 1979), at marxists.org, Part 8.

82. Mariana Mazzucato, *The Entrepreneurial State: Debunking Public vs. Private Sector Myths* (London: Anthem, 2013); Michael Hanlon, 'The Golden Quarter', *Aeon Magazine*, 3 December 2014, at aeon.co.

83. For a detailed account of this, see Mazzucato, *Entrepreneurial State*, Chapter 5.

84. Mariana Mazzucato, *Building the Entrepreneurial State: A New Framework for Envisioning and Evaluating a Mission-Oriented Public Sector*, Working Paper No. 824, Levy Economics Institute of Bard College, 2015, pdf available at levyinstitute. org, p. 9; Carlota Perez, *Technological Revolutions and Financial Capital: The Dynamics of Bubbles and Golden Ages* (Cheltenham: Edward Elgar, 2003).

85. Mazzucato, *Building the Entrepreneurial State*, p. 2.

86. For more, see missionorientedfinance.com.

87. Caetano Penna and Mariana Mazzucato, 'Beyond Market Failures: The Role of State Investment Banks in the Economy', paper presented at the Conference on Mission-Oriented Finance for Innovation, London, 24 July 2014, available on youtube.com.

88. Germany's major transformation towards renewable energy provides perhaps the best current example of this.

89. Nick Dyer-Witheford, 'Cycles and Circuits of Struggle in High-Technology Capitalism', in Jim Davis, Thomas Hirschl and Michael Stack, eds, *Cutting Edge: Technology, Information, Capitalism and Social Revolution* (London: Verso, 1997), pp. 206–7; Adrian Smith, *Socially Useful Production*, STEPS Working Paper 58 (Brighton STEPS Centre, 2014), at steps-centre.org, p. 2.

90. This shares some properties with Murray Bookchin's notion of liberatory technologies, though we are obviously less inclined towards his vision of a small-scale communitarian future. Murray Bookchin, 'Towards a Liberatory Technology', in *Post-Scarcity Anarchism* (Edinburgh: AK Press, 2004).

91. Hilary Wainwright and Dave Elliott, *The Lucas Plan: A New Trade Unionism in the Making?* (London: Allison & Busby, 1981), p. 16.

92. Ibid., pp. 10, 89.

93. Ibid., pp. 101–7.

94. Smith, *Socially Useful Production*, p. 5.

95. Ibid., p. 1.

96. Ibid., p. 2.

97. Wainwright and Elliott, *Lucas Plan*, p. 231.

98. Ibid., p. 157.

99. Tiqqun, *The Cybernetic Hypothesis*, n.d., at theanarchistlibrary.org.

100. Eden Medina, *Cybernetic Revolutionaries: Technology and Politics in Allende's Chile* (London: MIT Press, 2011), p. 26.

101. Ibid., p. 64.

102. Ibid., p. 72.

103. Ibid., p. 146.

104. Ibid., p. 150.

105. Ibid., p. 79.

106. Jameson, *Valences of the Dialectic*; Toscano, 'Logistics and Opposition'; Mike Davis, 'Who Will Build the Ark?', *New Left Review* II/61 (January–February 2010); Medina, *Cybernetic Revolutionaries*; Nick Dyer-Witheford, 'Red Plenty Platforms', *Culture Machine* 14 (2013); Terranova, 'Red Stack Attack!'; Evgeny Morozov, 'Socialise the Data Centres!' *New Left Review* 91 (January–February 2015).

107. For a sophisticated argument to the contrary, see Bernes, 'Logistics, Counterlogistics and the Communist Project'.

108. For a compelling quasi-fictional account of these problems, see Spufford, *Red Plenty*.

109. Caroline Saunders and Andrew Barber, *Food Miles – Comparative Energy/Emissions Performance of New Zealand's Agriculture Industry*, Agribusiness and Economics Research Unit, July 2006, pdf available at lincoln.ac.nz.

110. Feenberg, *Transforming Technology*, p. 58; Monika Reinfelder, 'Introduction: Breaking the Spell of Technicism', in Phil Slater, ed., *Outlines of a Critique of Technology* (London: Ink Links, 1980), p. 17.

111. There is an extensive literature on this political nature in the field of science and technology studies, but we would also add research on skill-biased and class-biased technical change. David Autor, Frank Levy and Richard Murnane, 'The Skill Content of Recent Technological Change: An Empirical Exploration', *Quarterly Journal of Economics* 118: 4 (2003); Amit Basole, 'Class-Biased Technical Change and Socialism: Some Reflections on Benedito Moraes-Neto's "On the Labor Process and Productive Efficiency: Discussing the Socialist Project"', *Rethinking Marxism* 25: 4 (2013).

112. For one of the earliest arguments to this effect, see Raniero Panzieri, 'The Capitalist Use of Machinery: Marx Versus the "Objectivists"', in Slater, *Outlines of a Critique of Technology*.

113. David F. Noble, *Forces of Production: A Social History of Industrial Automation* (New York: Oxford University Press, 1986); Karl Marx, *Capital: A Critique of Political Economy, Volume I*, transl. Ben Fowkes (London: Penguin, 1990), p. 526.

114. Melvin Kranzberg, 'Technology and History: "Kranzberg's Laws"', *Technology and Culture* 27:3 (1986), p. 545.

115. George Basalla, *The Evolution of Technology* (Cambridge: Cambridge University Press, 1988), p. 7.

116. On how users shape technology, see Nellie Ooudshorn and Trevor Pinch, eds, *How Users Matter: The Co-Construction of Users and Technology* (Cambridge, MA: MIT Press, 2005).

117. Harry Cleaver, 'Technology as Political Weaponry', in *The Responsibility of the Scientific and Technological Enterprise in Technology Transfer*, American Association for the Advancement of Science, 1981, pdf available at academia.edu.

118. Even if never used, nuclear weapons are still fundamentally premised on this function.

119. For an incisive reflection on cognitive workers and their relation to other figures of the working class, see Matteo Pasquinelli, 'To Anticipate and Accelerate: Italian Operaismo and Reading Marx's Notion of the Organic Composition of Capital', *Rethinking Marxism* 26: 2 (2014).

8. BUILDING POWER

1. By 'power', we mean the capacity to bring about one's interests. Steven Lukes, *Power: A Radical View*, 2nd edn (Houndmills: Palgrave Macmillan, 2005).

2. John Holloway, *Change the World Without Taking Power: The Meaning of Revolution Today* (London/Sterling, VA: Pluto, 2002).

3. We focus on these three factors here, but there are undoubtedly numerous others – not least, unpredictable elements like luck and individual vision.

4. In terms of traditional class struggle, this category includes associational power, marketplace bargaining power and workplace bargaining power. Beverly Silver, *Forces of Labor: Workers' Movements and Globalization Since 1870* (Cambridge: Cambridge University Press, 2003), pp. 13–16.

5. Indeed, the unique feature of class conflict under capitalism was argued to be its tendency to simplify the antagonism. Karl Marx and Friedrich Engels, 'The Communist Manifesto', in *Economic and Philosophical Manuscripts of 1844, and the Communist Manifesto* (Amherst, NY: Prometheus Books, 1988), p. 210.

6. 'The Holding Pattern: The Ongoing Crisis and the Class Struggles of 2011–2013', *Endnotes* 3 (2013), at endnotes.org.uk, pp. 49–50.

7. Frances Fox Piven and Richard Cloward, *Poor People's Movements: Why They Succeed, How They Fail* (New York: Random House, 1988), p. 194.

8. Marx and Engels, 'Communist Manifesto', pp. 217–18.

9. As Beverly Silver reminds us, though, we should not assume that these tactics and leverage points were obvious from the beginning. They had to be invented and built up through practice and experimentation. Silver, *Forces of Labor*, p. 6.

10. 'Editorial', *Endnotes* 3 (2013), p. 7.

11. Göran Therborn, 'New Masses? Social Bases of Resistance', *New Left Review* II/85 (January–February 2014), p. 9.

12. Ching Kwan Lee, *Against the Law: Labor Protests in China's Rustbelt and Sunbelt* (Berkeley, CA: University of California Press, 2007); Kevin Hamlin, Ilya Gridneff and William Davison, 'Ethiopia Becomes China's China in Global Search for Cheap Labor', *Business Week*, 22 July 2014.

13. Silvia Federici, *Caliban and the Witch: Women, the Body and Primitive Accumulation* (New York: Autonomedia, 2004), pp. 63–4; Zak Cope, *Divided World, Divided Class: Global Political Economy and the Stratification of Labour Under Capitalism* (Montreal: Kersplebedeb, 2012).

14. To give just a sample of how this topic has been broached, we can point to the problem of building the common, the problem of articulating a hegemony, the problem of the party, the problem of composition and the problem of framing. See, respectively, Michael Hardt and Antonio Negri, *Multitude: War and Democracy in the Age of Empire* (New York: Penguin, 2005); Ernesto Laclau, *On Populist Reason* (London: Verso, 2007); Jodi Dean, *The Communist Horizon* (London: Verso, 2012); 'The Holding Pattern'; Sidney Tarrow, *Power in Movement: Social Movements and Contentious Politics*, 2nd edn (Cambridge: Cambridge University Press, 1998).

15. Badiou, for example, offers a critique of the tendency of minimal rights to reduce the human down to its animalistic basis. Alain Badiou, *Ethics: An Essay on the Understanding of Evil*, transl. Peter Hallward (London: Verso, 2002), pp. 11–13.

16. Anna Feigenbaum, Fabian Frenzel and Patrick McCurdy, *Protest Camps* (London: Zed, 2013), p. 176.

17. In more classical language, we might say that objectivite unity is faced with subjective plurality.

18. While populist movements are often set in opposition to class movements, it is more accurate to say that populist movements *encompass* class movements. As Laclau argues, what populism denies is not class struggle, but instead the ahistorical necessity of class struggle as the only motor of social change. But within a populist movement, certain struggles can be more relevant than others, and under contemporary conditions of surplus populations, we believe class is again emerging as the dominant – though repressed – locus of struggle of our times. As understood here, populism therefore expresses a connective logic rather than a specific content. The 'people' is therefore not a subject, nor a substantial entity, but an emergent collective formed by a particular logic of connection. Linda Zerilli, 'This Universalism Which Is Not One', *Diacritics* 28: 2 (1998); Laclau, *On Populist Reason*, p. 236.

19. For a useful genealogy of the changing valence of 'populism', see Marco D'Eramo, 'Populism and the New Oligarchy', transl. Gregory Elliot, *New Left Review* II/82 (July–August 2013).

20. Laclau, *On Populist Reason*, p. 117.

21. Yannis Stavrakakis and Giorgos Katsambekis, 'Left-Wing Populism in the European Periphery: The Case of Syriza', *Journal of Political Ideologies* 19: 2 (2014); Pablo Iglesias, 'The Left Can Win', *Jacobin*, 9 December 2014, at jacobinmag.com; Dan Hancox, 'Why Ernesto Laclau Is the Intellectual Figurehead for Syriza and

Podemos', *Guardian*, 9 February 2015; Laclau, *On Populist Reason*; George Ciccariello-Maher, *We Created Chavez: A People's History of the Venezuelan Revolution* (Durham, NC: Duke University Press, 2013).

22. Ernesto Laclau, 'Why Constructing a People Is the Main Task of Radical Politics', *Critical Inquiry* 32: 4 (2006), p. 655.

23. Enrique Dussel, *Twenty Theses on Politics*, transl. George Ciccariello-Maher (Durham, NC: Duke University Press, 2009), p. 83.

24. For example, the *Wall Street Journal* estimated that anyone in the United States earning under $500,000 would be in the 99 per cent. It would be difficult to imagine that many earning a little under that were aligned with the project expressed by Occupy Wall Street. See Phil Izzo, 'What Percent Are You?', *WSJ Blogs – Real Time Economics*, 19 October 2011, at blogs.wsj.com.

25. Referring back to the discussion of universalism in Chapter 4, this is the way in which universalism becomes contaminated with the particular, and vice versa.

26. Therborn, 'New Masses?', pp. 8–9.

27. Bertie Russell, 'Demanding the Future? What a Demand Can Do', *Journal of Aesthetics and Protest*, 2014, at joaap.org.

28. Ben Trott, 'Walking in the Right Direction?', *Turbulence* 1 (2007), at turbulence. org.uk.

29. This also has resonances with what Plan C has called a 'community of reference'. Russell, 'Demanding the Future?'.

30. Tiziana Terranova, 'Red Stack Attack!', in Robin Mackay and Armen Avanessian, eds, *#Accelerate: The Accelerationist Reader* (Falmouth: Urbanomic, 2014), p. 387.

31. William K. Carroll, 'Hegemony, Counter-Hegemony, Anti-Hegemony', *Socialist Studies/Études Socialistes* 2: 2 (2006), pp. 30–2; Richard Day, *Gramsci Is Dead: Anarchist Currents in the Newest Social Movements* (London: Pluto, 2005).

32. David Harvey, *Rebel Cities: From the Right to the City to the Urban Revolution* (London: Verso, 2013), p. 125.

33. The Free Association, 'Rock 'n' Roll Suicide: Political Organisation in Post-Crisis UK', *Freely Associating*, n.d., at freelyassociating.org.

34. For a discussion of 'vanguard functions', see Rodrigo Nunes, *Organisation of the Organisationless: Collective Action After Networks* (London: Mute, 2014), pp. 34–40.

35. For an argument about the importance of multiple organizational forms, see Tarrow, *Power in Movement*, Chapter 8.

36. Carroll, 'Hegemony, Counter-Hegemony, Anti-Hegemony', p. 22.

37. Nunes, *Organisation of the Organisationless*, p. 30.

38. This is what is termed a 'network-system' by Rodrigo Nunes. Ibid., p. 20. Nunes's work also highlights an important area for more research – namely, a comparative network topology of movements. In this endeavour, the mathematical tools of graph theory will be indispensable.

39. Brian Steensland, *The Failed Welfare Revolution: America's Struggle over Guaranteed Income Policy* (Princeton, NJ: Princeton University Press, 2007), p. 22.

40. Henry Farrell and Cosma Shalizi, 'Cognitive Democracy', *Crooked Timber*, 23 May 2012, at crookedtimber.org.

41. Zeynep Tufekci, 'After the Protests', *New York Times*, 19 March 2014.

42. Manuel Castells, *Networks of Outrage and Hope: Social Movements in the Internet Age* (Cambridge: Polity, 2012), pp. 34–5.

43. Jane McAlevey, *Raising Expectations (and Raising Hell): My Decade Fighting for the Labor Movement* (London: Verso, 2014), p. 312.

44. Steensland, *Failed Welfare Revolution*, p. 230.

45. Roger Simon, *Gramsci's Political Thought* (London: Lawrence & Wishart, 1991), Chapter 12.

46. Antonio Gramsci, *Selections from the Prison Notebooks*, ed. Quintin Hoare and Geoffrey Nowell-Smith (London: Lawrence & Wishart, 1971), pp. 5–6.

47. SomeAngryWorkers, 'Gr***ford? Where the Hell's That?!', *Libcom*, 14 September 2014, at libcom.org.

48. McAlevey, *Raising Expectations*, p. 37.

49. This is what has been called 'whole-worker organising'. See ibid., pp. 14–16.

50. Erik Olin Wright, *Envisioning Real Utopias* (London: Verso, 2010), p. 223.

51. Alain Badiou, *The Rebirth of History: Times of Riots and Uprisings* (London: Verso, 2012), p. 30.

52. Harvey, *Rebel Cities*, p. 132.

53. McAlevey, *Raising Expectations*, p. 51.

54. Bill Fletcher and Fernando Gapasin, *Solidarity Divided: The Crisis in Organized Labor and a New Path Toward Social Justice* (London: University of California Press, 2009), p. 174.

55. Guy Standing, *The Precariat: The New Dangerous Class* (London: Bloomsbury Academic, 2011), p. 1.

56. Steven Greenhouse, 'The Nation: The $100,000 Longshoreman; A Union Wins the Global Game', *New York Times*, 6 October 2002.

57. Nina Power has recently suggested that UBI should be a global demand, rather than a national demand. While in agreement in principle, we believe current political conditions make it inevitable that these demands will have to first pass through individual states. Nina Power, 'Re-Engineering the Future,' presented at *Re-Engineering the Future*, Tate Britain, London, UK, 10 April 2015.

58. In recent years it has been common to argue that there is a crisis of the party-form, yet these announcements overlook the ways in which the party-form has been continually reinvented as conditions have changed. In simple terms, we can say there has been a breakdown of the vanguard party and the social democratic party. The former is predicated on a small elite group of intellectuals telling the masses what their interests are and inciting them to revolution. Lars T. Lih, *Lenin Rediscovered: 'What Is to Be Done?' in Context* (Chicago: Haymarket, 2008), pp. 13–18. The latter, on the other hand, is predicated on mass support, electoral politics, an independent financial base and a central position in a network of traditional workers' organisations. Gerassimos Moschonas, *In the Name of Social Democracy: The Great Transformation, 1945 to the Present*, transl. Gregory Elliott (London: Verso, 2002), p. 35. Both are unfit for contemporary conditions in the advanced capitalist countries, but we believe the Gramscian concept of the party as a modern Prince may hold value and help to clarify the structure of a party like Podemos. A full discussion of the party would go beyond what can be included

here, but we follow Peter Thomas in seeing this party as (1) only one section of a broader populist movement; (2) a form of self-governance of the movement; (3) an organisation that institutionalises difference rather than imposing identity; and (4) an organisation that can both synthesise the movement's demands and act as an experimental apparatus to lead it. Peter Thomas, 'The Communist Hypothesis and the Question of Organization', *Theory & Event* 16: 4 (2013), at muse.jhu.edu.

59. Dario Azzellini, 'The Communal State: Communal Councils, Communes, and Workplace Democracy', *North American Congress on Latin America*, Summer 2013, at nacla.org.

60. Dan Hancox, 'Podemos: The Radical Party Turning Spanish Politics on Its Head', *Newsweek*, 22 October 2014.

61. Specifically, in the case of Podemos these include 'open citizen primaries, the constitution and proliferation of the circles, the editing and approval of a participative programme, collective funding, transparent accounting, agreement on the revocability of roles, the limitation of mandates and salaries of representatives'. Germán Cano, Jorge Lago, Eduardo Maura, Pablo Bustinduy and Jorge Moruno, 'Podemos: Overcoming Representation', *Cunning Hired Knaves*, 31 May 2014, at hiredknaves. wordpress.com.

62. There is, however, much internal debate within Podemos about the direction in which the movement should move forward. Broadly, we can distinguish between those who appear to want more state-based and centralized power, and those who want more power delegated to decentralized and local social movements. See Luke Stobart, 'Understanding Podemos (2/3): Radical Populism', *Left Flank*, 14 November 2014, at left-flank.org.

63. Gary Genosko, *The Party Without Bosses: Lessons on Anti-Capitalism from Félix Guattari and Luís Inácio 'Lula' Da Silva* (Winnipeg: Arbeiter Ring, 2003), p. 19.

64. Ciccariello-Maher, *We Created Chavez*, p. 16.

65. Mark Levinson, *The Box: How the Shipping Container Made the World Smaller and the World Economy Bigger* (Princeton, NJ: Princeton University Press, 2008), p. 10.

66. Ibid., p. 27.

67. Silver, *Forces of Labor*, p. 47.

68. Timothy Mitchell, *Carbon Democracy: Political Power in the Age of Oil* (London: Verso, 2013), p. 19.

69. Ashok Kumar, '5 Reasons the Strike in China Is Terrifying! (to Transnational Capitalism)', *Novara Wire*, April 2014, at wire.novaramedia.com.

70. SomeAngryWorkers, 'Gr***ford?'.

71. Deborah Cowen, *The Deadly Life of Logistics: Mapping Violence in Global Trade* (Minneapolis, MN: University of Minnesota Press), pp. 41–5.

72. This is what is described by Erik Olin Wright as a type of structural power. Erik Olin Wright, 'Working-Class Power, Capitalist-Class Interests, and Class Compromise', *American Journal of Sociology* 105: 4 (2000), p. 962.

73. Jonathan Cutler and Stanley Aronowitz, 'Quitting Time', in Stanley Aronowitz and Jonathan Cutler, eds, *Post-Work: The Wages of Cybernation* (New York: Routledge, 1998), pp. 9–11.

74. Cynthia Cockburn, *Brothers: Male Dominance and Technological Change* (London: Pluto, 1991).

75. McAlevey, *Raising Expectations*, p. 28.

76. Cutler and Aronowitz, 'Quitting Time', p. 17.

77. Ibid., pp. 12–13; Noam Chomsky, *Occupy* (London: Penguin, 2012), p. 34.

78. Murray Wardrop, 'Boris Johnson Pledges to Introduce Driverless Tube Trains Within Two Years', *Daily Telegraph*, 28 February 2012.

79. Paul Einzig, *The Economic Consequences of Automation* (New York: W. W. Norton, 1957), p. 235.

80. David Autor, *Polanyi's Paradox and the Shape of Employment Growth*, Working Paper, National Bureau of Economic Research, September 2014, at nber.org, p. 26.

81. Anh Nguyen, Jason Yosinski and Jeff Clune, 'Deep Neural Networks Are Easily Fooled: High Confidence Predictions for Unrecognizable Images', *arXiv*, 2015, at arxiv.org.

82. A classic resource here is Piven and Cloward, *Poor People's Movements*. See also Liz Mason-Deese, 'The Neighborhood Is the New Factory', *Viewpoint* 2 (2012), at view-pointmag.com.

83. Day, *Gramsci Is Dead*, p. 42.

84. Jael Vizcarra and Troy Andreas Araiza Kokinis, 'Freeway Takeovers: The Reemergence of the Collective Through Urban Disruption', *Tropics of Meta: Historiography for the Masses*, 5 December 2014, at tropicsofmeta.wordpress.com.

85. For instance, in order to uncover the effects of a West Coast port stoppage, a general equilibrium model has been used to forecast the effects for individual industries, along with the impacts from items like perishable goods and rerouted goods. The model further disaggregates these effects into impacts on exports, imports and consumer purchasing power, pinpointing the precise targets of any political pressure exerted through a blockade. 'The National Impact of a West Coast Port Stoppage', National Association of Manufacturers and the National Retail Federation, June 2014, pdf available at nam.org, p. 9.

86. See, for example, the development of new forms of organising around logistics networks. Jane Slaughter, 'Supply Chain Workers Test Strength of Links', *Labor Notes*, April 2012.

87. McAlevey, *Raising Expectations*, p. 37.

CONCLUSION

1. This is a point implied by Marx when he writes that 'the realm of freedom actually *begins* only where labour which is determined by necessity and mundane considerations ceases'. Karl Marx, *Capital: A Critique of Political Economy, Volume III* (London: Lawrence & Wishart, 1977). Emphasis added.

2. The tenacity of the gendered division of society is amply demonstrated in Maria Mies, *Patriarchy and Accumulation on a World Scale: Women in the International Division of Labour* (London: Zed, 1999).

3. Kathi Weeks, *The Problem with Work: Feminism, Marxism, Antiwork Politics, and Postwork Imaginaries* (Durham, NC: Duke University Press, 2011), p. 216.

4. Robert J. Van Der Veen and Philippe Van Parijs, 'A Capitalist Road to Communism', *Theory and Society* 15: 5 (1986), p. 637.

5. Gregory N. Mandel and James Thuo Gathii, 'Cost-Benefit Analysis Versus the Precautionary Principle: Beyond Cass Sunstein's Laws of Fear', *University of Illinois Law Review* 5 (2006).

6. For an essential meditation on this, see Benedict Singleton, 'Maximum Jailbreak', in Robin Mackay and Armen Avanessian, eds, *#Accelerate: The Accelerationist Reader* (Falmouth: Urbanomic, 2014).

7. Paul Mason, 'What Would Keynes Do?', *New Statesman*, 12 June 2014.

8. Singleton, 'Maximum Jailbreak'; Nikolai Federovich Federov, 'The Philosophy of the Common Task', in *What Was Man Created For?*, transl. Elisabeth Kouitaissof and Marilyn Minto (London: Honeyglen, 1990).

9. For an accessible articulation of this position, see W. Brian Arthur, *The Nature of Technology: What It Is and How It Evolves* (London: Penguin, 2009).

10. Tony Smith, 'Red Innovation', *Jacobin* 17 (2015), p. 75.

11. Mariana Mazzucato, Erik Brynjolfsson and Michael Osborne, 'Robot Panel', presented at the FT Camp Alphaville, London, 15 July 2014, available at youtube.com.

12. Michael Hanlon, 'The Golden Quarter', *Aeon Magazine*, 3 December 2014, at aeon.co; Tyler Cowen, *The Great Stagnation: How America Ate All the Low-Hanging Fruit of Modern History, Got Sick, and Will (Eventually) Feel Better* (New York: Dutton, 2011), p. 13.

13. This is one of the primary conclusions of Mariana Mazzucato's important book *The Entrepreneurial State: Debunking Public vs. Private Sector Myths* (London: Anthem, 2013).

14. For a lengthy analysis of how Apple cynically deployed state-developed technologies to build the iPhone, see ibid., Chapter 5.

15. The fact that so many megaprojects continue to go ahead despite their history of cost overruns and lack of profitability is deemed a paradox by one study: Bent Flyvbjerg, Nils Bruzelius and Werner Rothengatter, *Megaprojects and Risk: An Anatomy of Ambition* (Cambridge: Cambridge University Press, 2003), pp. 3–5.

16. André Gorz, *Paths to Paradise: On the Liberation from Work*, transl. Malcolm Imrie (Boston, MA: South End, 1985), p. 61.

17. As Marx and Engels write, 'this development of productive forces . . . is an absolutely necessary practical premise because without it privation, *want* is merely made general, and with *want* the struggle for necessities would begin again, and all the old filthy business would necessarily be restored'. Karl Marx and Friedrich Engels, *The German Ideology* (London: Prometheus, 1976), p. 54.

18. This appeal to a humanity outside of capitalism is one of the more problematic aspects of Jacques Camatte's work, for instance. See Jacques Camatte, *This World We Must Leave* (Brooklyn: (Semiotexte), 1996).

19. Weeks, *Problem with Work*, p. 169.

20. Ernest Mandel, *Late Capitalism* (London: Verso, 1998), pp. 394–5.

21. Translation slightly modified – from 'human energy' to 'human powers'. Marx, *Capital, Volume III*, p. 820.

22. Federico Campagna, *The Last Night: Anti-Work, Atheism, Adventure* (Winchester: Zero, 2013), p. 68.

23. For some investigations into what these could look like, however, see Alexandra Kollontai, *Selected Writings*, transl. Alix Holt (London: Allison & Busby, 1977).

24. Stephen Eric Bronner, *Reclaiming the Enlightenment: Toward a Politics of Radical Engagement* (New York: Columbia University Press, 2004), p. 15.

25. Weeks, *Problem with Work*, p. 103.

26. Benjamin Bratton, *The Stack: On Software and Sovereignty* (Cambridge, MA: MIT Press, 2015).

27. Tiziana Terranova, 'Red Stack Attack!', in Robin Mackay and Armen Avanessian, eds, *#Accelerate: The Accelerationist Reader* (Falmouth: Urbanomic, 2014), pp. 391–3.

28. Accounts of daily life under participatory economics make for sobering reading. See Michael Albert, *Parecon: Life After Capitalism* (London: Verso, 2004), Part 3.

29. Nick Dyer-Witheford, 'Red Plenty Platforms', *Culture Machine* 14 (2013), p. 13.

30. Measured in terms of floating operations per second, the difference between 1969 and what is expected by 2019 is 10^7 versus 10^{18}. Ibid., p. 8.

AFTERWORD: REINVENTING THE FUTURE

1. In particular the report issued by the Royal Society for the Encouragement of Arts, Manufactures and Commerce, while unambitious in its scope, played an important role in normalising the policy within discussions in the UK. See Anthony Painter and Chris Thoung, *Creative Citizen, Creative State: The Principled and Pragmatic Case for a Universal Basic Income* (London: Royal Society for the Encouragement of Arts, Manufactures and Commerce, 2015), at thersa.org. For a more ambitious take on costing UBI within the UK, see Howard Reed and Stewart Lansley, *Universal Basic Income: An Idea Whose Time Has Come?* (London: Compass, 2016).

2. Helen Hester has been one of the few to examine in depth the implications of automation for reproductive labour – both its limits and its possibilities. In a talk entitled 'Obstinate Gender', she points out the limits of many discussions of post-work: 'Forms of work that are mainly (and problematically) associated with cis men are explicitly treated as labour that must be resisted, refused, and (through automation) transcended. The response to forms of work that have conventionally (and, again, problematically) been gendered as "feminine", meanwhile, involves not denunciation but valorisation. In this sense, post-work societies are also pre-work societies, because they herald new forms of social organization in which reproductive labour proliferates. "Masculinized" labour is escaped, whilst "feminized" labour multiplies – all in a fashion that (supposedly) marks the end of work.' Helen Hester, 'Obstinate Gender: Technopolitics and the Limits of Transformation', The Academy Lectures, Oslo National Academy of the Arts, Oslo, 9 September 2015.

3. Indeed, while the book is often rightly represented as a book about technology, the phrase 'surplus populations' appears just as many times in the body of the text as 'technology' does.

4. For a brilliant complementary piece to this chapter, see Bue Rübner Hansen, 'Surplus Population, Social Reproduction, and the Problem of Class Formation', *Viewpoint* 5 (2016).

5. This historically constructed character is why we used the term 'folk' in the 'folk psychology' sense – as an intuitive relation to the world which is socially constructed and historically mutable.

6. We would also like to reiterate that while nearly all the focus today is on UBI as a magic bullet to all our problems, this is fundamentally misguided. UBI is a contestable object, and we should be mobilising around it, but we should not put all of our resources and hopes into it. Post-work is a much larger demand that just this one issue.

7. Rodrigo Nunes, *Organisation of the Organisationless: Collective Action after Networks* (London: Mute, 2014), pp. 38–9.

8. Ibid., p. 35.

9. Nunes has also recently had some important thoughts on what strategy means in a complex world, which nicely complement the ideas proposed in the book: Rodrigo Nunes, 'Beneath the Control Board, the Breach', *Plan C* 1 (2015).

Index